GREAT 2x4

Projects for Indoor Living

GREAT 2x4
Projects for Indoor Living

Making Stylish Furniture from Standard Lumber

Stevie Henderson & Mark Baldwin

STERLING INNOVATION
An imprint of Sterling Publishing Co., Inc.

New York / London
www.sterlingpublishing.com

In Loving Memory of
Stevie P. Henderson
1943–2007

STERLING and the distinctive Sterling logo are registered trademarks of
Sterling Publishing Co., Inc.

Library of Congress Cataloging-in-Publication Data
Henderson, Stevie, 1943-2007
Great 2 x 4 projects for indoor living : making stylish furniture from standard lumber
/ Stevie Henderson and Mark Baldwin.
p. cm.
Includes index.
ISBN-13: 978-1-4027-5338-1
ISBN-10: 1-4027-5338-1
1. Furniture making--Amateurs' manuals. I. Baldwin, Mark, 1975- II. Title. III. Title: Great two by four
projects for indoor living. IV. Title: 2x4 projects for indoor living.
TT194.H4622 2008
684'.08--dc22

2007032208

2 4 6 8 10 9 7 5 3 1

Published 2008 by Sterling Publishing Co., Inc.
387 Park Avenue South, New York, NY 10016

© 2008 by Stevie Henderson and Mark Baldwin

This book is comprised of materials from the following Sterling/Lark books:
Great 2x4 Accessories for Your Home © 1999 by Stevie Henderson and Mark Baldwin
Great Looking 2x4 Furniture © 1996 by Stevie Henderson

Distributed in Canada by Sterling Publishing
C/o Canadian Manda Group, 165 Dufferin Street
Toronto, Ontario, Canada M6K 3H6
Distributed in the United Kingdom by GMC Distribution Services
Castle Place, 166 High Street, Lewes, East Sussex, England BN7 1XU
Distributed in Australia by Capricorn Link (Australia) Pty. Ltd.
P.O. Box 704, Windsor, NSW 2756, Australia

Sterling ISBN-13: 978-1-4027-5338-1
ISBN-10: 1-4027-5338-1

Design by StarGraphics Studio

For information about custom editions, special sales, premium and
corporate purchases, please contact Sterling Special Sales
Department at 800-805-5489 or specialsales@sterlingpublishing.com.

Contents

Home Office & Accessories 215

Introduction

This book was written with one clear goal in mind: to give readers who have longed to try their hand at woodworking a way to jump right in. If you think that woodworking is a mysterious pastime practiced only by kindly, gray-haired men with leather tool aprons and fifty years' practice, you're about to discover that you're wrong. Master woodworkers aren't the sole keepers of the flame. If you can imagine yourself cutting a board, hammering nails, and driving screws, you can work with wood. Although you probably won't be capable of making reproductions of Chippendale chairs in the first two weeks, you certainly will be able to construct good-looking, sturdy, and useful furniture and accessories for your home. Everyone has to have basic furniture—a bed, a table, and somewhere to sit. But the space becomes your own when you add an ottoman, a folding screen, a wooden valance, or a grandmother clock. The accessory pieces we added to this book are not essential to furnishing a home, but—we're willing to bet you'll find something in this book that you just have to have!

These projects, which range from incredibly simple to slightly more complex, are designed to eliminate the need for advanced woodworking skills. Many of them also take advantage of pre-made materials now available to the do-it-yourselfer—materials that make it easier to have fun while you learn. Why drive yourself crazy with complex wood-joinery techniques to make a cabinet door, when shutter doors are available at building-supply stores? Or worry about turning a table leg on a lathe when you can add a purchased finial to the end of a 4x4 instead? Woodworking—especially when you're first starting out—should be a pleasure, not a stress-inducing puzzle.

This was a particularly enjoyable book to put together, because the projects are just plain fun. It contains "bread and butter" projects—basic furniture that everyone needs and also what we call "icing on the cake" projects—pieces that add flair and style to your home and make it unique and inviting.

You've never used a saw before? Start by reading the first section of the book, where you'll find descriptions of basic tools and how to use them, advice on purchasing lumber and materials, and important safety tips. With the help of step-by-step instructions, detailed illustrations, and complete lists of required materials, you'll soon be standing back to admire your finished handiwork.

If you're an advanced woodworker with a workshop full of high-powered and high-priced stationary tools, don't despair. You, too, can make these projects! You may need to modify the instructions to accommodate your tools and knowledge, but this won't be difficult to do.

As experts already know, the best aspect of "doing-it-yourself" isn't just producing high-quality products for a very low price. It's the sense of accomplishment that making them yourself brings. Developing your skills won't take fifty years of practice, either. Why? Because woodworking skills and enthusiasm tend to build themselves. The more you work with wood, the more eager (and able) you'll be to tackle increasingly challenging projects and to enjoy the increasingly significant rewards.

Materials, Tools, & Techniques

Like every craft, woodworking has its own language and its own set of specialized tools, but rest assured. Learning to speak the language and use the tools is several thousand times easier than going to medical school or studying nuclear fission. Once in a rare while, of course, you'll run into an employee at a building-supply store or lumberyard who'd like to make you believe you're too young, too old, too stupid, or the wrong gender to practice "his" craft. Ignore folks like these, and head for the hundreds of others who haven't forgotten that they started out where you probably are now. You'll discover that most woodworkers who know their stuff are a remarkably helpful, humble, and friendly lot.

Read this section carefully. You won't find every answer to every question, but you will find the information you'll need to build your first several projects. By the time you've finished reading it, you'll be calling a circular saw a circular saw instead of "one of those electric cutting things with a blade that goes round and round," and you won't feel cheated when the 2x4s that you buy turn out to be 1½" thick and 3½" wide.

Materials

Lumber

Regardless of your skill level or the complexity of the chosen project, it's a good idea to have some basic knowledge about the characteristics of various types of wood and which woods are most suitable for the chosen project. Different wood types have different grain patterns, fiber density, odors, and appearances. On the most basic level, all woods are classified as either *hardwood* or *softwood*. Softwood is cut from coniferous trees (or evergreens), such as pine, redwood, and cedar. Softwood is a good choice for the projects in this book—projects designed for the beginning woodworker—as it is easier to cut, drill, and nail than hardwood and has the added advantage of being much less expensive.

Hardwood, on the other hand, comes from deciduous trees (trees that shed their leaves annually), such as maple, cherry, and walnut. Though we have constructed the projects in this book from white pine, a readily available softwood, you can certainly use any hardwood of your choice (see page 12 for more information on substituting hardwood).

For purposes of clarity, this book refers to each surface of a board by a specific name. The broadest part of a board is called a face; the narrow surface along the length of the board is an edge; and the smallest surfaces on the extremities of each board are the ends.

Buying Lumber

Softwood is sold in standard dimensional sizes (2x4, 1x4, and 1x12, for example), and in specific lengths (6, 8, and 10 feet are common lengths). When you are searching for specific sizes in your local hardware store, a bin labeled 2x4x6 contains 2x4s that are 6 feet in length.

A word about dimensions; Although it might appear that a 2x4 should be 2 inches thick and 4 inches wide, this is not the case. In fact, the term 2x4 describes the dimensions of the piece before it was planed to a smooth surface on all four sides. There is some method to the madness, however, and you can take comfort in knowing that all stock lumber is planed to the same dimensions—a 2x4 is (or very close to) 1½ inches thick and 3½ inches wide. See below for a chart lists nominal sizes and actual sizes for softwood stock lumber.

Nominal Size	Actual Size
1x2	³/₄"x1½"
1x3	³/₄"x2½"
1x4	³/₄"x3½"
1x6	³/₄"x5½"
1x8	³/₄"x7¼"
1x10	³/₄"x9¼"
1x12	³/₄"x11¼"
2x2	1½"x1½"
2x4	1½"x3½"
2x6	1½"x5½"
2x8	1½"x7¼"
2x10	1½"x9¼"
2x12	1½"x11¼"
4x4	3½"x3½"
4x6	3½"x5½"
6x6	5½"x5½"
8x8	7½"x7½"

Softwood is graded according to its quality. The higher the quality, the higher the price. Though it may be tempting to buy the highest quality wood, keep in mind that small imperfections can be covered with paint. Don't buy better quality than you need for the specific project. Softwood grades are as follows:

Common Grades

No. 1 COMMON contains knots and few imperfections, but should have no knotholes.
No. 2 COMMON is free of knotholes, but contains some knots.
No. 3 COMMON contains larger knots and small knotholes.
No. 4 COMMON is used far construction only. It contains large knotholes.
No. 5 COMMON is the lowest grade of lumber; it is used only when strength and appearance aren't important.

Select Grades

B AND BETTER (OR 1 AND 2 CLEAR) are the best and most expensive grades used for the finest furniture projects.
C SELECT may have a few small blemishes.
D SELECT is the lowest quality of the better board grades; it has imperfections that can be concealed with paint.

Select wood is higher quality than common wood and is more expensive. Clear boards come from the inner section of the tree, or the heartwood, and are nearly free of imperfections. Sapwood, or the outer portions of the tree, yields boards with more knots and other flaws.

Please read through the instructions and cutting list for your project before shopping for materials. Each materials list specifies the total number of linear feet of particular wood required to make the project. So if the total linear feet required is 40 feet, you can purchase five 8-foot length, four 10-foot lengths, and so on. When you arrive at the lumberyard or store, you may find that the 8-foot lengths of wood are of lesser quality than the 6-foot lengths. You could then buy seven 6-foot lengths and have a little left over, but you must first check to make certain that no single piece required by the project is over 6 feet long.

It is also wise to keep transportation abilities in mind. If you own (or can borrow) a pickup truck to transport your materials, board lengths are not a factor. But it's pretty difficult to get a 12-foot length of wood into a small car. Most building-supply stores will be happy to give you one free cut on in individual piece of lumber; some charge a fee.

Unless you have chosen a very expensive wood with which to build your project, it makes sense to slightly overbuy your materials. That way, if you do make a mistake, you have a reserve board to bail you out. Returning to the store for just one more board is frustrating, time consuming, and (depending upon how far you drive) sometimes more expensive than if you had purchased an extra board in the first place. We have built some overage into the materials list to accommodate squaring the piece and allowing for the width of saw cuts.

Selecting Lumber

Before purchasing any stock lumber, inspect each board for any defects and imperfections. It makes the trip to the lumber store more time consuming, but saves hours of frustration later. If the building-supply store will not allow you to hand-pick individual boards, consider purchasing the lumber elsewhere. Some defects in wood can be corrected, but such corrections are time consuming—and choosing the wood carefully in the first place is the best way to get blemish-free boards. There is no reason to buy unusable wood, regardless of how low the price.

If you plan to paint the wood, small knots or blemishes are acceptable. (Bear in mind also that small knots on the ends of boards can sometimes be cut off; be sure to purchase a large enough board to allow for the waste.) Large knotholes should be avoided; there is always the chance that they will fall out and leave a large hole behind.

Since some building-supply stores purchase wood from many different suppliers, the board widths may vary slightly between boards. Although this may seem to be a minor point, know that even $1/64$ of an inch difference may mean that pieces will not fit together properly.

To make sure the boards are all the same length, simply position the boards on top of each, other to make certain they are all exactly the same.

Another common problem with stock lumber is that it has a tendency to warp and bow. Though it is possible to straighten warped wood, purchasing straight wood is much easier. To check for warping or bowing, place one end of the board on the floor and look down the length of its face. Next, turn the board and look down its edge. By examining the board in this way, any warps or bows will be obvious.

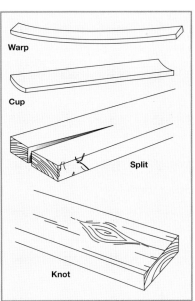

Warp

Cup

Split

Knot

Avoid split boards; check the ends as well as the rest of the board. Split boards do tend to separate lengthwise into two (unusable) boards. Again, it is possible to cut off end splits, but be sure you purchase enough wood to allow for the waste.

Substituting Hardwood

Any of the projects in the book can he built with hardwood, though you'll need to make some extra calculations to do so. Hardwood will resist scratches and dents much better than softwood, but it is more difficult to work with and significantly more expensive.

Because it is cut from logs as wide and as long as possible, hardwood is normally sold in random widths and lengths. Consequently, hardwood is sold by a measure called the *board foot*, which represents a piece of lumber 1 inch thick (or less), 12 inches wide, and 1 foot long. Board foot measurements usually indicate that the lumber is rough, not surfaced.

Hardwood thicknesses are measured in quarter inches; the standard thicknesses are $4/4$, $5/4$, $6/4$, and $8/4$ (pronounced "four-quarter," "five-quarter," and so forth, not "four-fourths").

To calculate board feet, multiply the thickness by the width in inches, then multiply the length in feet and divide by 12. A $4/4$ oak plank 6 inches wide and 10 feet long is 5 board feet (BF). The board-foot measurement is doubled for boards thicker than 1 inch. *Note:* Even if the boards you buy have been thickness-planed to $3/4$ inch, you pay for $4/4$ lumber.

Plywood

As you might expect, plywood is made from, several plies, or layers, of wood that are glued together. You can find two principal kinds of plywood: veneer-core and lumber-core. Because they are unattractive, the edge of veneer-core plywood must be either filled or covered. Lumber-core plywood is higher in quality, and the edges can be worked just as you would any solid wood.

Plywood is usually sold in sheets measuring 4 feet by 8 feet, though in some building-supply stores, it is available in half-sheets measuring 4 feet by 4 feet. A variety of thicknesses are available; the standard thicknesses are $1/8$, $1/4$, $3/8$, $1/2$, $5/8$, $3/4$ inch.

Another indicator of plywood quality is the grade of its outer veneer. You will find plywood in grades A through D, with A representing the best quality. In addition, each piece of plywood has two grades, one for each face. Thus, an A-C piece has one surface that is A quality and one that is C. Check also to see if plywood is designated exterior or interior. Exterior-grade has waterproof glue between the plies; do not use interior-grade plywood for outside projects, as it will warp and split when exposed to the elements for even a short period of time.

Finishes

Paint

One of the biggest advantages of painting your project is that paint will cover or camouflage most flaws in the wood. You will be surprised at how fabulous a not-so-attractive piece will look once you've applied a coat of high-quality paint. The downside is that wood needs to be thoroughly filled, sanded, and primed before you paint—which takes time and effort. If you plan to paint your project, you can buy a lower grade of wood.

Purchase high-quality paint—it pays off, since it looks much better and often requires less paint. When shopping for paint, look for special characteristics that protect local weather problems. For example, here in Florida, many paints protect against mildew, which occurs in areas with high humidity. (The paint store can sometimes add a mildew-resistant substance to regular paint.) Also look to see how long the paint is warranted.

Stain

If you plan to stain your project, you will need to make this decision before you purchase the wood. Buy boards that have few imperfections and similar grain patterns.

Stains have come a long way. They used to come only in shades of brown and be very difficult to apply evenly. These days, stains are available in a terrific variety of colors, from the palest white to the darkest black. They can be extremely translucent or nearly opaque. And best of all, most stains are now quite easy to apply, usually requiring only one coat.

Although most manufacturers suggest applying stain with a brush, we have found that a clean rag provides a very smooth, even appearance. The degree of success using this technique varies among different types of stains, so make sure you test first on a scrap piece of wood or on a surface of your project that will not show before you begin. Before using any product, read the instructions carefully and follow them explicitly.

FINISHING MATERIALS
Clockwise from left: wood filler and putty knife, assortment of finishes and stains, disposable foam brushes, and a natural-bristle brush

Brushes

Though some experts swear by expensive paintbrushes, we use foam brushes almost exclusively, since they are extremely cheap and can be thrown away after each use. This helps with cleanup and makes the entire process more simple. Look for the ones that have a smooth surface (like a cosmetic sponge) and a wooden handle. Don't buy the ones that look like kitchen sponges with visible holes on their surfaces.

A tip: If you need to interrupt the job temporarily, simply insert the brush into an airtight plastic sandwich bag. You can leave it there for several days, and it will remain pliable and ready to use.

Adhesives

Aliphatic resin, which is commonly marketed as wood glue or carpenter's glue, is the most widely used woodworking adhesive. The main consideration when using wood glue is quantity. Do not overdo it. If too much glue is used, the glue will squeeze out of the joint and drip onto your project when pressure is applied.

Apply a small ribbon of glue down the center of one surface then rub the adjoining surface against the ribbon to distribute the glue evenly. Coat both surfaces with a uniform, thin coating. Wipe off drips quickly with a damp cloth. If drips are allowed to dry on the surface of the wood, they will harden and require sanding to remove. Do not leave glue drips; they will not accept most stains and will always show up as a different color, even under a clear finish.

Fasteners

Nails

An assortment of screws, (top), nails (left), and brads (right)

The list of nail varieties is long: common, large flathead, duplexhead, and oval head are just a sampling. The type most commonly used in woodworking is the finish nail. Finish nails have a much smaller head than the common nail, making them easy to recess below the surface of the wood, or countersink. When a finish nail is countersunk, the small hole remaining on the surface of the wood is easily concealed with wood filler.

Nail sizes are designated by "penny" (abbreviated as "d"). A nail's penny size corresponds directly to its length, although the nail diameter is larger for longer nails. Finish nails range in length from 1 inch to 6 inches. An easy way to determine the penny size of a nail up to 3 inches (10d): take the length of the nail you need, subtract $^1/_2$ inch, and multiply by 4. For example, if you need a $2^1/_2$ inch nail, subtract $^1/_2$ inch, leaving 2. Next, multiply by 4. What you need is an 8-penny nail (8d). Refer to the table below for commonly used nail sizes:

Penny Size	Length (in inches)
2d	1
3d	$1^1/_4$
4d	$1^1/_2$
5d	$1^3/_4$
6d	2
7d	$2^1/_4$
8d	$2^1/_2$
9d	$2^3/_4$
10d	3
12d	$3^1/_4$
16d	$3^1/_2$
20d	4

A good general rule to follow when choosing a nail is to use a nail that will provide the greatest amount of holding power without penetrating the opposite surface. For example, if you are joining two 1x4s, each piece of wood is $^3/_4$ inch thick—a total of $1^1/_2$ inches of wood. For such a project, you should choose a $1^1/_4$-inch (3d) nail.

Keep in mind that nails driven at an angle provide more holding power than those driven straight into the wood. The term *toenailing* refers to the method of driving a nail into wood at an extreme angle to secure two pieces together. The most difficult part of toenailing comes when the nail is nearly into the wood and only the head and a bit of the shank are visible.

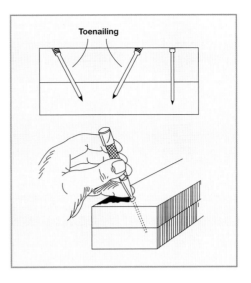

To avoid making hammer marks on the wood, hammer the nail into the piece until the head is still slightly above the surface. Then use a nail set to finish the job and countersink the nail (see illustration, right). Indeed, the best way to avoid leaving hammer marks on the wood is to use a nail set. The trick to using a nail set effectively is holding it in the proper manner. The set should be steadied with the hand by gripping it firmly with all four fingers and the thumb. Rest the little finger on the surface of the wood for added stability.

It is a good idea to predrill nail holes, especially if you are working with hardwood, a very narrow piece of softwood, or any other wood that has a tendency to split. Use a drill bit that is just barely smaller than the diameter of the nail, and drill a pilot hole about two-thirds the diameter of the nail.

Brads

Wire brads, which are a thinner and smaller version of finish nails, are extremely useful for attaching trim and molding, as well as for very small projects. They are designated in length in inches and wire gauge numbers from 11 to 20. The lower the gauge number, the larger the diameter.

Screws

Screws have more holding power than nails and have the additional advantage of being easily removed (when used without glue) at a later date. However, screws are more difficult to insert.

There are many kinds of screws. In woodworking, flathead Philips screws are most commonly used. This type of screw has a flat head that can be countersunk. It is most often labeled as a "drywallscrew" and can be driven with a power drill.

Screws are designed by length and diameter. As with nails, you want to use the longest screw possible that won't penetrate the opposite surface. Screw diameter is designated by gauge numbers, with the most common gauge numbers ranging from #2 to #16. Larger diameters have higher gauge numbers. The projects in this book use screws with gauge numbers from #6 to #10.

Do not be stingy with screws; that being said, you do not want to insert so many screws into your project that the metal outweighs the wood. If there is any chance that the joint is not secure, add extra screws. Your project, after all, may need to hold up to several moves over the course of the years, which will place additional strain on the joints.

It is possible to countersink a screw in very soft wood simply by driving it with a power drill. However, the resulting surface hole must be covered, either with wood filler or by predrilling the screw hole and inserting a wood plug on top of the countersunk screw head.

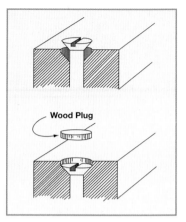

Predrilling is normally a two-step operation. First drill the larger, countersunk portion at a diameter just larger than the diameter of the screw head and deep enough to accommodate it. If a wood plug is to be used, use a bit with the same diameter as the plug. Next, drill the pilot hole in the center of the larger hole, using a drill bit the same diameter as the solid portionof the screw (minus the threads). If you use the same size screws on a regular basis, you may wish to invest in a combination pilot/countersink bit for your drill, which will perform both functions at the same time.

Wood plugs can be purchased, or you can cut your own by slicing a wooden dowel. The only disadvantage to plugs you make is that the plug will show the end grain and will be visible if the wood is stained. An alternative is to cut wood plugs using a plug cutter, but that method requires a drill press.

Screws can be inserted at an angle, the same way that nails are, to toenail two pieces of wood together (see page 15). It takes a little practice, but inserting a screw at an angle gets easier. A drill or a screw starter makes this process easier by beginning the screw hole.

Staple Guns & Staples

Staples are light-duty fasteners that are often used to attach fabric to wood. It is a good idea to invest in a staple gun—it's a useful tool to have around the house for a variety of jobs. They are available in a variety of sizes, styles, and price ranges. Electric staple guns are handy, to be sure, but a simple, heavy-duty gun is a good beginning. Purchase staples in a variety of lengths to accommodate different thicknesses of wood.

Tools
Work Surface

A smooth and level work surface is essential in woodworking. It is nearly impossible to get table legs perfectly even on an uneven surface. Your work surface does not have to be elaborate or professional-quality (or even attractive)—it just has to be level and even. It can be as simple as an old, unpaneled door or a piece of thick plywood.

To make sure your work surface is level, simply set a long level in various spots on the surface, turning it so that it faces several directions. In addition, stand back and sight along the surface to make sure it isn't twisted. If you need to lift the surface to make it perfectly level, attach a shim with glue and nails or screws.

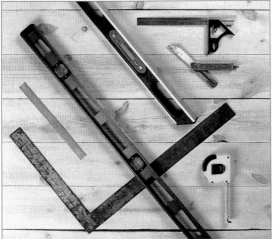

MEASURING TOOLS

Clockwise from top right: combination square, adjustable bevel, carpenter's square, measuring tape, conventional level, straightedge, and electronic level

CUTTING TOOLS

Clockwise from top: squaring jig, jigsaw, miter box and saw, backsaw, coping saw and blades, carpenter's handsaw, and circular saw

Measuring Tools

An **adjustable bevel** is a useful measuring tool; it helps establish bevel angles, and checks and transfers bevels and mitered ends. It has a steel blade that pivots and slides within a handle, and can be locked into position to form an angle.

Squares are important tools in woodworking, as they make it easier to mark an accurate cutting line and to obtain a right angle. They are also useful for performing many additional functions, such as checking the outer or inner squareness of a joint and guiding a saw through a cut. The most commonly used types are the combination square and the framing square (or carpenter's square).

A **straightedge**, or a steel ruler 12 to 24 inches long, is a great tool to have on hand for quick measurements.

A **wide steel tape rule** works much better than a narrow tape, because its rigidity allows for more accurate cuts. (A narrow tape will bend more easily along the length of the board.)

Cutting Tools

A **circular saw** has a blade that can be adjusted to cut a 90° angle, a 45° angle, or any angle in between. It is probably the most popular power cutting tool.

A **crosscut saw** is made for crosscutting, or cutting across the width (and the grain) of the wood. They are available with 7 through 12 points per inch, depending on how coarse or fine you wish the cut to be. The greater the number, the smoother (and slower) the cut.

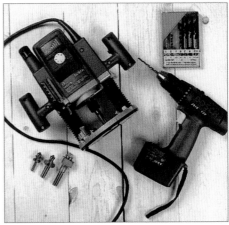

Left: router and bits. Right: battery operated power drill with drill bits

A **rip saw** has teeth designed for ripping, or cutting along the length of the board (with the grain). It comes with 4¹⁄₂ though 7 points per inch, the latter being the smoothest cut.

Although there are **saw blades** designed specifically for ripping and crosscutting, the most practical blade for general woodworking projects (such as the ones in this book) is the combination blade, which rips and crosscuts with equal ease. Carbide-tipped blades are more expensive, but well worth the cost, since they last much longer than regular blades.

The hand held **jigsaw**, or **saber saw**, is used to cut curves, shapes, and large hole in panels or boards up to 1¹⁄₂ inches in thickness. Its cutting action comes from a narrow reciprocating "bayonet" blade that moves up and down very quickly. The most useful jigsaws have a variable speed control and an orbital blade action, which swings the cutting edge forward into the work and back again during the blade's up-and-down cycle—and a dust blower that keeps the sawdust away from the cut.

A **power miter saw** is one of our favorite tools. It can be used to efficiently cut boards to length and can be adjusted both horizontally and vertically from 0° to 45°. It is especially useful for cutting 45° miters, though an inexpensive miter box and saw also work for this purpose.

Chisels are useful for performing unique woodworking tasks, such as hollowing out a small section of wood. Using chisels takes some practice, but is worth the effort. Make sure your chisels are sharp and that you have at least two: one very narrow one and one about ¹⁄₂ inch wide.

A **plane** is useful for shaving a small section of wood from the end or the edge of a board when the need arises. Buy a high-quality plane and keep it very sharp. Practice with it until you feel comfortable with cutting technique.

An assortment of screwdrivers

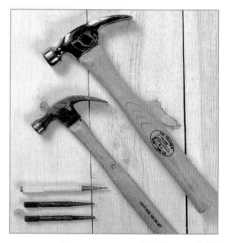

An assortment of nail sets (left) and hammers (right)

Clamps

You will need a variety of clamps to make the projects in this book. Clamps are valuable tools in assembling projects, because they apply pressure and hold joints together until the glue sets. Clamps are generally used in pairs, so always buy two of any particular style of clamp.

Clamps make working alone much easier, since they allow a single person to assemble a large project. A new type of clamp is now available that can be operated with one hand. This type, which comes in a variety of lengths, looks similar to a regular bar clamp (see below), but instead of tightening it by turning a screw mechanism, you squeeze its double handle as you would that of a caulk gun. They are easy to use, work well, and have a quick-release mechanism.

When working with clamps, always insert a scrap piece of wood between the clamp and your work to act as a cushion, especially when working with softwoods. This technique prevents clamp marks on the surface of the wood.

Old-fashioned **wood clamps** are great, since they can be adjusted to clamp offsetting surfaces. You should have several around your workshop to use for this purpose.

Spring Clamps are useful when you need to quickly hold a piece of wood while you saw or keep two thin boards positioned. The 2-inch size is most useful because yon can operate it with one hand.

Bar clamps and **pipe clamps** are useful for holding assemblies together temporarily while you add the fastener. They can also be used to apply pressure to laminates. Bar clamps and pipe clamps look very similar and function in essentially the same way, though pipe clamps are significantly less expensive. The fittings for pipe clamps are sold separately—and they can be used for various lengths of pipe. You can also purchase rubber "shoes" that fit over the pipe-clamp fittings, which will prevent clamp marks on wood. Remember to put pieces of plastic or wax paper between the pipes and any glue lines they come in contact with, because a chemical reaction between the glue and the pipe can leave a dark stain on the surface of the wood.

Web clamps, also called **band clamps**, are used for clamping such things as chairs, or drawers, where a uniform pressure needs to be exerted completely around a project. They consist of a continuous band with an attached metal mechanism that can be ratcheted to pull the band tightly around the object.

C Clamps are inexpensive and quite useful for a number of woodworking tasks. They can hold two thicknesses of wood together, secure a piece of wood to a work surface, and perform many other functions. One end of the C-shaped frame is fixed, and the other end is fitted with a threaded rod and swivel pad that can be clamped tightly across an opening ranging from zero to several inches or more, depending on the size of the clamp.

An assortment of chisels and a plane (center)

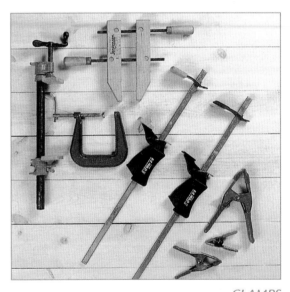

CLAMPS
Clockwise from top: wood clamps, light-duty bar clamps, spring clamps, pipe clamp, and C clamp (center)

Sanding Tools

There are variety of options for sanding projects. Of course, any wood surface can be sanded by hand, though hand-sanding may prove-time consuming. For sanding by hand, any inexpensive plastic sanding block will work just fine on a level surface. An even more inexpensive version is to wrap a block of wood with a piece of sandpaper. For sanding moldings, curves, or any other small spaces, wrap a pencil or other appropriately sized object with sandpaper.

SANDING TOOLS

Clockwise from top right: orbital sander, finishing sander, an assortment of sandpaper, sanding block (center), and belt sander

The amount of sanding required for any given project depends on, to a large degree, the intended use of the project and the kind of finish you plan to use. If you prefer a rustic look, the project need not be sanded completely smooth. (However, a rustic chair requires more sanding than a rustic table, since someone will be sitting on it.)

An **orbital sander** is useful for beginning the sanding process, but it may leave circular marks that must be sanded out by hand.

A **finishing sander** is probably the most practical power sander for furniture projects. It can smooth the surface of the wood very quickly, and it does not leave circular marks.

For large jobs, a **belt sander** may be the best choice. It sands quickly, but it is difficult to control on softwood, such as pine. Because of its power, a belt sander can easily gouge softwood or, if you don't watch carefully, it can remove more of the wood than you wish.

Regardless of the sanding tool you choose, begin sanding with coarse grit and gradually progress to sandpaper with a fine grit. An open-coat aluminum oxide paper is best for sanding both softwoods and hardwoods. Throw sandpaper away as soon as it quits working; there's no sense prolonging the job to save a few cents.

Tools Checklist

The Essentials

- Work surface that is smooth and level
- Measuring tools: tape measure, level, and combination square
- Hammers and nails: large hammer, small hammer, tack hammer, and nail set
- Screwdrivers (hand and/or power): assortment of flathead and Phillips sizes
- Saws: combination saw (or ripsaw and crosscut saw), circular saw, and a selection of blades
- Drill: hand or power drill and a variety of bits
- Clamps: two "quick clamps," two wood hand clamps, and a few 2-inch spring clamps
- Sanding tools: sanding block and an assortment of sandpaper (from fine to coarse)

Optional Tools

- Measuring tools: framing square
- Saws: saber saw, circular saw, and a selection of blades
- Chisels: $1/4$-inch, $3/4$-inch, and 1-inch wide
- Finishing sander
- Router
- Safety equipment: goggles and dust mask (for use with power tools)
- Miter box
- Woodworking vise or portable vise/work table
- Clamps: two C clamps, a web clamp, two light-duty bar clamps, and two pipe clamps

Advanced Tools

- Belt Sander
- Table saw
- Band saw
- Drill press

Techniques

Measuring Lumber

Nothing is more frustrating than gathering the necessary materials and embarking upon a project only to find that inaccurate cutting has made it impossible for the pieces to fit together properly—and thus for the project to look right. Woodworking projects, regardless of the skill level, go much more smoothly if you follow the old adage "measure twice-cut once."

The best way to make good cuts is to measure accurately. There are a number of tools that will help with this: a wide steel tape rule, a square, and a variety of saws (see page 16 for more information on choosing tools). It is essential that you buy or borrow quality tools. Whatever tools you choose, use the same measuring device throughout the project, as two instruments may vary enough to make a difference.

Cutting Lumber

The most important rule in cutting lumber is to cut the longest piece first. If you botch the cut, then you can still cut smaller pieces from the remaining board. It is also important to re-examine each piece of lumber one last time before you cut; this is useful in spotting end splits or knots that can be cut off.

If you plan carefully, you can cut so that all the best sides of the wood are facing out—this makes for the best possible use of your wood, and saves you from having to fill and sand any imperfections after the project is finished.

Every time you use a blade to cut wood, the blade removes an amount of wood equal to the width of its saw blade called the *kerf*. After you have precisely measured for a cut and marked it with a sharp pencil, set the saw so that the blade will exactly remove the waste side of the mark. Cut along the mark, trying to remove just half of your pencil line.

There are two types of cuts that can be made to a piece of wood: a rip or a crosscut. A rip is a cut along the length of the board, and a crosscut is a cut across the width of the board. There are specific hand tools for each procedure; see page 16 for detailed information on these cutting tools.

When you are cutting either lumber or plywood, note the type of cut that your tool is making, and use it to your advantage. For example circular saws and jigsaws cut on the upstroke, so they may leave ragged edges on the upper surface of the wood. When using these saws, you should position the wood with the better surface facing down when cutting.

There is an accurate method for cutting a length of wood to fit between two existing pieces in an assembly. After you square off the wood you are cutting, simply hold it up to the actual space, and mark it for cutting.

Making Wood Joints

Though there are hundreds of different kinds of wood joints—from plain butt joints to incredibly intricate and complex joints the projects in this book are constructed with only the simplest joints, secured with glue and either nails or screws. No matter what kind of joint you're making, it is advisable to use both glue and fasteners (nails or screws) whenever possible. The only exception, when you may want to omit the glue, is on joints that you wish to disassemble at a later date.

Butt Joints

The simplest of joints, butt joints are formed when one board abuts another at a right angle. Though butt joints are easy, they offer the least amount of holding power of any joint and must be reinforced with a fastener, usually screws.

Edge-to-Edge Joint

Edge-to-edge joints are used when laminating boards together edge to edge to obtain a wider piece of wood. To create an edge-to-edge joint, a minuscule amount of wood should be ripped from, the first edge of each board in order to ensure a perfect meeting between boards. The boards should be flipped widthwise and the second edge ripped.

Once the edges of the boards have been ripped, apply glue to the adjoining edges and clamp the boards together. Apply even clamping pressure along the length of the piece. Wipe off any excess glue that is squeezed out in the clamping process. The boards should be firmly clamped, but not so tightly that all of the glue is forced out or that the lamination starts to bow

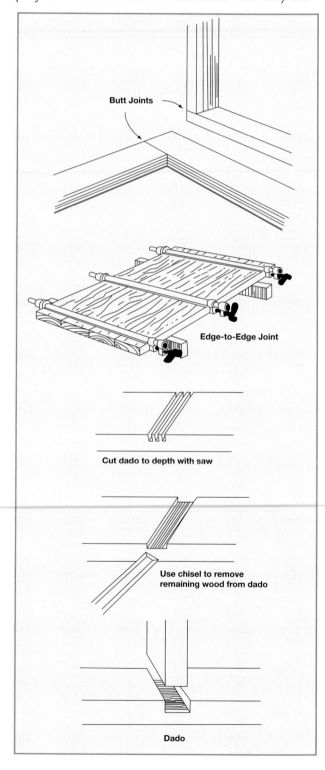

Butt Joints

Edge-to-Edge Joint

Cut dado to depth with saw

Use chisel to remove remaining wood from dado

Dado

across its width. On a long lamination, extra boards may be placed across the width above and below the lamination. The extra boards are then clamped, with C clamps or wood clamps. (It is a good idea to place a piece of plastic or wax paper between the work piece and any wood clamped across the joints; this will prevent the clamped board from becoming a permanent part of the finished lamination.)

Dado

A dado is a groove cut in the face of one board to accommodate the thickness of another board. It can be cut with a handsaw and a chisel (see below), with a router, or with a dado set on a table saw.

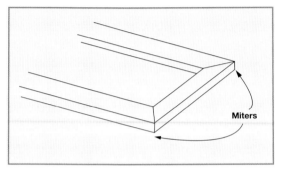

Miters

Miter

A miter is an angle cut across the width of a board. It is used to join the ends of two pieces of wood at an angle without exposing the end grain of either piece. A mitered joint must also be reinforced with nails or screws and is most often cut to 45°. Two boards mitered to 45° angles are then used to construct a right angle.

The most important consideration when making miters is careful measurement. When cutting and applying molding, begin at one end, cut the first piece and attach it. Then cut the first angle on the second piece, hold it in place, and mark the cut (and the direction of that cut) on the other end. Since you are usually switching directions of 45° on each successive cut, this method avoids confusion. Attach the second piece, and continue the process for each subsequent piece. A helpful tip to make your miter joints look more perfect than they are: Firmly rub the length of the completed joint with the side of a pencil to smooth the two edges together.

Miters on Crown Moldings

Crown molding, which have curves on one face and two bevels on the other, can be tricky to miter. We have come up with a simple, shop-made jig to make this process much easier. To make the fabulous Crown Molding Mitering Jig, follow these steps:

1 Cut two bases from 1x6 pine, each measuring 24 inches long.

2 Place one base on a level surface, as shown in *figure 1*.

3 Place the second base on edge against one edge of the first base, as shown in *figure 1*. Apply glue to the meeting surfaces, and screw through the second base into the edge of the first base. Use $1^5/8$-inch screw spaced about every 4 inches.

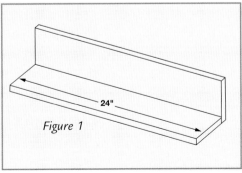

24"

Figure 1

If you don't reload your stamp with paint the second time you use it, the image will be lighter and will produce a different look. Using two different colors of paint on the same stamp also gives an interesting contrast. Or try stamping with one color first, then clean your stamp and use the same stamp with a different color, as we did with the Folding Screen (page 237).

You can also create stamps by cutting up ordinary commercial sponges, as we did for the Wooden Window Valance (page 110). For that project, we cut a square out of a dishwashing sponge, then used the sponge to stamp.

SAFETY EQUIPMENT
Clockwise from top left:
ear protectors,
commercial first-aid kit,
safety goggles, safety
glasses, and dust mask

Safety

Woodworking, particularly working with power tools, can be very dangerous. It is not uncommon for woodworkers to have missing digits. It pays to treat power tools with respect— and be a little scared of them. Keep a first-aid kit and a phone handy. Read the instructions that are provided with every tool and follow them religiously. The instructions in this book are written for the beginner using hand tools and must be altered when using power tools. Never attempt a maneuver that is not appropriate to the power tool you are using. Misuse of power tool equipment can lead to serious injury to yourself or damage to the tool.

When using power tools, it is essential to remember that you should never take your eyes off what you are doing. Always concentrate on the work at hand, and take the necessary safety precautions as outlined in the tool's owner's manual. Just a moment of lost concentration or not following the safety rules can result in frightful consequences. Develop the habit of avoiding the path of the saw; do not stand directly behind it or directly in front of it. Power saws can flip a piece of wood back at you with incredible force.

Safety goggles or glasses should be worn at all times when working with wood. If you manage to avoid just one splinter aimed at your eye, you will be happy you bothered. Wearing a dust mask is also a good idea, since sawdust can be very irritating to your eyes and your lungs. There are several types of dust masks available, from a simple paper mask to those with replaceable filters.

Once you've taken steps to protect your digits, your eyes, and your lungs, invest in a pair of earplugs. Prolonged exposure to loud noise—like that from a circular saw, for example—can have harmful effects on your hearing.

One last plug for using protective gear: Safe practice in the workshop allows you to insulate yourself from the irritating aspects of woodworking, and to concentrate better on (and enjoy more fully) the work at hand.

The Projects

You're anxious to get started on your first project, to buy the lumber, then begin cutting and hammering and building something fabulous. Take just a few minutes more to read this section. We've included some basic information on how the instructions are organized—as well as a few tips that will save you time, money, and frustration.

Skill Level

This is a book designed for beginning woodworkers, although experienced woodworkers will enjoy building the projects, too. If we didn't think someone new to woodworking could handle all the projects, we wouldn't have included all of them in the book. But some of the projects demand more time, patience, and technique to accomplish than others. As is true of other skills, woodworking skills are developed with practice. We suggest that you begin by constructing one or two of the quick-to-build projects. You will soon acquire the necessary skills and confidence to tackle projects that are more challenging.

Special Tools & Techniques

When applicable, we have provided a list of special tools that you may not have and techniques that you may need to learn. Check the list before you go shopping. If it calls for a staple gun and you don't own one, you need to decide whether to purchase (or borrow) a staple gun or select another project. If the project calls for dados and you aren't familiar with the term, read through that portion of the techniques section before you begin the project.

If you are an advanced woodworker who possesses large stationary power tools, it is particularly important to read through the project instructions before beginning, since you will probably want to modify the procedures to accommodate your advanced knowledge and tools. Bear in mind that these instructions are written for very basic tools, and some techniques may need to be "translated" in order to use your tools safely. For instance, a dado may be cut by hand, on a table saw, or with a router, but each of these methods requires a different setup and specific knowledge of the tools involved. Know the capabilities of your tools, and don't exceed them.

Materials

The list of materials for each project specifies in linear feet the amount of wood you will need. Where we have specified pine, we simply mean a decent grade of dimensional lumber. Feel free to use whatever lumber is more readily available in your area. We have allowed slight overage in the number of feet required, to square the ends of each board and to cover waste, but it is always prudent to overbuy slightly. A trip back to the store to buy another 2x4 is frustrating.

For purposes of clarity in the project instructions, each board surface has been named. The broadest board surface is called its face, and the narrow surface along the length is its edge. The ends, obviously, are the smallest surfaces at each end of the board.

Hardware

We have also specified the number of nails, screws, and other hardware you will need for the project you have chosen. We recognize that you will purchase nails and screws by the box, and will not actually buy "12 nails," but our total will give you a reference amount. Again, it is always prudent to have extra supplies on hand.

Cutting List

We have provided an exact guide for cutting each piece of wood for your project. Don't cut all the pieces right away. The instructions will walk you through cutting each piece as it is required in the building process. Do, however, read through the cutting list before you shop for your materials. If your project calls for an 8-foot length, you shouldn't purchase all your 1x4s in 6-foot lengths.

Inspect each piece of wood before you buy it. Avoid buying wood that is warped, twisted, or cupped. The easiest way to check a board is to place one end on the floor and look down the length of its face. Then turn the board and look down its edge. Any unwanted curves will be obvious immediately. See page 9 for more information on inspecting and purchasing lumber.

Also keep in mind that you will have to transport the lumber home. If your project requires 10-foot lengths of wood, and you drive a small car, call a friend to borrow a pickup truck or have the wood delivered. It is also important to consider how you want to finish the surface of the project. Lower grades of wood can be used if you plan to paint, because wood filler and paint will cover many imperfections. If you plan to stain the wood, choose a better grade and pick boards with similar grain patterns.

A cutting hint: Cut the longest project pieces first. If you miscut, you'll still have plenty of wood to cut another piece. Pay some attention to the size of waste wood. Try to produce cutoffs that can be used for other pieces in the project.

Before You Begin

Read and review all the instructions carefully, and visualize the process before you begin. The more you understand about the project you are going to make and how the process should proceed, the smoother the work will go. Woodworking is a step-by-step process, in which one step must be completed before the next one is begun. The slightest error in one step can drastically change the outcome of a project. If you understand where the next piece goes and cut it just before you use it, you can check to make sure that your assembly is truly accurate and adjust any small imperfections.

You will not avoid making mistakes in woodworking. The key is to learn from them. Consider woodworking to be a constantly evolving process. If you slip up several times in a row, take a break and come back to it. Your projects will turn out better, and you will be a safer and more satisfied woodworker.

Living Room
& Hallway

Butler's Chest

Because it's designed to suit a variety of purposes, this butler's chest (see page 33) is a piece of furniture that absolutely anyone can appreciate. Used by itself, it can serve as an end table or can befit under a window. Two chests placed back-to-back form a great-looking coffee table. For extra storage space, you can even stack two or three chests on top of one another.

Special Tools & Techniques

- Beveling
- Mitering

Materials

- 9 linear feet of 1x3 pine
- 10 linear feet of 1x4 pine
- 16 linear feet of 2x4 pine
- 1 piece of $^1/_4$"-thick plywood, 14"x25"
- 1 sheet of $^3/_4$"-thick plywood, 4'x 8'
- 20 linear feet of $^3/_4$"-wide decorative molding

Hardware

- Approximately 20 #6x$^3/_4$" flathead wood screws
- Approximately 100 #6x1$^1/_4$" flathead wood screws
- Approximately 20 #6x2" flathead wood screws
- Approximately 20 #6x2$^1/_2$" flathead wood screws
- Approximately 30 wire brads
- 4 offset door hinges
- 2 decorative cabinet-door pulls

Cutting List

Code	Description	Qty.	Material	Dimensions
A	Long Inner Support	4	2x4 pine	34$^1/_2$" long
B	Short Inner Support	4	2x4 pine	12$^1/_2$" long
C	Side	2	$^3/_4$" plywood	16$^1/_4$"x20$^1/_2$"
D	Back	1	$^3/_4$" plywood	20$^1/_2$"x36"
E	Vertical Trim	3	1x4 pine	20$^1/_2$" long
F	Horizontal Trim	4	1x4 pine	12$^3/_4$" long
G	Top/Bottom	2	$^3/_4$" plywood	18"x38"
H	Cabinet Door	2	$^1/_4$" plywood	12$^1/_4$"x13"
I	Top/Bottom Trim	4	1x3 pine	14$^1/_4$" long
J	Side Trim	4	1x3 pine	10" long

Making the Inner Frame

1 The inner frame of the butler's chest, which is covered with $^3/_4$"-thick plywood, consists of two rectangular inner support assemblies connected to each other by two sides and a back. Start by cutting four long inner supports (A) from 2x4 pine, each measuring 34$^1/_2$" long.

2 Cut four short inner supports (B) horn 2x4 pine, each measuring 12$^1/_2$" long.

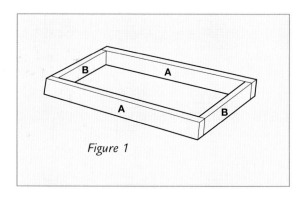

Figure 1

3 Place two long inner supports (A) on a level surface, parallel to each other, on edge, and 12¹/₂" apart. Fit two short inner supports (B) between the two long inner supports (A), as shown in *figure 1* on page 32. Glue the supports together and insert two 2¹/₂" screws through the long inner supports (A) into the ends of the short inner supports (B) at each joint. You now have one inner support assembly.

4 Repeat Step 3, using the remaining two short inner supports (B) and two long inner supports (A) to construct a second inner support assembly.

Adding the Sides and Back

1 Cut two 16¹/₄"x20¹/₂" sides (C) from ³/₄"-thick plywood.

2 Bevel one 20¹/₂"-long edge of each side (C) at a 45-degree angle, as shown in *figure 2* on page 34.

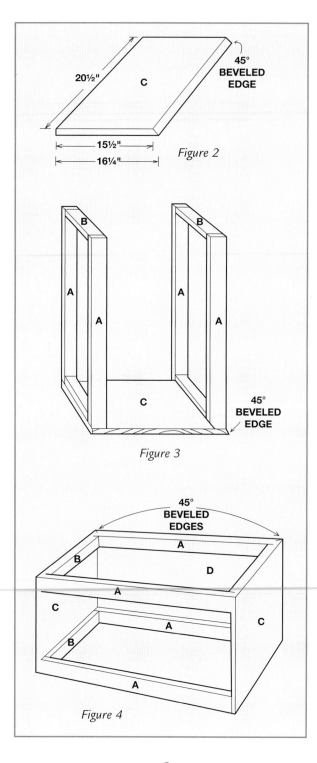

20½"

C

45°
BEVELED
EDGE

15½"

16¼"

Figure 2

Figure 3

B   B

A   A

A   A

C

45°
BEVELED
EDGE

45°
BEVELED
EDGES

A

B   D

A

C   C

A

B

A

Figure 4

3 Glue one side (C) to the two inner support assemblies, as shown in *figure 3*. Note that the two assemblies fit flush with the 15½"-long, non-beveled edge of the side (C) and that the beveled portion of the side (C) extends past the assemblies. Secure with 2" screws inserted through the side (C) and into each of the assemblies; space the screws about 4" apart.

4 Repeat Step 3 to attach the remaining side (C) to the opposite side of the inner support assemblies.

5 Cut one 20½"x36" back (D) from ³/₄"- thick plywood.

6 Bevel each of the 20½"-long edges of the back (D) at a 45-degree angle, in the same manner that you did on one edge of each side (C).

7 Glue the back (D) over the beveled edges of the sides (C), matching the bevels as shown in *figure 4*. Insert 1¹/₄" screws, spaced about 6" apart, through the back (D) and into both of the long inner supports (A).

Adding the Front Trim

1 Cut three 20¹/₂"-long vertical trim pieces (E) from 1x4 pine.

2 Glue one vertical trim piece (E) to the left side of the cabinet, as shown in *figure 5* on page 35, and insert 1¹/₄" screws, spaced about 6" apart, through the vertical trim piece (E) and into the long inner supports (A) and the edge of the side (C).

3 Repeat Step 2 to attach a second vertical trim piece (E) to the right side of the cabinet.

4 Attach the third vertical trim piece (E) in the center of the cabinet, as shown in *figure 5* on page 35, inserting two 1¹/₄" screws through the top and bottom of the vertical trim piece (E) into the long inner supports (A) at each joint. Note that the spacing between the vertical trim pieces (E) should be exactly 12³/₄".

5 Cut four 12³/₄"-long horizontal trim pieces (F) from 1x4 pine.

6 Using *figure 5* on page 35 as a guide, glue the four horizontal trim pieces (F) flush with the top and bottom of the cabinet, between the vertical trim pieces (E). Secure with three 1¹/₄" screws driven through each of the four horizontal trim pieces (F). Note that the opening between the top and bottom horizontal trim pieces (F) should be exactly 12³/₄"x13¹/₂".

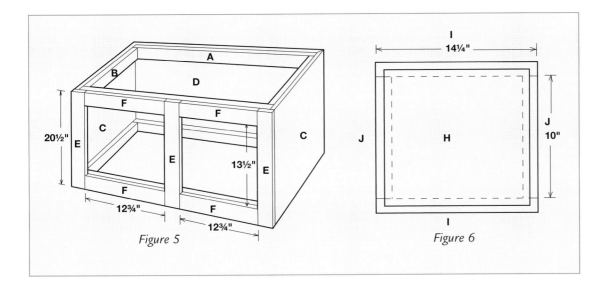

Figure 5

Figure 6

Adding the Top & Bottom

1 Cut two 18"x38" top/bottom pieces (G) from ³/₄"-thick plywood.

2 Center one top/bottom (G) over the cabinet assembly so that it's flush with the edge of the back (D) and overhangs by 1" at the front and at each side. Glue the top/bottom (G) in place and insert 1¹/₄" screws through it and into the inner support assemblies, spacing the screws about 6" apart.

3 Turn the cabinet upside-down and repeat Step 2 to attach the remaining top/bottom (G) to it.

4 To cover the exposed edges and ends of the plywood top/bottom pieces (G), cut and fit ³/₄"-wide decorative molding, mitering the molding at the corners. Glue the molding in place and secure with wire brads spaced about 6" apart.

Making the Cabinet Doors

1 The cabinet doors are nothing more than pieces of ¹/₄"-thick plywood trimmed with borders of 1x3 pine. They're easy to make, but do be certain that the finished doors are perfectly square. Start by cutting two 12¹/₄"x13" cabinet door pieces (H) from ¹/₄"-thick plywood.

2 Cut four 14¹/₄" long top/bottom trim pieces (I) from 1x3 pine.

3 Cut four side trim pieces (J) from 1x3 pine, each measuring 10" long.

4 Place two top/bottom trim pieces (I) and two side trim pieces (J) on a level surface, as shown in figure 6. Center the cabinet door (H) over the trim pieces. There should be a 1"-wide

border of trim visible along each of the four edges of the cabinet door (H). Glue the pieces together and insert $^3/_4$" screws through the door (H) and into the trim pieces, spacing the screws about 4" apart.

5 Repeat Step 4 to assemble the second cabinet door.

Finishing

1 Fill any cracks, crevices, or holes with wood filler.

2 Sand all surfaces thoroughly.

3 Paint or stain the cabinet and doors the color of your choice.

4 Install the hinges on each of the doors, first measuring carefully to ensure that the hinges are positioned the same distance from the top and bottom of each door.

5 Have someone help you support the doors while you hold them over the door openings. Line up each door evenly with the door next to it and make sure that neither door scrapes any surface of its opening. Then attach the remaining sides of the hinges to the cabinet.

6 Attach the pulls to each of the cabinet doors, spacing them evenly and aligning them with each other.

Occasional Table

Everyone can use an extra table somewhere in the house, and because this occasional table is only 21" high and about 24" square, it will fit almost anywhere, too. If you have enough space, make a couple of these tables and place them side-by-side to create a good-looking coffee table.

Special Tools & Techniques

- Bar clamps
- Mitering

Materials

- 18 linear feet of 1x4 pine
- 7 linear feet of 1x6 pine
- 1 piece of laminated pine, 17"x17"
- 4 table legs, each 20" long

Hardware

- Approximately 40 #6x1¼" flathead wood screws
- Approximately 8 #10x3" flathead wood screws

*Notes on Materials

The center top (A) of this occasional table is made from laminated pine boards. Most building-supply stores sell sections of wood that have already been laminated. You can laminate the boards yourself, of course, but we don't recommend doing so unless you're an experienced woodworker and own the necessary tools. The monetary savings aren't that significant, and you'll save a lot of time by purchasing the laminated pine.

If you don't have a lathe or don't want to turn the legs yourself, just purchase four turned legs from a building-supply store. The shape of the legs isn't important, but the four faces at the top of each one must be flat in order to provide proper connections for the rails that abut them.

Cutting List

Code	Description	Qty.	Material	Dimensions
A	Center Top	1	Laminated	17"x17" pine
B	Top Trim	4	1x4 pine	24" long
C	Long Base	2	1x6 pine	24" long
D	Short Base	2	1x6 pine	13" long
E	Leg	4	Purchased	20" long
F	Rail	4	1x4 pine	Cut to fit (approx.16¾" long)
G	Corner Support	4	1x4 pine	10" long

Constructing the Table Top

1 Cut one 17"x17" center top (A) from laminated pine.

2 Cut four 24"-long top trim pieces (B) from 1x4 pine.

3 Set each top trim piece (B) on its face and miter each end of all four pieces at a 45-degree angle, as shown in *figure 1*. When you're finished, one edge of each top trim piece should be 17" long and the opposite edge should be 24" long.

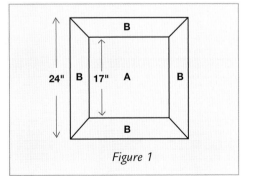

Figure 1

4 Glue and clamp the top trim pieces (B) to the edges of the table top (A) and leave the assembly undisturbed for at least 24 hours. The framed top should measure 24"x24".

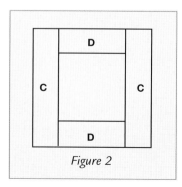

Figure 2

Constructing the Base Frame and Legs

1 Cut two long base pieces (C) from 1x6 pine, each 24" long.

2 Cut two short base pieces (D) from 1x6 pine, each 13" long.

3 To assemble the base frame, place the two long base pieces (C) on a level surface, parallel to each other and 13" apart. Place the two short base pieces (D) between the long base pieces (C) to form a 24"x24" square, as shown in *figure 2*. Glue and clamp the four pieces together. Leave the assembly undisturbed for at least 24 hours.

4 To add the four 20"-long legs, you must first center each one in a corner of the base frame. To locate the center point for a leg, draw a line across a long base piece (C) 5¹⁄₂" from the end, as shown in *figure 3*, to form a 5¹⁄₂"x5¹⁄₂" square. Then draw two lines to connect each set of opposite corners in that square. The inter section of these two lines is the center point for the leg.

5 Most purchased legs come with a metal screw in the center of the top of the leg. At the marked center point on the long base (C), drill a hole slightly smaller in diameter than the metal screw. Apply glue to the meeting surfaces and hand-screw the leg (E) into the drilled hole. Make certain that the leg is positioned so that the flat faces at its top are parallel to the edges of the table.

6 Repeat Step 5 to attach the remaining three legs (E) to the other three corners of the base frame.

7 Make certain that all four legs (E) are perfectly straight. Then let the assembly dry overnight until the glue sets.

8 To reinforce the leg joints, turn the base assembly right-side up. Insert two 3" screws through the each long base (C) and into each leg (E).

Adding the Rails

1 Before cutting the four rails (F) from 1x3 pine, measure the distance between each set of table legs. This measurement will vary, depending upon the diameter of the legs you purchased. Then cut each rail piece (F) to that length.

2 Glue one rail (F) between each set of two adjacent legs (E), as shown in *figure 4*. Then insert 1¹⁄₄" screws, spaced 6" apart, through the long bases (C) and short bases (D) and into the edges of the rails (F).

3 Cut four 10"-long corner supports (G) from 1x4 pine. Set the corner supports on their faces and miter the ends of each one at 45-degree angles.

4 To further reinforce the rails (F) and legs (E), glue a corner support (G) between each set of two rails (F), as shown in *figure 4*. Insert 1¹⁄₄" screws through the corner support and into the base frame.

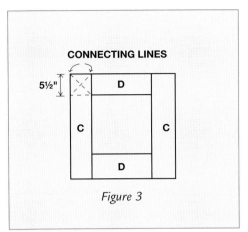

CONNECTING LINES

5½"

D

C

C

D

Figure 3

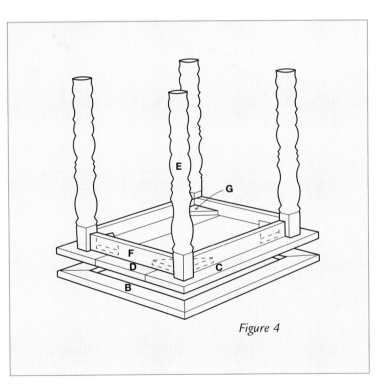

E

G

F

D

B

C

Figure 4

Adding the Table Top

1 Place the center top (A) and attached trim pieces (B) upside down on a level surface.

2 Center the base assembly over the top assembly, so that the sides of the assemblies are exactly flush (see *figure 4* on page 39). Glue the assemblies together and insert 1¼" screws, spaced 6" apart, through the long and short base pieces (C and D) into the top assembly.

Finishing

1 Fill any cracks, crevices, or screw holes with wood filler. Then sand all surfaces of the occasional table thoroughly.

2 Paint or stain the completed project the color of your choice.

Coffee Table

This simple-to-make coffee table is guaranteed to perk up the living room, and can be coordinated to any color scheme. The decorative trim pieces are painted wooden drawer pulls.

Special Tools & Techniques

- Bar clamps
- Miter

Materials

- 35 linear feet of 1x4 pine
- 2 linear feet of 1x6 pine
- 3 linear feet of 1x8 pine
- Premade pine laminate, 21½"x45½", approx, ¾" thick
- 28 square wooden drawer pulls

Hardware

- 85 1½" (4d) finish nails
- 15 2" (6d) finish nails
- 30 1⅝" wood screws

Cutting List

Code	Description	Qty.	Material	Dimensions
A	Leg Side	4	1x4 pine	17" long
B	Small Base	4	1x6 pine	5½" long
C	Large Base	4	1x8 pine	7¼" long
D	Short Base Side	2	1x4 pine	21½" long
E	Long Base Side	2	1x4 pine	47" long
F	Center Top	1	laminate	21½"x45½"
G	Long Top Side	2	1x4 pine	52½" long
H	Short Top Side	2	1x4 pine	28½" long

Constructing the Legs

1 Cut four Leg Sides (A) from 1x4 pine, each measuring 17 inches.

2 Assemble the four Leg Sides (A), overlapping each piece in rotation, as shown in *figure 1*. With the four sides (A) in position, the leg should measure 4¼ inches wide on all sides. Apply glue to the meeting surfaces, and nail all four sides (A) along their entire length. Use 1½-inch nails, spacing nails about 6 inches apart.

3 Cut four Small Bases (B) from 1x6 pine, each measuring 5½ inches.

4 Cut four Large Bases (C) from 1x8 pine, each measuring 7¼ inches.

5 Center one Small Base (B) over one Large Base (C), as shown in *figure 2* on page 42. Apply glue to the meeting surfaces, and nail the two pieces together using four 1½-inch nails.

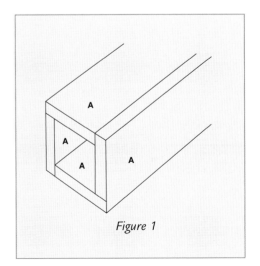

Figure 1

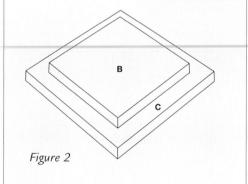

Figure 2

6 Repeat step 5 three times, using the remaining Small Bases (B) and Large Bases (C).

7 Center one base assembly (B and C) on top of one leg assembly, as shown in *figure 3* on page 43. The Large Base (C) should be facing up with the small base (B) below it. Wipe glue on the meeting surfaces, and attach the base assembly to the leg using four 2-inch nails.

8 Repeat step 7 three times to attach the remaining base assemblies to the remaining three legs.

Constructing the Base Frame

1 Cut two Short Base Sides (D) from 1x4 pine, each measuring 21^1/$_2$ inches.

2 Cut two Long Base Sides (E) from 1x4 pine, each measuring 47 inches.

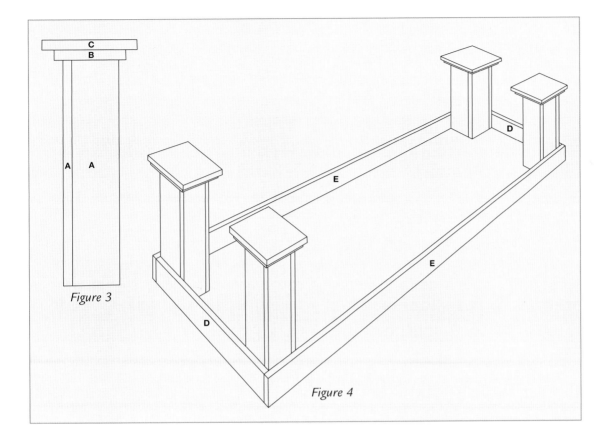

Figure 3

Figure 4

3 Place the two Short Base Sides (D) on edge, parallel to each other and 45$^1/_2$ inches apart. Place the two Long Base Sides (E) over the ends of the two Short Base Sides (D) to form a rectangle, as shown in *figure 4*.

4 Place the legs upside down inside each corner of the assembled base frame, as shown in *figure 4*. Apply glue to the meeting surfaces, and attach the legs to the base frame using two 1$^5/_8$-inch screws on each side of each leg. Screw through the base frame into the legs.

Constructing the Table Top

1 Trim the laminated Center Top (F) to 21$^1/_2$x45$^1/_2$ inches.

2 Cut two Long Top Sides (G) from 1x4 pine, each measuring 52$^1/_2$ inches.

3 Cut two Short Top Sides (H) from 1x4 pine, each measuring 28$^1/_2$ inches.

4 Place the Center Top (F) on a level surface. Place the two Long Top Sides (G) on the long

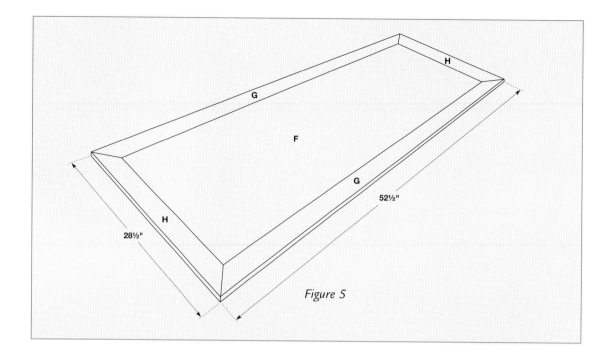

Figure 5

sides of the Center Top (F), as shown in *figure 5*. Place the two Short Top Sides (H) on the short sides of the laminate Center Top (F). Apply glue to the meeting surfaces. Hold the assembled top in place using bar clamps, and set aside to dry for 24 hours.

5 Center the table top over the base. Apply glue to the meeting surfaces, and nail through the Sides (G and H) into the Base Sides (D and E) using $1^{1}/_{2}$-inch nails spaced every 5 inches.

Finishing

1 Fill any holes, cracks, or crevices with wood filler.

2 Thoroughly sand all areas of the completed coffee table.

3 Paint or stain the coffee table with the color of your choice. We chose a clear stain and sealer.

4 Paint 28 drawer pulls the color of your choice. Here, we've used a salmon color.

5 Referring to *figure 6*, drill 10 holes on each of the Long Base Sides (E) and four holes on each of the Short Base Sides (D). Insert the drawer pull screws through the holes and attach the drawer pulls.

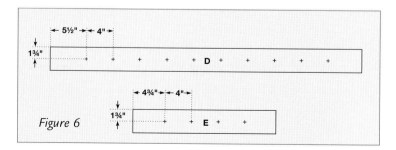

Figure 6

Wall Ledge

This simple ledge is one of our favorite projects, and can be constructed in only a few hours. Top it with anything that needs a home—from a row of picture frames to your collection of candlesticks—and your friends will think you hired a master decorator!

Special Tools & Techniques

- Miter

Materials

- 4 linear feet of 1x6 pine
- 4 linear feet of 2x4 pine
- 4 linear feet of ³/₄"-wide cove molding
- 3 linear feet of 1x2 pine

Hardware

- 10 2" wood screws
- 20 1⁵/₈" wood screws
- 15 1" (2d) finish nails

Cutting List

Code	Description	Qty.	Material	Dimensions
A	Top Ledge	1	1x6 pine	36" long
B	Front Support	1	2x4 pine	34" long
C	Side Support	2	2x4 pine	4¹/₂" long
D	Long Trim	1	³/₄"-wide cove molding	35¹/₂" long
E	Short Trim	2	³/₄"-wide cove molding	5¹/₄" long
F	Ledge Mount	1	1x2 pine	25" long

Making the Ledge

1 Cut one Top Ledge (A) from 1x6 pine, measuring 36 inches.

2 Cut one Front Support (B) from 2x4 pine, measuring 34 inches.

3 Miter both ends of the Front Support (B) at opposing 45° angles, as shown in *figure 1*.

4 Cut two Side Supports (C) from 2x4 pine, each measuring 4¹/₂ inches. Miter one end of both Side Supports (C) at a 45° angle, as shown in *figure 2*.

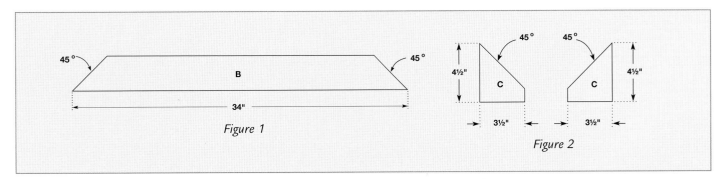

Figure 1

Figure 2

5 Using *figure 3* as a guide, place the Front Support (B) face down on a level surface. Place a Side Support (C) at both ends of the Front Support (B), so that the miters of the Front Support (B) meet the Side Support (C) miters. Apply glue to the meeting surfaces. Connect the Side Supports (C) to the ends of the Front Support (B), using two 2-inch screws.

6 Place the Top Ledge (A) over the assembled Front and Side Supports (B and C), as shown in *figure 4*. The edge of the Top Ledge (A) should overhang the ends and front sides of the Side Supports (C). Apply glue to the meeting surfaces, and screw through the face of the Top Ledge (A) into the Front and Side Supports (B and C), using 1⁵/₈-inch screws.

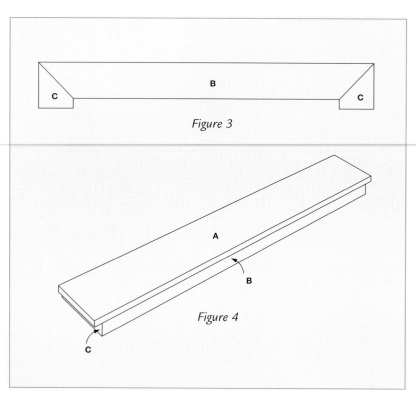

Figure 3

Figure 4

7 Cut one Ledge Mount (F) from 1x2 pine, measuring 25 inches. This board will be mounted to the wall with screws, and the ledge will be attached to it.

Adding the Trim

1 Cut one Long Trim (D) from ³/₄-inch-wide cove molding, measuring 35¹/₂ inches.

2 Miter both ends of the Long Trim (D) at opposing 45° angles.

3 Apply glue to the meeting surfaces, and nail the Long Trim (D) to the front of the assembly, just below the Top Ledge (A), using 1-inch nails spaced about every 4 inches.

4 Cut two Short Trims (E) from $^3/_4$-inch-wide cove molding, each measuring $5^1/_4$ inches long.

5 Miter one end of each of the two Short Trims (E) at a 45° angle.

6 Apply glue to the meeting surfaces, and nail one Short Trim (E) to the side of the assembly, just below the end of the Top Ledge (A). Nail through the Short Trim (E) into the Side Supports (C) using three 1-inch nails.

7 Repeat step 6 to attach the remaining Short Trim (E) to the other side of the assembly.

Finishing

1 Fill any cracks, crevices, or screw holes with wood filler.

2 Thoroughly sand all surfaces of the completed ledge.

3 Seal and paint or stain your completed ledge the color of your choice.

4 Locate wall studs and attach the Ledge Mount (F) to the wall using $1^5/_8$-inch screws. Make certain that the Ledge Mount (F) is perfectly level, then set the assembled ledge on top of the Ledge Mount (F), flush against the wall. Secure the ledge to the Ledge Mount (F) by screwing through the ledge into the Ledge Mount (F) using $1^5/_8$-inch screws about every 10 inches.

Triangular Table

Every so often a very easy project turns out to be an all-time favorite. That's the case with this small triangular table (see page 49). Although it takes almost no time to put together, we've received more than our share of "attaboys" for the finished product. We wanted a triangular table to fit next to our couch, which is positioned diagonally in the family room. Here's the result!

Special Tools & Techniques

- Mitering

Materials

- 8 linear feet of 1x4 pine
- 6 linear feet of 4x4 pine
- 1 piece of ³/₄" plywood, 24"x24"
- 3 fence finials

Hardware

- Approximately 50 #6x1¹/₄" flathead wood screws

*Notes on Materials

We made the legs on this table by purchasing screw-in finials (sold at building-supply stores as decorative additions for porch posts) and inserting them into lengths of 4x4 pine. Our finials are approximately 4¹/₂" long and 3" in diameter.

Cutting List

Code	Description	Qty.	Material	Dimensions
A	Top	1	³/₄" plywood	See *figure 1*
B	Short Trim	1	1x4 pine	25¹/₂" long
C	Medium Trim	1	1x4 pine	26¹/₂" long
D	Long Trim	1	1x4 pine	37¹/₂" long
E	Leg	3	4x4 pine	Cut to fit (approx. 72" total)

Making the Table Top

1 Using *figure 1* as a guide, cut one triangular top (A) from ³/₄"-thick plywood. The simplest way to do this is to start by marking off a 24" square on the plywood. Then draw a line to connect either set of opposite corners. Cut along the lines, and your triangle is complete.

2 Cut one short trim piece (B) from 1x4 pine, measuring 25¹/₂" long.

3 Miter one end of the short trim piece (B) at a 45-degree angle, as shown in *figure 2* on page 49.

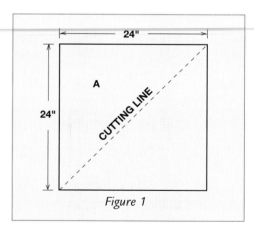

Figure 1

4 To add the short trim piece (B) to the outer edge of the top (A), first place the top upside down on a level surface. Glue the short trim piece (B), on edge, to a 24"-long edge of the top (A)

and secure it by driving 1¹/₄" screws, spaced about 6" apart, through the trim (B) and into the edge of the plywood.

5 Cut one 26¹/₂"-long medium trim piece (C) from 1x4 pine.

6 Miter one end of the medium trim piece (C) at a 45-degree angle, as shown in *figure 2*. Note that the medium trim piece (C) overlaps the short trim piece (B) at the 90-degree corner.

7 Attach the medium trim piece (C) to the top (A), in the same way that you attached the short trim piece. Use two additional screws to connect the two trim pieces at the 90-degree corner.

8 Cut one long trim piece (D) from 1x4 pine, measuring 37¹/₂" in length.

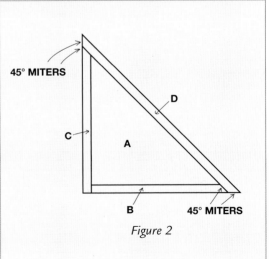

45° MITERS

D

C

A

B   **45° MITERS**

Figure 2

9 Miter both ends of the long trim piece (D) at 45-degree angles. Before attaching it, check to make certain that this piece fits perfectly along the long edge of the top (A).

10 Attach the long trim piece (D) to the top (A) in the same way that you attached the other two trim pieces. Then insert four additional 1¼" screws to secure the long trim piece to the other two trim pieces (B and C).

Adding the Legs

1 The legs are made by attaching decorative finials to the ends of pine 4x4s (E). To find the bottom center of each 4x4, simply draw two lines to connect the opposing corners at one end (see *figure 3*). The point at which the two lines intersect is the center. Apply glue to the meeting surfaces of the 4x4 and one finial; then hand-screw the, finial into the marked center of the 4x4.

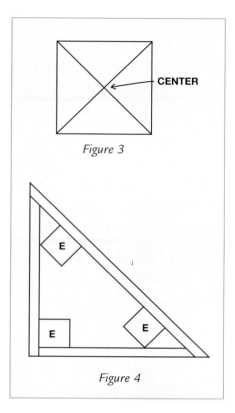

Figure 3

Figure 4

2 Measure and mark a point 25" from the end of the finial down the leg (E). Cut the leg to this length.

3 Repeat Steps 1 and 2 to make two more legs (E).

4 Using *figure 4* as a placement guide, glue the three legs (E) to the bottom face of the top (A). To secure the legs, first insert two 1¼" screws through each abutting trim piece (B, C, and D) and into each leg. Also insert four 1¼" screws through the top (A) and into the end of each leg, positioning the screws at the corners of the legs, but not so close to the corners that you split the wood.

Finishing

1 Fill all holes, cracks, and crevices with wood filler.

2 Sand the entire table thoroughly.

3 Paint or stain the finished table the color of your choice. We decided to sponge-paint our table to simulate the plaid in our furniture. Although doing this looks difficult, it's actually quite easy. Start by painting the table with the base color of your choice. Next, sponge-paint stripes in one direction and let them dry. Then sponge-paint stripes in the opposite direction. We were really pleased with the results.

Ottoman

You've long admired that high-priced ottoman/coffee table in the furniture store. Why not make your own? It's an easy project to construct, and you can pick and choose the fabric and paint colors to match your décor.

Special Tools & Techniques

- Miter
- Staple gun and staples
- Bar clamps

Materials

- 28 linear feet of 2x4 pine
- 4-x-8-foot sheet of $^3/_4$" plywood
- 15 linear feet of $^3/_4$"-wide beaded trim
- 1$^1/_2$ yards of 45" upholstery fabric
- 3$^1/_2$ yards of 1$^1/_2$" fringe (optional)
- 31" square of 2" thick foam
- 4 fabric-covered buttons (optional)

Hardware

- 8 corrugated metal fasteners
- 30 2$^1/_2$" wood screws
- 35 2" wood screws
- 60 wire brads

Cutting List

Code	Description	Qty.	Material	Dimensions
A	Inner Frame	4	2x4 pine	29$^1/_2$" long
B	Inner Legs	4	2x4 pine	29$^1/_2$" long
C	Sides	4	$^3/_4$" plywood	31"x16"
D	Trim	4	$^3/_4$"-wide trim	cut to fit
E	Middle Frame	4	2x4 pine	31" long
F	Top	1	$^3/_4$" plywood	31" square

Constructing the Inner Frame

1 Cut four Inner Frames (A) from 2x4 pine, each measuring 29$^1/_2$ inches.

2 Miter the ends of each of the four Inner frames (A) at opposing 45° angles.

3 Place the four Inner Frames (A) on a flat surface, mitered ends together, to form a 29$^1/_2$-inch square, as shown in *figure 1*. Hammer a corrugated metal fastener across each mitered joint to temporarily hold the frame together.

4 Cut four Inner Legs (B) from 2x4 pine, each measuring 14$^1/_2$ inches.

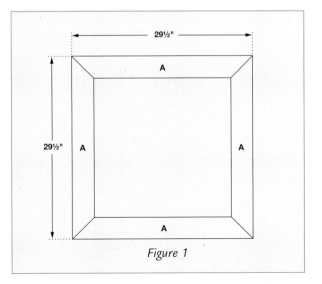

Figure 1

5 Attach one Inner Leg (B) to the assembled frame, covering the outer edge of the mitered joint, as shown in *figure 2* on page 53. Make certain that the leg is exactly square to the inner frames. Screw through the Inner Frames (A) into the Inner Leg (B) using four 2½-inch screws on each joint. Don't be concerned if the structure is not very stable at this time—the stability will come when the sides are added.

Adding the Sides

1 Cut four Sides (C) from ¾-inch plywood, each measuring 31x16 inches.

2 Bevel the 16-inch edges of each of the four Sides (C) at opposing 45° angles.

3 Lay one Side (C) with the bevels down. Referring to *figure 3* on page 53, mark a cutout on one 31-inch edge. Cut out along the marked lines.

4 Repeat step 3 to mark and cut out the same edge on each of the remaining three Sides (C).

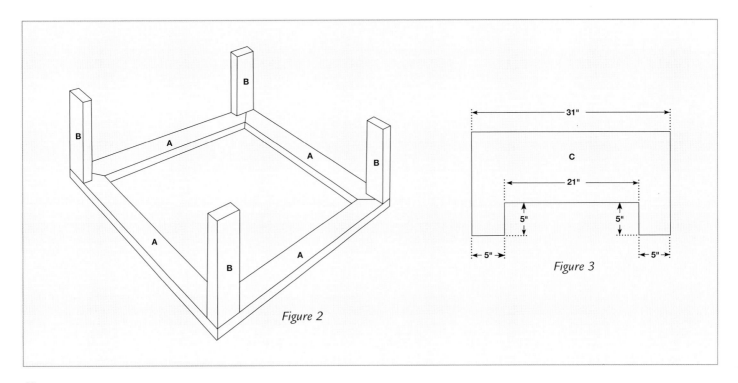

Figure 2

Figure 3

5 Place the Inner Frame and Leg assembly (A and B) upside down on a level surface. Apply glue to the meeting edges, and fit the four Sides (C) (matching beveled edges and placing the cutout at the top) around the assembly, as shown in *figure 4* on page 54. Make certain that all of the mitered joints fit together perfectly along the entire length. Use bar clamps to hold the Sides (C) in place. Screw through the edges of the Sides (C) into the Inner Legs (B) and Inner Frame (A), using 2-inch screws spaced about 5 inches apart.

Adding the Trim

1 Miter lengths of ³/₄-inch beaded Trim (D) to fit around the lower cutout edges of the ottoman, as shown in *figure 5* on page 54. Notice that the Trim (D) is mitered across the width to fit around the cutout, and mitered on its edge to fit around the corners.

2 Apply glue to the meeting surfaces, and attach the trim to the Sides (C) using small wire brads placed about every 3 inches.

Constructing the Middle Frame

1 Cut four Middle Frames (E) from 2x4 pine, each measuring 31 inches.

2 Miter each of the four Middle Frames (E) at opposing 45° angles.

3 Place the four Middle Frames (E) on a flat surface, mitered ends together, to form a 31-inch square, as for the Inner Frames (A) (see *figure 1*). Hammer a corrugated metal fastener across each mitered joint to temporarily hold the frame together.

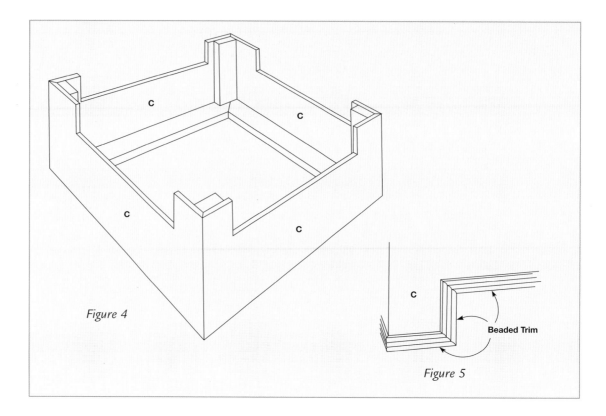

Figure 4

Beaded Trim

Figure 5

4 Cut and piece together a strip of your chosen fabric 4 inches wide and 10$^1/_2$ feet long. This will be used to cover the outer edges of the Middle Frame (E).

5 Beginning at one corner, staple the fabric strip to the frame assembly so that 1 inch of fabric is on the top, and 3 inches overhangs the edges, as shown in *figure 6* on page 55. When you reach the end, fold the end of the strip under, and staple securely in place.

6 Turn the entire frame assembly over, pull the fabric around the outer edges, and staple the fabric to the opposite side of the frame.

7 Add fringe at this point, if you wish. We stapled the fringe around the outer edges of the middle frame assembly.

Making the Top Cushion

1 Cut a Top (F) from $^3/_4$-inch plywood, measuring 31 inches square.

2 Place a 31-inch square of 2-inch foam over the Top (F).

3 Cut a 38-inch square of your chosen fabric. Place the fabric, wrong side up, on a level surface.

4 Center the cushion and Top (F) upside down over the fabric square.

5 Pull the fabric tightly over the cushion and edge of the Top (F) and staple the fabric in place. Staple the center of each side first, then work out to each corner.

6 If you want to add buttons, follow the measurements given in *figure 7* for positioning. Mark the button positions, and staple through the fabric and cushion on each of the marks. Then glue a button of your choice over each of the staples.

Finishing

1 Paint the frame assembly (sides and beaded trim) the color of your choice. We used a dark marbleizing kit (available at craft stores). Let the paint dry overnight.

2 Place the top cushion upside down and center the middle frame over it.

3 Screw through the middle frame into the Top (F) at all four corners and the center of each side, using 2-inch screws.

4 Center the painted frame assembly over the assembled top and middle frame. Screw through the Inner Frames (A) into the Middle Frames (E), using 2¹/₂-inch screws about every 8 inches.

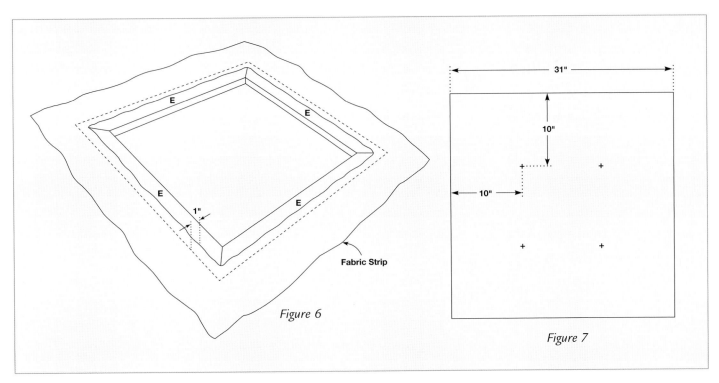

Figure 6

Fabric Strip

31"

10"

10"

Figure 7

House Numbers

Here's a quick and easy way to add a face-lift to the outside of your house: Replace those old house numbers from the hardware store with this great-looking project. The numbered tiles are readily available at most building-supply stores. To give our project some pizzazz, we added a border of 1"-square tiles to the design.

Special Tools & Techniques

- Small mastic trowel
- Rubber-surfaced grout trowel
- Mitering

Materials

- 9 linear feet of 1x4 pine
- 1 piece of $^3/_4$"-thick plywood, 22"x26"
- 9 linear feet of $^3/_4$"-wide decorative molding
- 2 pieces of $^3/_4$"x$^3/_4$" scrap wood, 22" long
- 2 pieces of $^3/_4$"x$^3/_4$" scrap wood, 26" long
- House-number tiles
- 1"x1" border tiles (optional)
- Small containers of tile grout, mastic, and sealer

Hardware

- Approximately 20 #6x1$^1/_4$" flathead wood screws
- Approximately 30 wire brads

*Notes on Materials

Purchase exterior-grade plywood for the base (A), and if you plan to place your finished project outdoors, be sure to use exterior-grade wood components and galvanized hardware. Also be sure to use paint, grout, and sealer that are rated for exterior use.

Because the number of digits in house numbers varies, so will the total number of tiles and the amount of wood you need; this project must be personalized for each residence. The materials specified here will be sufficient for a tile design that measures 20"x24", or less. If your design is larger, just add to the wood materials specified. If you decide to include the border tiles, buy a few extra in case you break any of them.

Most tiles sold at building-supply stores are now "self-spacing"; they come with small projections on their edges so that when you lay them out, the grout lines between the tiles will be even. We suggest that you spend some time at the tile supplier laying out the numbered tiles—and the border tiles if you decide to use them—to make certain that you like the design and that it completes a rectangle. The exact size doesn't matter; all of the wood pieces can be adjusted to fit.

Cutting List

Code	Description	Qty.	Material	Dimensions
A	Base	1	$^3/_4$" plywood	Cut to fit
B	Side	2	1x4 pine	Cut to fit
C	Top/Bottom	2	1x4 pine	Cut to fit

Cutting the Plywood

1 In order to determine the precise size of your project, you'll need to lay out your design on the $^3/_4$"-thick plywood. Place the tiles on the plywood exactly as you want them to look in the finished project, making certain that they're spaced correctly and that the sides of the tile rectangle are absolutely straight. If your tiles aren't self-spacing, don't forget to leave gaps for the grout.

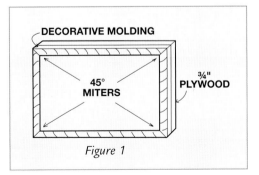

2 Place a ³/₄"x³/₄" piece of scrap wood along each of the four sides of the tile design. The scrap wood will align the tiles and will add a ³/₄" width on all four sides. Use a framing square to make certain that the outer edges of the four scrap pieces are exactly square with one another.

3 Use a pencil to mark the outer perimeter of the scrap wood onto the plywood. To form the plywood base (A) of the project, carefully cut out the marked rectangle.

4 Cut four pieces of ³/₄"-wide decorative molding to fit exactly around the perimeter of the upper face of the base (A), mitering the corners of the molding as shown in *figure 1*. Check to see that the tiled design will fit exactly inside the decorative molding that you have cut—now is the time to make any necessary adjustments.

DECORATIVE MOLDING

45°
MITERS

³/₄"
PLYWOOD

Figure 1

5 Glue the mitered decorative molding to the upper face of the base (A) and secure it with small wire brads. Use a tack hammer to insert the brads and recess them into the molding with a nail set.

6 Measure the length and width of the base (A). Cut two sides (B) from 1x4 pine to the exact width of the rectangle.

7 Add 1½" to the length of the rectangle and cut two top/bottom pieces (C) from 1x4 pine to that measurement.

8 Place the two sides (B) on one top/ bottom piece (C), as shown in *figure 2*. Make certain that the assembly is perfectly square. Glue the pieces together and insert two 1¼" screws through the top/bottom piece (C) and into the side (B) at each joint.

9 Fit the plywood assembly into the two sides (B) and top/bottom piece (C), as shown in *figure 3*, adjusting the plywood so that it is inset 1½" from the back edges of the sides and top/bottom piece.

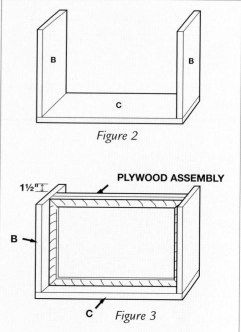

Figure 2

PLYWOOD ASSEMBLY

Figure 3

10 Glue the remaining top/bottom piece (C) to the two sides (B) and secure it in place with two 1¼" screws at each joint.

11 To hold the plywood assembly in place, insert three 1¼" screws through each side (B) and each top/bottom piece (C) into the edges of the plywood.

Finishing the Wood Frame

1 Fill any holes, cracks, or crevices with wood filler.

2 Sand the project thoroughly.

3 Paint the wood frame the color of your choice. Do not paint the plywood face that will receive the tiles.

Adding the Tiles

1 Following the manufacturer's directions carefully, use a small trowel to spread an even coat of tile mastic over the surface of the plywood base. Take care not to get the mastic on any of the painted decorative molding.

2 Place the tiles on the mastic one at a time, making sure that they are absolutely straight. Do not slide them, or the mastic will be forced up onto the sides of the tiles. Let the mastic dry overnight.

3 Mix the tile grout according to the manufacturer's directions (or use pre-mixed grout).

4 Using a rubber-surfaced grout trowel, spread the grout over the tiles with arc-like motions. Hold the trowel at an angle so that it forces the grout evenly into the spaces between the tiles.

5 When the grout begins to set up, use a damp rag to wipe the excess from the tiles and the joints. Don't let the grout dry completely before doing this, or it will be very difficult to remove. Use as little water as possible during this process so that you don't thin the grout that remains. Let the grout dry overnight.

6 Wipe the remaining film from the tiles with a damp rag.

7 Apply grout sealer, following the manufacturer's directions. (These directions often recommend that you wait several days before applying the sealer to the project.)

Wall Table

This suspended table is a nice addition to a neglected area in an entryway. It takes up no floor space, is only about 9 inches deep, and makes a perfect surface for a small plant and a few odd decorative items

Materials

- 11 linear feet of 1x8 pine
- 5 linear feet of 1x4 pine
- 3 linear feet of 1x2 pine*

Hardware

- 35 1½" (4d) finish nails
- 12 1½" wood screws

*Notes on Materials

Because 1x2 pine will be used as the inner support for the table, you may substitute any scrap wood for this piece, as long as it is approximately 30 inches long.

Cutting List

Code	Description	Qty.	Material	Dimensions
A	Top/Bottom	2	1x8 pine	36" long
B	Front	1	1x8 pine	36" long
C	Sides	2	1x8 pine	7¼" long
D	Triangular Trim	8	1x4 pine	6¼"x4⅞"x4⅞"
E	Support	1	1x2 pine	30" long

Constructing the Table

1 Cut two Top/Bottoms (A) from 1x8 pine, each measuring 36 inches.

2 Cut one Front (B) from 1x8 pine, measuring 36 inches.

3 Place the Top/Bottoms (A) and the Front (B) on a level surface, parallel to each other and 5½ inches apart.

4 Apply glue to the top edges of the Top/ Bottoms (A). Place the Front (B) over the top edges of the Top/Bottoms (A) as shown in *figure 1*. Nail through the Front (B) into the edges of the Top/Bottoms (A), using 1½-inch nails spaced 5 inches apart.

5 Cut two Sides (C) from 1x8 pine, each measuring 7¼ inches.

6 Apply glue to the meeting surfaces, and attach one Side (C) to one open end of the assembly as shown in *figure 2* on page 62. Nail through the Side (C) into the edges of the Top/Bottoms (A) and Front (B), using two 1¼-inch nails on each joint.

7 Repeat Step 6 to attach the remaining Side (C) to the other (open) end of the assembly.

Adding the Triangular Trim

1 Cut eight Triangular Trims (D) from 1x8 pine, each measuring $6^{1}/_{4}$ x $4^{7}/_{8}$ x$4^{7}/_{8}$ inches.

2 Sand all edges of each of the Triangular Trims (D).

3 Place the table assembly front side up on a level surface. Place six evenly spaced Triangular Trims (D) across the Front (B), even with the top edge of the table, as shown in *figure 3* on page 62. After sanding, you will have minuscule spaces between the Triangular Trims (D).

4 Apply glue to the meeting surfaces, and attach the six Triangular Trims (D) to the Front (B) using two $1^{1}/_{2}$-inch nails for each Trim (D). Nail through the Triangular Trims (D) into the Front (B).

5 Center one Triangular Trim (D) on the top edge of one Side (C).

6 Apply glue to the meeting surfaces, and attach the Triangular Trim (D) to the Side (C) using two 1½-inch nails. Nail through the Triangular Trim (D) into the Front (B).

7 Repeat Steps 5 and 6 to attach the remaining Triangular Trim (D) to the opposite Side (C).

Finishing

1 Fill any nail holes or imperfections in the wood with wood filler.

2 Thoroughly sand all parts of the table.

3 Stain or paint the finished table the color(s) of your choice. We chose a mauve paint for the top and triangular trims, and a pale green for the remaining portions of the table.

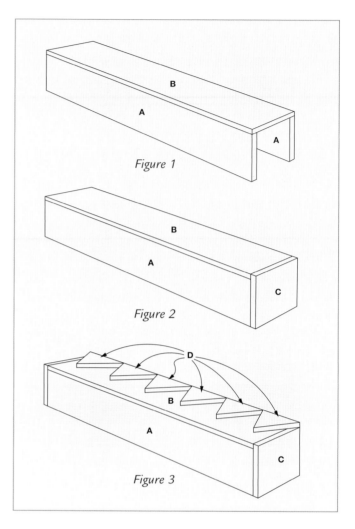

Figure 1

Figure 2

Figure 3

Attaching the Table to the Wall

1 Cut one Support (E) from 1x2 pine, measuring 30 inches (or substitute any other material that is approximately the same length).

2 Attach the Support (E) to the wall ¾ inch lower than you want the table height to be, and centered horizontally where the table will hang. Given the length of the Support (E), you should be able to locate at least one stud. If your walls are plaster or concrete, you will need to use special screws for hanging.

3 It is helpful to have an assistant to mount the table. Position the table over the Support (E), making sure that it is in the correct horizontal position. Have your helper hold the table in place while you screw through the top of the table into the Support (E). Use three or four 1¹/₂-inch wood screws spaced evenly across the top. Countersink the screws.

4 Fill the screw holes with wood filler, and use matching paint or stain to cover the filled holes.

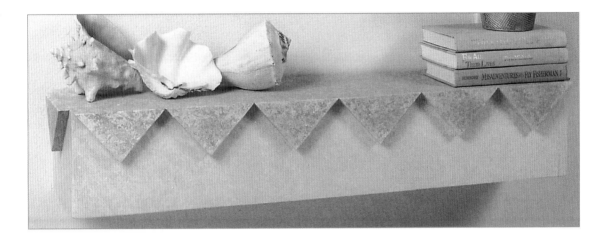

Coatrack

Attach purchased gingerbread brackets to a premade porch post to create a decorative and functional coatrack for your hallway. The entire project can be completed in just one day!

Materials

- 1 premade porch post, at least 6' long
- 3 linear feet of 1x3 pine
- 4 linear feet of 1x4 pine
- 4 gingerbread brackets, each measuring 6¼"x8½" on the straight sides
- 1 fence post finial

Hardware

- 30 1½"(4d) finish nails
- 15 1¼" (3d) finish nails
- 4 metal coat hooks

Cutting List

Code	Description	Qty.	Material	Dimensions
A	Post	1	porch post	at least 6' long
B	Trim	4	1x3 pine	6½" long
C	Long Base	1	1x4 pine	24" long
D	Short Base	2	1x4 pine	10¼" long

Constructing the Coatrack

1 Cut the Post (A) to the length you desire—we cut ours to 65 inches. First cut the top of the post so the upper square with flat sides will measure 5 inches. Then cut the other end of the post to the desired length.

2 Fill any cracks or imperfections with wood filler, and thoroughly sand the entire post.

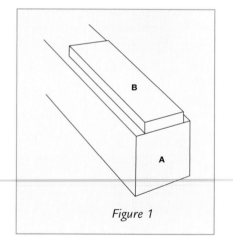

Figure 1

3 Cut four Trims (B) from 1x3 pine, each measuring 6½ inches.

4 Center one Trim (B) on one flat side of the Post (A), flush with the bottom of the Post (A), as shown in *figure 1*. Apply glue to the meeting surfaces, and nail through the Trim (B) into the Post (A) using three 1½-inch nails.

5 Center one 6¼-inch side of a gingerbread bracket over the Trim (B), flush with the bottom of the Trim (B), as shown in *figure 2*. Apply glue to the meeting surfaces, and nail through the bracket into the Trim (B) using four 1½-inch nails.

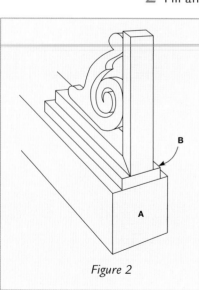

Figure 2

6 Repeat Steps 4 and 5 three times to attach the remaining Trims (B) and gingerbread brackets to the Post (A).

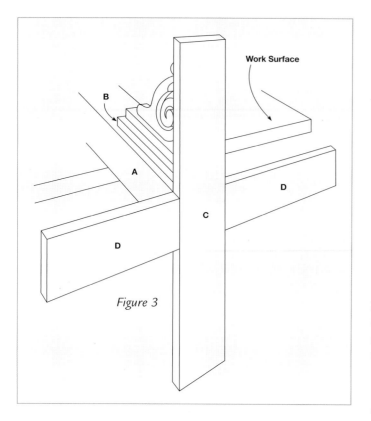

Work Surface

Figure 3

7 Cut one Long Base (C) from 1x4 pine, measuring 24 inches long.

8 Place the Post (A) on a flat surface, so that the Trims (B) overhang the work surface. Center the Long Base (C) over opposing 8½-inch sides of the gingerbread brackets, as shown in *figure 3*. Apply glue to the meeting surfaces, and nail through the Long Base (C) into the gingerbread brackets and the Post (A). Use four 1¼-inch nails on each joint.

9 Cut two Short Bases (D) from 1x4 pine, each measuring 10¼ inches long.

10 Center one Short Base (D) over one of the gingerbread brackets, perpendicular to the Long Base, as shown in *figure 3*. Apply glue to the meeting surfaces, and nail through the Short Base (D) into the brackets using four 1¼-inch nails.

11 Repeat Step 10 to attach the remaining Short Base (D) over the remaining gingerbread brackets.

Finishing

1 Mark the center top of the Post (A) and screw in a fence post finial.

2 Fill all remaining nail holes, cracks, and crevices with wood filler.

3 Sand all parts of the coatrack that remain unsanded.

4 Stain or paint your coatrack the color of your choice. We painted the coatrack white, and then decorated the individual parts with different designs using a paint pen.

5 Install four coat hooks—one on each flat side of the top of the coatrack.

Shell Mirror

Are you trying to decide what to do with all those shells you collected on vacation? Take them out of the box in your closet and create a unique hall mirror. It is sure to brighten up a neglected spot in your hall—and to be a constant reminder of your fun on the beach.

Special Tools & Techniques

- Bar or pipe clamps

Materials

- 4- x4-foot sheet of $3/4$" plywood
- 5 linear feet of 1x8 pine
- 8 linear feet of 1x4 pine
- 5 linear feet of 1x2 pine
- Mirror, approximately $24^1/2$"x34"*
- Construction glue

Hardware

- 8 corrugated metal fasteners
- 40 $1^1/4$" wood screws
- Picture hanging wire kit*
- Picture hangers

*Notes on Materials

We suggest that you purchase a mirror after you have assembled the mirror frame. That way, you can be certain that all of your measurements are correct, and that the mirror will fit the frame you have built. When specifying the size of the mirror, we suggest that you carefully measure the inner frames, and order a mirror at least $1/4$ inch smaller in each dimension than your opening.

When purchasing the picture hanging wire kit, buy one that will support your finished mirror. With the shells attached, ours was very heavy, and we used two 50-pound hangers, and wire that would support the same weight.

Cutting List

Code	Description	Qty.	Material	Dimensions
A	Top	1	$3/4$" plywood	$10^3/4$"x 36"
B	Bottom	1	$3/4$" plywood	$6^1/2$"x36"
C	Sides	2	1x8 pine	30" long
D	Side Frame	2	1x4 pine	38" long
E	Top/Bottom Frame	2	1x2 pine	$25^1/2$" long

Transferring the Patterns

1 Enlarge the pattern for the Top (A) (shown in *figure 1* on page 69) to full size on butcher paper or paper bags, and cut the pattern out carefully.

2 Tape the enlarged paper pattern to $3/4$-inch plywood, and trace around the pattern with a pencil.

3 Remove the paper pattern, and cut out the Top (A).

4 Repeat steps 1 through 3 to enlarge the pattern for the Bottom (B), transfer the pattern to $3/4$-inch plywood, and cut out the Bottom (B). See *figure 1* on page 69.

Constructing the Mirror Frame

1 Cut two Sides (C) from 1x8 plywood, each measuring 30 inches.

2 Position the two Sides (C) on their wide surfaces, parallel to each other and approximately 18 inches apart.

3 Position the Top (A) at the ends of the two Sides (C), as shown in *figure 2* on page 69.

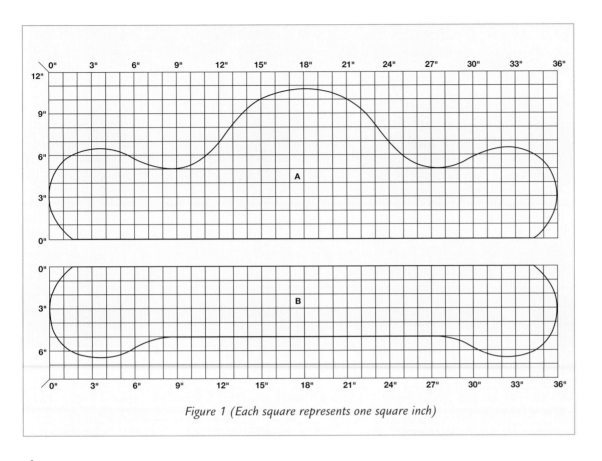

Figure 1 (Each square represents one square inch)

4 Place the Bottom (B) at the opposite ends of the two Sides (C), as shown in *figure 2*.

5 Measure the center opening (where the mirror will fit) in several places, to make absolutely certain that both the distance from Top (A) to Bottom (B) and the distance from Side (C) to Side (C) are equal at all points. Apply glue to the meeting surfaces, and clamp the Top (A), Bottom (B), and two Sides (C) together.

6 Use two corrugated metal fasteners across each of the joints to hold the pieces together temporarily.

Adding the Inner Frames

1 Cut two Side Frames (D) from 1x4 pine, each measuring 38 inches.

2 With the assembly (Top [A], Bottom [B], and Sides [C]) on the working surface and the corrugated fasteners visible, place one Side Frame (D) over one Side (C), flush with the outer edges, as shown in *figure 2*. The ends of the Side Frame (D) should extend over the Top (A) and Bottom (B) by approximately 4 inches.

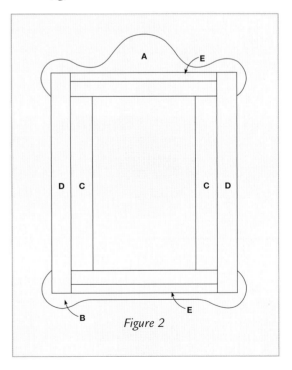

Figure 2

3 Place the two Base Sides (B) on a level surface, parallel to each other and 14³/₄ inches apart. Apply glue to the meeting surfaces, and place one Base Front/Back (A)

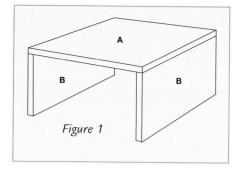

Figure 1

over the edges of the two Base Sides (B), as shown in *figure 1*. Nail through the Base Front/Back (A) into the edges of the Base Sides (B) using four 1¹/₂-inch nails evenly spaced along each joint.

4 Cut one mock Drawer Front (C) from 1x8 pine, measuring 12 inches.

5 Apply glue to the meeting surfaces, and center the Drawer Front (C) over the remaining Base Front/Back (A), as shown in *figure 2* on page 73. Nail through the Drawer Front (C) into the Base Front/Back (A) using three 1¹/₂-inch nails on each 12-inch side.

6 Turn the assembly upside down, and repeat Step 3 to attach the remaining Base Front/Back (A) (with attached Drawer Front [C]) to the assembly.

7 Cut two Base Top/Bottoms (D) from ³/₄-inch plywood, each measuring 11¹/₂x16¹/₄ inches.

8 Place the assembly on a level surface with the Drawer Front (C) facing you. Apply glue to the meeting surfaces, and nail one Base Top/ Bottom (D) over the edges of the Base Sides (B) and Base Front/Back (A), as shown in *figure 3* on page 73. Nail through the Base Top/Bottom (D) into the Base Sides and Front/Back (A and B) using four 1¹/₂-inch nails on each side.

9 Set the remaining Base Top/Bottom (D) aside. It will be added during the final assembly.

Building the Middle Section

1 Cut one Middle Front (E) from ³/₄-inch plywood, measuring 33¹/₂x16¹/₄ inches.

2 Cut two Middle Sides (F) from ³/₄-inch plywood, measuring 33¹/₂x2 inches.

3 Place the two Middle Sides (F) on edge on a level surface, parallel to each other and 14³/₄ inches apart. Apply glue to the meeting surfaces, and place the Middle Front (E) over the edges of the Middle Sides (F), as shown in *figure 4*. Nail through the Middle Front (E) into the edges of the Middle Sides (F), using 1¹/₂-inch nails spaced about every 5 inches.

4 Cut two Middle Top/Bottoms (G) from ³/₄-inch plywood, each measuring 16¹/₄x2³/₄ inches.

5 Apply glue to the meeting surfaces, and attach one Middle Top/Bottom (G) over the edges of the two Middle Sides (F) and Middle Front (E), as shown in *figure 4*. Nail through the Middle Top/Bottom (G) into the edges of the two Middle Front and Sides (E and F) using two 1¹/₂-inch nails on the Middle Sides (F) and three nails on the Middle Front (E).

6 Turn the assembly around, and repeat step 5 to attach the remaining Middle Top/Bottom (G).

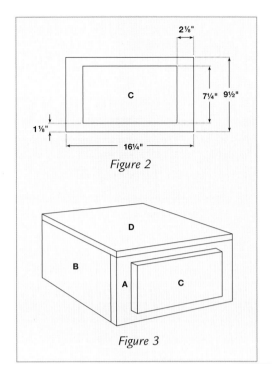

Figure 2

Figure 3

Building the Clock Case

1 The last section is the clock case, which will house the battery-operated clock. Cut two Case Front/Backs (H) from ³/₄-inch plywood, each measuring 14³/₄x16¹/₄ inches.

2 Enlarge the pattern shown in *figure 5* and transfer it to the two Case Front/Backs (H). Designate one as the Case Front (H) and one as the Case Back (H). The clock opening should be transferred to only the Case Front (H), to accommodate the battery-operated clock. Check to make certain that the clockwork portion of the clock you purchased will fit snugly into the opening; alter the size of the opening if necessary.

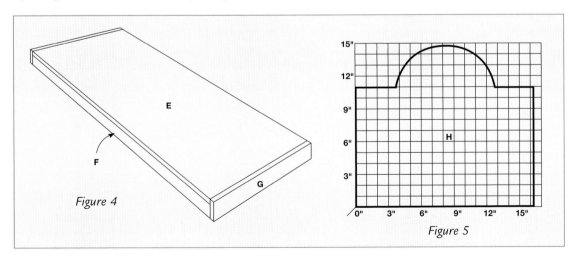

Figure 4

Figure 5

3 Cut two Case Sides (I) from ³/₄-inch plywood, each measuring 10¹/₄x10 inches.

4 Cut one Case Top (J) from ³/₄-inch plywood, measuring 10x16¹/₄ inches.

5 Place the two Case Sides (I) on a level surface, parallel to each other and 14³/₄ inches apart. Apply glue to die meeting surfaces, and place the Case Top (J) over the edges of the two Case Sides (I) as you did in *figure 1*. Nail through the Case Top (J) into the edges of the Case Sides (I). Use four 1¹/₂-inch nails evenly spaced along each joint.

6 Apply glue to the meeting surfaces and center the Case Front/Back (H) over the Case Sides and Top (I and J), as shown in *figure 6*. Nail through the Case Front (H) into the Case Sides and Top (I and J) using 1¹/₂-inch nails spaced every 5 inches.

7 Turn the assembly upside down, and repeat Step 6 to attach the remaining Case Back (H) to the assembly.

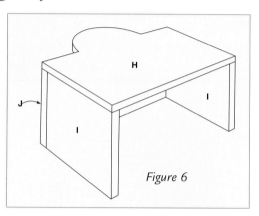

Figure 6

Connecting the Three Sections

1 Place the clock base, middle, and case on their sides, with the fronts facing away from you and the backs flush with each other, as shown in *figure 7* on page 75. Make certain that each of the pieces is perfectly aligned with the adjoining one. Apply glue to the meeting surfaces, and screw through the Middle Top (G) into the edge of the Case Back (H), using four or five 1¹/₂-inch screws. Apply glue to the meeting surfaces and screw through the opposite Middle Top (G) into the Base Top (D), using four or five 1¹/₂-inch screws.

2 Cut two Columns (K) from 1¹/₂ -inch-diameter fluted wooden curtain rods, each measuring 37 inches.

3 Cut two Column Supports (L) from 1x2 pine, each measuring 6¹/₄ inches.

4 Miter each of the Column Supports (L) at opposing 45° angles, as shown in *figure 8* on page 75.

5 Turn the clock assembly around so the front is facing you. Insert one Column- (K) inside the front bottom corner of the clock case, and adjust it so that the opposite end of the Column (K) is tight against the Base Top (D).

6 Place one Column Support (L) inside the clock case across the Column (K). If necessary, trim the Column Support (L) so that it fits snugly against the Case Front (H), the Column (K), and the Case Side (I). To hold the Column (K) tightly in place, apply glue to the meeting surfaces, and nail through the Case Front and Side (H and I) into the Column Support (L), using two 1¹/₄-inch nails.

7 Make sure that the opposite end of the Column (K) is exactly square against the Base Top (D), and screw through the Base Top (D) into the center bottom of the Column (K) using a 1¹/₂-inch screw.

8 Turn the assembly to its other side, and repeat Steps 5 through 7 to attach the remaining Column (K) and Column Support (L) to the opposite side of the clock.

9 Cut one Pendulum Support (M) from 1x2 pine, measuring 10 inches.

10 Apply glue to the meeting surfaces and fit the Pendulum Support (M) between the two Case Front/Backs (H) at the center bottom of the clock case. Nail through both Case Front/Backs (H) into the Pendulum Support (M) using two 1¹/₂-inch nails on each joint.

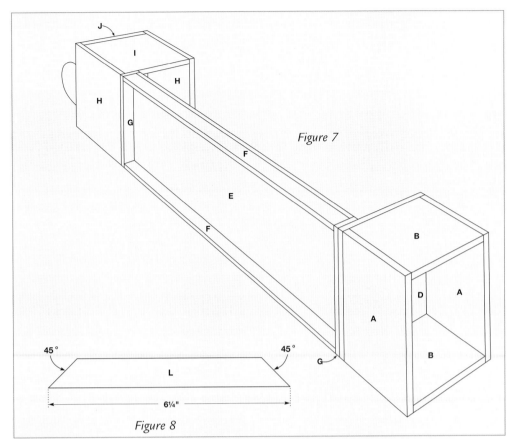

Figure 7

Figure 8

11 Drill a hole through the center of the Drawer Front (C) and Base Front (A), just large enough to accommodate the doorknob or drawer pull that you have selected. Install it on the Drawer Front (C).

12 Locate the remaining Base Top/Bottom (D) that was set aside. Apply glue to the meeting surfaces, and attach the Base Bottom (D) over the bottom of the assembly. Nail through the Base Bottom (D) into the Base Sides and Front/Back (A and B) using four 1¹/₂-inch nails on each joint.

Making the Pendulum

1 Cut one Pendulum Rod (N) from 1x1 pine, measuring 22¹/₂ inches.

2 Cut one Pendulum Circle (O) from ¹/₄-inch plywood, measuring 5 inches in diameter.

3 Place the center of the Pendulum Circle (O) on top of the Pendulum Rod (N), and 1 inch from the end of the Pendulum Rod (N). Apply glue to the meeting surfaces, and nail through the center of the Pendulum Circle (O) into the Pendulum Rod (N) using a 1-inch finish nail.

Finishing the Clock

1 Fill any holes, cracks, or crevices with wood filler.

2 Thoroughly sand all areas of the completed clock.

3 Attach a curtain rod finial in each of the four corners of the Base Bottom (D).

4 Attach a curtain rod finial in each of the four corners of the Case Top (J).

5 Paint or stain the clock and pendulum the color of your choice. We painted our clock with a different pattern on each of the individual surfaces. Refer to the photograph or choose your own patterns and colors. See page 24 for more information on decorative painting.

6 Install the battery-operated clock in the opening of the clock case. This clock is one that is simply hung on the wall, and only required inserting the clock into the hole.

7 Screw one brass cup hook into the end of the pendulum, and another into the center of the Pendulum Support (M). Hang the pendulum on the cup hook.

Bedroom
& Bath

Rustic Armoire

Most of our favorite project designs result from satisfying our own needs. The one shown on the next page 80 is no exception. This armoire was designed and built to fit in a small room in our house that was designated by the builder to be a "study." He must have pictured the future owners installing floor-to-ceiling bookshelves, a massive globe, and leather-covered easy chairs. What we needed, however, was a guest room—ahh, reality! The problem was that the room had no closet and not much space left over when the sleeper sofa was open for guests. This armoire neatly solved both of the problems. Although it's only 12" deep, it has a small hanging closet for clothes and enough drawer space to accommodate guests' necessities. Because the armoire is so narrow, it must be attached to the wall to provide stability when the doors and/or drawers are open.

Special Tools & Techniques

- Mitering
- Dadoes
- Ripping

Materials

- 80 linear feet of $3/4$"x$3/4$" pine
- 44 linear feet of 1x3 pine
- 37 linear feet of 1x4 pine
- 13 linear feet of 1x6 pine
- 15 linear feet of 1x8 pine
- 33 linear feet of 1x12 pine
- 2 pieces of laminated pine or oak, each 20"x72"
- 1 piece of $1/4$"-thick plywood, 20"x34"
- 2 sheets of $3/4$"-thick plywood, each 4'x8'
- 10 linear feet of 5" crown molding

Hardware

- 2 lbs. #6x$1^1/4$" flathead wood screws
- 1 lb. #6x2" flathead wood screws
- Approximately 50 2d finishing nails
- Approximately 200 3d finishing nails
- 6 offset door hinges
- 7 drawer pulls

*Notes on Materials

The armoire drawers and doors shown here are constructed from laminated pine boards. Most building-supply stores sell sections of wood that have already been laminated. You can laminate the boards yourself, of course, but we don't recommend doing this unless you're an experienced woodworker and own heavy-duty tools. Due to the number of boards and the overall size of the project, laminating is a bigger job than it may appear to be.

Although this armoire isn't wide enough to accommodate clothes hangers suspended parallel to its sides, you can certainly hang clothes parallel to its front and back. Just purchase a wooden towel rod with removable arms, attach the arms to the inside top of the armoire, and cut the rod down to a length that will fit between the arms.

Constructing the Back

1 The basic supporting frame for the armoire is nothing more than a large box. Although it requires quite a bit of space to construct, the actual assembly is very straightforward. Start by cutting one $41^1/8$"x$70^1/2$" wide back (A) and one $23^1/8$"x$70^1/2$" narrow back (B) from the $3/4$"-thick plywood.

Cutting List

Code	Description	Qty.	Material	Dimensions
A	Wide Back	1	3/4" plywood	41 1/8"x70 1/2"
B	Narrow Back	1	3/4" plywood	23 1/8"x70 1/2"
C	Inner Vertical Support	8	3/4"x3/4" pine	70 1/2" long
D	Shelf Support	3	3/4"x3/4" pine	39 5/8" long
E	Side	2	1x12 pine	72" long
F	Inner Divider	1	1x12 pine	70 1/2" long
G	Top/Bottom	2	1x12 pine	65" long
H	Narrow Front Vertical	2	1x4 pine	72" long
I	Center Front Vertical	1	1x6 pine	72" long
J	Narrow Horizontal Frame	2	1x4 pine	36" long
K	Short Horizontal Frame	2	1x4 pine	18" long
L	Horizontal Inner Support	4	3/4"x3/4" pine	39 5/8" long
M	Shelf	1	1x12 pine, ripped	41 1/8" long
N	Wide Horizontal Frame	2	1x6 pine	36" long
O	Short Inner Support	4	3/4"x3/4" pine	21 5/8" long
P	Drawer Front/Back	4	1x8 pine	35" long
Q	Drawer Side	4	1x8 pine	9" long
R	Drawer Bottom	2	1/4" plywood	9 3/8"x33 7/8"
S	Drawer Front	2	Laminated pine	8 1/2"x35 1/2"
T	Top/Bottom Trim	4	1x3 pine	33" long
U	Side Trim	4	1x3 pine	11" long
V1	Upper Drawer Guide	4	1x4 pine	10 1/2" long
V2	Lower Drawer Guide	4	1x4 pine	9" long
W	Cabinet Door	2	Laminated pine	17 1/2"x35 1/2"
X	Top/Bottom Door Trim	4	1x3 pine	15 1/4" long
Y	Side Door Trim	3	1x3 pine	37 1/2" long
Z	Wardrobe Door	1	Laminated pine	17 1/2"x64"
AA	Top/Bottom Wardrobe Door Trim	2	1x3 pine	15" long
BB	Side Wardrobe Door Trim	2	1x3 pine	66 1/4" long
CC	Top Side Trim	2	1x4 pine	12" long
DD	Top Front Trim	1	1x4 pine	68" long

2 Cut eight 70 1/2"-long inner vertical supports (C) from 3/4"x3/4" pine.

3 Using *figure 1* on page 91 as a guide, glue two inner vertical supports (C) to the wide back (A), positioning the supports flush with the long edges of the wide back (A). Use 3d finishing nails, spaced about 6" apart, to secure the supports in place.

4 Cut three 39 5/8"-long shelf supports (D) from 3/4"x3/4" pine.

5 Glue one shelf support (D) to the wide back (A), between the two vertical supports (C) and 39 3/4" down from what will be the top of the finished armoire, as shown in *figure 1* on page 81. Secure the shelf support with 3d finishing nails, spaced about 6" apart. It doesn't make any difference which end of the wide back (A) you choose as the top, but now is the time to decide.

6 Glue a second shelf support (D) to the wide back (A), 12 7/8" down from the first support, in the same manner that you attached the first one, as shown in *figure 1* on page 81.

7 Nail and glue the remaining shelf support (D) 2" from the bottom edge of the wide back (A).

8 Glue and nail one inner vertical support (C) to the narrow back (B), flush with one long edge, as shown in *figure 1* on page 81. Secure the support with 3d finishing nails spaced about 6" apart.

Adding the Sides & Inner Divider

1 Cut two 72"-long sides (E) from 1x12 pine

2 Glue one inner vertical support (C) flush with one 70½"-long edge of one side (E), as shown in *figure 2*. Center the inner vertical support (C), leaving a ³/₄" gap at each end of the side (E). Secure the support with 3d finishing nails, spaced about 6" apart.

3 Repeat Step 2 to attach another inner vertical support (C) to the remaining side (E).

4 Cut one 70½" long inner divider (F) from 1x12 pine.

5 Glue an inner vertical support (C) to each side of the inner divider (F), flush with one edge, as shown in *figure 3*. Secure with 3d finishing nails spaced about 6" apart.

6 Glue a third inner vertical support (C) to the inner divider (F), offsetting it ³/₄" from the other long edge, as shown in *figure 3*. Secure the support with 3d finishing nails spaced about 6" apart.

7 Place the inner divider (F) along the edge of the wide back assembly, facing its offset inner vertical support (C) away from the wide back (A), as shown in *figure 4* on page 82. Glue the inner divider (F) and wide back assembly together. Then insert 2" screws at an angle through the bottom ³/₄"-wide offset on the inner divider (F) and into the inner vertical support (C) that is attached to the wide back (A). Space the screws-about 4" apart.

8 Fit the narrow back (B) underneath the offset inner vertical support (C) on the inner divider (F), as shown in *figure 4*. Glue the narrow back in place and insert 1¹/₄" screws, spaced about 4" apart, through the inner vertical support (C) on the inner divider (F) and into the narrow back (B).

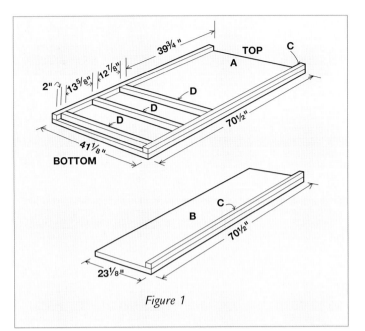

Figure 1

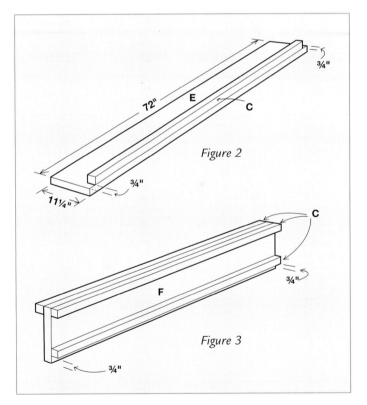

Figure 2

Figure 3

9 Center one side (E) on the wide back (A), leaving a ³/₄" gap at each end, as shown in *figure 4* on page 82. Glue the side (E) in place and insert screws, spaced about 4" apart, through the side (E) to attach it alternately to both the inner vertical support (C) and to the edge of the wide back (A). Use 2" screws to attach it to the wide back (A) and 1¹/₄" screws to attach it to the inner vertical support (C).

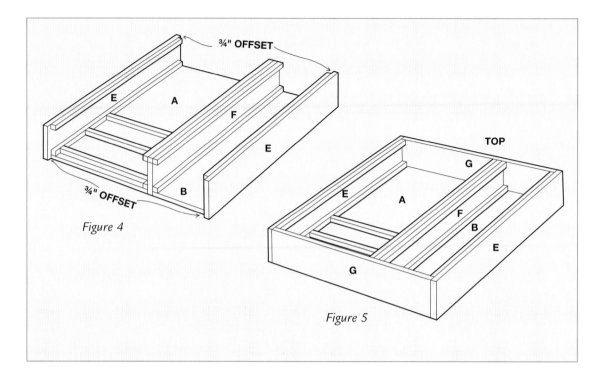

Figure 4

Figure 5

10 Center the remaining side (E) along the edge of the narrow back (B), leaving a ³/₄" gap at each end, as shown in *figure 4*. Glue the side in place and secure with screws, just as you secured the side (E) in Step 9.

Adding the Top and Bottom

1 Cut two top/bottom pieces (G) from 1x12 pine, each measuring 65" long.

2 Fit one top/bottom piece (G) between the two sides (E), as shown in *figure 5*. Note that the top/bottom piece (G) fits over the ends of the wide and narrow backs (A and B) and the inner divider (F). Glue the top (G) in place and insert 2" screws, spaced about 3" apart, through the sides, (E) and into the ends of the top/bottom piece (G). Also attach the top/bottom piece (G) to the inner divider (F) and to the wide and narrow backs (A and B) by inserting 2" screws, spaced about 3" apart, through the top piece (G) and into the ends of pieces A B, and F.

3 Repeat Step 2 to attach the other top/bottom piece (G) at the other end of the assembly, as shown in *figure 5*.

Adding the Front Frame Pieces

1 The front frame pieces are not difficult to add, but do take the time to make certain that all the pieces are absolutely square. One piece of the frame that is off will affect the way the shelves and drawers fit, so before you attach each piece, double-check your work. Start by cutting two 72"-long narrow front verticals (H) from 1x4 pine.

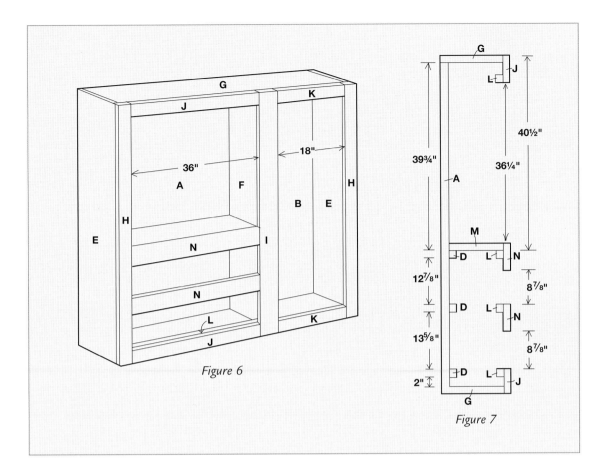

Figure 6

Figure 7

2 Glue the narrow front verticals (H) to the frame assembly, fitting them over the edges of the sides (E) and the top/bottom pieces (G), as shown in *figure 6*. Insert 2" screws, spaced about 4" apart, through each narrow front vertical (H) and into the edges of the sides (E) and top/bottom pieces (G).

3 Cut one 72"-long center front vertical (I) from 1x6 pine.

4 Center the center front vertical (I) over the edge of the inner divider (F). It should extend 2³/₈" on either side of the inner divider (F). At this point, check the spacing on the front of your armoire. (Well, it's almost an armoire by now!) The distance between the center front vertical (I) and the narrow front vertical (H) on the side of the armoire that contains the wide back (A) should be exactly 36". The distance between the center front vertical (I) and the narrow front vertical (H) on the other side of the armoire should be exactly 18". Measure across each of the openings at the top, bottom, and at least two midpoints. If your measurements are off, alter the remaining front frame pieces, drawers, and doors so that they'll fit properly.

5 Cut two 36"-long narrow horizontal frames (J) from 1x4 pine.

6 Glue one narrow horizontal frame (J) at the top of the 36"-wide opening on the left side of the armoire, between the center front vertical (I) and the narrow front vertical (H), as shown

in *figure 6* on page 83. Insert 2" screws, spaced about 4" apart, through the narrow horizontal frame (J) and into the edge of the top (G).

7 Repeat Step 7 to attach the remaining narrow horizontal frame (J) at the bottom of the 36"-wide opening, as shown in *figure 6* on page 83.

8 Cut two 18"-long short horizontal frames (K) from 1x4 pine.

9 Glue one short horizontal frame (K) at the top of the 18"-wide opening on the right side of the armoire, between the center front vertical (I) and the narrow front vertical (H), as shown in *figure 6* on page 83. Insert 2" screws through the short horizontal frame (K) and into the edge of the top (G).

10 Repeat Step 10 to attach the remaining short horizontal frame (K) at the bottom of the 18"-wide opening on the right side of the armoire, as shown in *figure 6* on page 83.

Adding the Inner Supports and Shelves

1 Cut four $39^5/_8$" horizontal inner supports (L) from $^3/_4$"x$^3/_4$" pine. These will fit behind the narrow and wide horizontal frames (J and N) and will support the inner shelves as well as stabilizing the narrow horizontal frames (J) which you just attached. A cutaway view of the placement of the inner supports on the left side of the armoire is provided in *figure 7* on page 83.

2 Glue one horizontal inner support (L) onto the inner edge of each of the narrow horizontal frame pieces (J), positioning them as shown in *figure 7* on page 83. Secure the supports with 3d finishing nails, spaced about 6" apart.

3 Attach a third horizontal inner support (L) $40^1/_2$" from the top edge of the armoire, across the front opening. It should be exactly level with the shelf support (D) which you previously attached to the wide back (A). Use 3d finishing nails to secure it to the back faces of the narrow front vertical (H) and the center front vertical (I).

4 Cut one $41^1/_8$" upper shelf (M) from 1x12 pine, and rip the shelf to $10^1/_2$" in width. The shelf will fit on top of the horizontal inner support (L) which you just attached and the shelf support (D) on the wide back (A), as shown in *figure 7* on page 83. In order to make the shelf fit, each of the corners must be cut out to accommodate the inner vertical supports (C) inside the armoire. Cut out a square from each corner of the upper shelf (M), measuring just over $^3/_4$"x$^3/_4$", as shown in *figure 8* on page 85.

5 Fit the upper shelf (M) over the horizontal inner support (L) and the shelf support (D). Glue the shelf in place, and secure with 3d finishing nails spaced about 6" apart.

6 Cut two 36"-long wide horizontal frames (N) from 1x6 pine.

7 Glue one wide horizontal frame (N) over the raw edge of the upper shelf (M), between the center front vertical (I) and the narrow front vertical (H), as shown in *Figures 6* and *7* on page 83. Insert 1¼" screws, spaced about 6" apart, through the face of the wide horizontal frame (N) and into the edge of the upper shelf (M).

8 We're finally going to use that fourth horizontal inner support (L) that you've been so worried about! Bet you thought we forgot. Attach this support (L) across the 36"-wide opening, 12⅞" below the horizontal inner support (L) that is under the upper shelf (M), as shown in *figure 7* on page 83. Nail and glue the support (L) to the inner faces of the center front vertical (I) and the narrow front vertical (H).

9 Glue the remaining wide horizontal frame (N) to the horizontal inner support (L) which you just attached. The long upper edge of the wide horizontal frame (N) should be flush with the top edge of the horizontal inner support (L).

10 Cut four 21⅝"-long short inner supports (O) from ¾"x¾" pine. These will fit behind each of the short horizontal frames (K) on the right side of the armoire to stabilize the joints.

11 Glue and nail one short inner support (O) to the inner face of the short horizontal frame piece (K) at the top of the armoire, flush with its edge. Secure the support with 3d finishing nails spaced about 6" apart.

12 Repeat Step 11 to attach the second short inner support (O) to the short horizontal frame piece (K) at the bottom of the armoire.

Making the Drawers

1 There are two identical drawers in this armoire. Both are constructed as shown in *figure 9*. Start by cutting the following parts from 1x8 pine: two 35"-long drawer front/back pieces (P) and two 9"-long drawer sides (Q).

2 To accommodate the plywood drawer bottoms, cut a ¼"x¼" dado on the inside of each drawer piece (P and Q), ⅜" from its lower edge.

3 Cut two 9⅜"x33⅞" drawer bottoms (R) from ¼"-thick plywood. Assemble each drawer as shown in *figure 9*. Note that the drawer front/back pieces (P) overlap the ends of the drawer sides (Q). Use glue and 3d finishing nails at each end of the overlapping boards; leave the drawer bottoms (R) floating freely within their dadoes. The drawer fronts (S) will be added later.

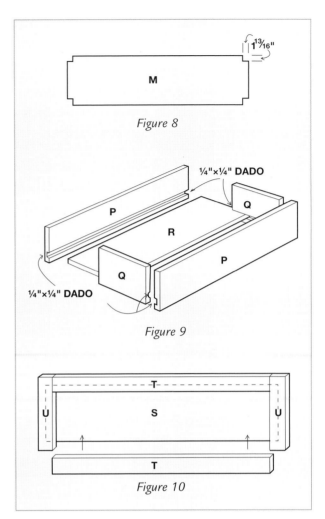

Figure 8

Figure 9

Figure 10

Making the Drawer Fronts

1 The drawer fronts are nothing more than rectangles of laminated pine trimmed with a border of 1x3 pine. You'll need to make sure that each finished assembly is perfectly square. Start by cutting one $8^1/_2$"x$35^1/_2$" drawer front (S) from laminated pine.

2 Cut two 33"-long top/bottom trim pieces (T) from 1x3 pine.

3 Cut two 11"-long side trim pieces (U) from 1x3 pine.

4 Using *figure 10* on page 85 as a guide, place the four trim pieces (T and U) on a level surface. Center the drawer front (S) over the trim pieces, leaving a $1^1/_4$" border of trim visible on each of the four sides of the drawer front (S). Glue and nail the pieces together, using 3d finishing nails spaced about 4" apart.

5 Repeat Steps 1 through 4 to assemble the second drawer front. Set the drawer fronts aside.

Adding the Drawer Guides

1 Cut four $10^1/_2$"-long upper drawer guides (V1) from 1x4 pine. Also cut four 9"-long lower drawer guides (V2) from 1x4 pine.

2 Glue one upper guide (V1) and one lower guide (V2) together, as shown in *figure 11*, leaving a $^3/_4$" space at each and of the upper guide. Note that the back face of the upper guide should be flush with the back edge of the lower guide. Secure the pieces with three $1^1/_4$"-long screws spaced evenly along the joint.

3 Repeat Step 2 three more times, using the remaining six drawer guide pieces (V1 and V2), to make a total of four assembled drawer guides.

4 Fit the first two L-shaped drawer guides between the horizontal inner support (L) and the shelf support (D) on the sides of the drawer opening, with their open sides facing each other and positioned so that the drawer is centered, as shown in *figure 12*. Check to make certain that the drawer fits snugly between them. Remove the drawer; then glue and nail the guides in place.

5 Repeat Step 4 to attach the remaining two drawer guides in the second opening.

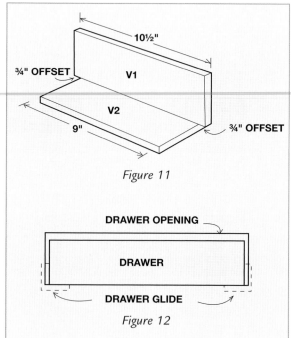

Figure 11

Figure 12

Making the Cabinet Doors

1 The cabinet doors are constructed in the same manner as the drawer fronts, with the exception that the right-hand cabinet drawer has no trim on the edge that sits next to the left-hand door. Start by cutting two 17$\frac{1}{2}$"x35$\frac{1}{2}$" cabinet doors (W) from laminated pine.

2 Cut four 15$\frac{1}{4}$"-long top/bottom door trim pieces (X) from 1x3 pine.

3 Cut three 37$\frac{1}{2}$"-long side door trim pieces (Y) from 1x3 pine.

4 Using *figure 13* as a guide, arrange the five trim pieces (X and Y) on a level surface. (Note the $\frac{1}{4}$" gap between the Y piece in the center and X pieces to the right of it.) Center the two door fronts (W) over the trim pieces, leaving a $\frac{1}{2}$" gap between the two. There should be a 1$\frac{3}{8}$" border of trim visible along each side of the doors (W) and a 1" border at the top and bottom. Glue and nail the door (W) on the left to the trim (X and Y) that it covers, using 3d finishing nails spaced about 4" apart. Glue and nail the door on the right to the two top/bottom trim pieces (X) and to the side door trim piece (Y) on the right, but do not attach this door to the piece of Y trim in the center.

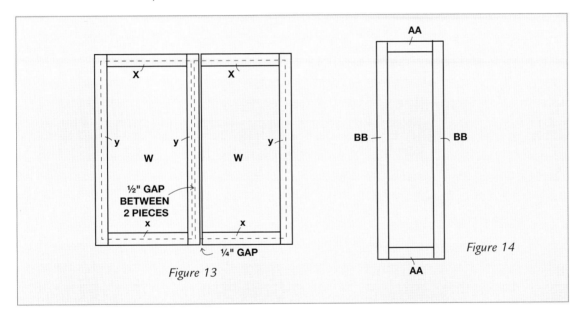

Figure 13

Figure 14

Making the Wardrobe Door

1 The wardrobe door is made in the same manner as the drawer fronts and the cabinet doors; only the measurements are different. Start by cutting one 17$\frac{1}{2}$"x64" wardrobe door (Z) from laminated pine.

2 Cut two 15"-long top/bottom wardrobe door trim pieces (AA) from 1x3 pine.

3 Cut two 66$\frac{1}{4}$"-long side wardrobe door trim pieces (BB) from 1x3 pine.

4 Using *figure 14* on page 87 as a guide, arrange the four trim pieces (AA and BB) on a level surface. Center the door front (Z) over the trim pieces, leaving a 1¼" border of trim visible on each side of the wardrobe door front and a 1⅛" border of trim visible at the top and bottom of the door front. Glue the pieces together and secure with 3d finishing nails spaced about 4" apart.

Installing the Doors

1 Slide the assembled drawers into their openings, placing a scrap piece of wood between the back of each one and the back of the armoire to hold the drawers flush with the front of the armoire. Use heavy-duty, double-sided tape to stick a drawer front temporarily in place on each drawer until you have both drawer fronts positioned exactly right. Then attach the fronts to the drawers by inserting three 1¼" screws through each drawer and into each drawer front.

2 First measuring carefully, install the hinges on the doors so that the hinges are positioned the same distance from the top and bottom of each door.

3 Have someone help you position the doors and attached hinges over the door openings. Line up each door so that it's even with the door and/or drawers next to it and make sure that none of the doors binds or scrapes against surrounding surfaces. When the doors are aligned, attach the hinges to the armoire.

4 Attach the drawer pulls to each of the drawers and cabinet doors, spacing them evenly and aligning them with one another.

Adding the Top Trim

1 The last step (whew!) is to add the top trim to the armoire. As you can see in the photo, we added two layers: a first layer of 1x4 pine and a second layer of crown molding. Be sure to take careful measurements for your trim pieces as they should be cut to fit exactly. Start by measuring and cutting two 12"-long top side trim-pieces (CC) from 1x4 pine and one 68"-long top front trim piece (DD) from 1x4 pine.

2 Glue the three trim pieces (CC and DD) to the top of the armoire so that each piece overlaps the armoire by 1" and extends above it by 2$^1/_2$". Secure the trim with 3d finishing nails spaced about 6" apart.

3 Measure and cut three pieces of crown molding to fit above the 1x4 pine trim, mitering the corners to fit perfectly. Glue the crown molding onto the 1x4 pine trim, overlapping the trim by only 1". Secure the molding to the trim with 2d finishing nails spaced about 4" apart.

Finishing

1 Countersink all nails. Fill any nail or screw holes with wood filler.

2 Sand all surfaces thoroughly.

3 Paint or stain the completed armoire the color of your choice. We used a light green wood stain.

4 Take an admiring look at your handiwork. Then figure how to get it moved to the room where you will use it! Don't forget that it should be attached to the wall for stability.

Padded Headboard

Here's an inexpensive and easy way to make a decorator headboard for your bed. Although we made ours for a queen-size bed, you can alter the dimensions to fit any bed from twin to king-size. We used two coordinating fabrics to match our duvet cover and bed pillows. The headboard shown in the photo, by the way, was customized to fit a waterbed with an existing wooden frame. It's just slightly different from the project described here, which is designed to fit a standard metal bed frame.

Special Tools & Techniques

- Staple gun and ⁵/₈" staples
- Saber saw

Materials

- 1 sheet of ³/₄"-thick plywood, 4'x8'
- 1 piece of 2"-thick foam rubber, 2'x5'
- 6 bags of polyester fiberfill
- 2 yards of 36"-wide decorator fabric
- 3¹/₂ yards of 36"-wide coordinating fabric
- 2 yards of 36"-wide backing fabric (optional)
- Decorative cording (optional)

Hardware

- 2 large bolts with matching nuts, 1¹/₂" long

*Notes on Materials

Standard metal frames come with holes in the metal brackets at the head of the bed; the holes accommodate the bolts with which you'll attach the leg portions of your headboard, so be sure to check the hole size before purchasing bolts.

Buy the cheapest plywood you can find; it will be covered with fabric, so its flaws will be invisible.

Because we wanted to stack pillows against the completed project, we made it taller than most headboards. Feel free to alter the specific dimensions to please your own taste.

To make certain that our headboard dimensions will fit your bed (see *figure 1* on page 92), we suggest that you cut a trial headboard shape out of heavy paper and tape it to the wall behind your bed. When you're certain you're pleased with the result, use the paper as a pattern for marking and cutting the plywood.

Cutting List

Code	Description	Qty.	Material	Dimensions
A	Headboard	1	³/₄" plywood	48"x65"

Cutting the Plywood

1 Cut out the plywood headboard first (see *figure 1* on page 92), leaving the top corners square. To round the corners, place any circular object (a round tray works well) on each upper corner, trace around it, and then follow the traced lines with your saber saw.

2 Measure 6" in from the edges of the plywood headboard (A) and draw a rough stapling line, as shown in *figure 1* on page 92.

3 Using *figure 1* as a guide, cut one piece of 2"-thick foam rubber to cover the upper portion of the headboard. The foam shouldn't extend all the way to the stapling line; leave about 1¹/₂" between that line and the cut edge of the foam.

4 Place the foam on the plywood head-board (A) and staple it in place along the stapling line by bending its upper edges down to meet the line, as shown in *figure 2* on page 92. Staple the foam at the bottom of the headboard, too.

Adding the Fabric

1 Cut one piece of 36"-wide decorator fabric large enough to cover all of the foam rubber and to overlap it by 2" on all edges.

2 Staple the decorator fabric over the foam rubber, placing the staples along the fabric stapling line.

3 To pad and cover the bare portions of plywood, first measure along the entire length of the stapling line and multiply the result by 2¹/₂. Seam together enough 15" lengths of 36"-wide coordinating fabric to obtain that result. (Be sure to seam the 15" edges together.)

4 Sew gathering stitches along one long edge of the seamed-together lengths. Pull the gathering stitches until the gathered edge is the same length as the stapling line.

5 Place the gathered edge right-side down, matching the gathering line and the stapling line. Let the fabric drape over the padded portion of the headboard. Then staple the gathered coordinated fabric to the stapling line. Don't be stingy with the staples—they should form an almost a solid line.

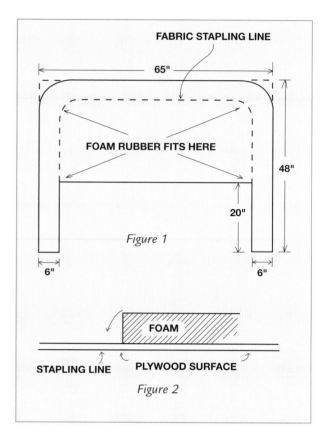

Figure 1

Figure 2

6 Now you'll pad the top portion of the headboard as you bring the stapled fabric up over it; you'll need to experiment to get just the right amount of fiberfill and to distribute it evenly over the top of the headboard. Beginning at one side of the headboard, cover a 2' section of the 6"-wide exposed wood and the edge of the plywood headboard with a generous amount of fiberfill. Then pull the gathered fabric up over the fiberfill and the edge of the headboard. (This will be easier if you can find a helper to hold the fabric in place while you evaluate your work.) Adjust the amount of fiberfill, if necessary. When you're satisfied with the way the headboard looks, staple the other edge of the fabric to the back of the headboard (A), adjusting the gathers evenly along the 2' section of the headboard.

7 Repeat this procedure to pad the remaining portion of the headboard, working in 2' sections all the way around.

8 Next, you'll cover the leg portions of the plywood. Cut two pieces of decorator fabric 2" wider than these leg portions.

9 Cover the front of one leg portion with one piece, turning under ¹/₂"-wide seams at the top and bottom edges of the fabric. Wrap the fabric around to the back of the plywood and staple it in place.

10 Repeat Step 9 to cover the front and edges of the remaining leg with fabric.

11 If you wish to finish the back of the headboard, simply cut a piece of backing fabric 2" larger than the headboard on all sides, turn under a 2"-wide hem, and staple the fabric to the back of the headboard. Cover the staples with decorative cording.

Finishing

1 Place the finished headboard behind the bed and align the legs with the metal brackets on the bed frame. Mark the position of the bed-frame holes on the headboard legs.

2 Drill holes through the headboard legs large enough to accommodate the bolts you've purchased. Insert the bolts through the headboard and through the holes in the metal bed frame. Tighten the nuts on the bolts.

Victorian Table

The four decorative quarter-circles that make up the surface of this lovely table were originally destined for use as gingerbread on house porches, but you'll use them—and a circular sheet of glass—to transform an easy-to-make stand into a lovely table. Once you've purchased the materials, you can probably construct the entire project in a couple of hours. Paint the finished table, add the glass to the top, and you're finished.

Materials

- 1 sheet of $^3/_4$"-thick plywood, 4'x8'
- 4 decorative gingerbread quarter-circles
- 1 circle of $^3/_8$"-thick glass, 36" in diameter
- 5 small felt or plastic pads to protect the glass

Hardware

- Approximately 30 #6x1$^1/_4$" flathead wood screws

Notes on Materials

For a table the same size as the one shown in the photo, the straight sides of each gingerbread quarter-circle that you purchase should measure 17$^1/_4$". If you'd like to use larger or smaller quarter-circles, just alter the measurements of the plywood to match the size of the gingerbread that you find.

When you buy the circular piece of glass, be sure that its edges have been beveled or sanded in some manner so that no one is injured by sharp glass.

The table supports (A) will support a glass circle of up to 40" in diameter.

Cutting List

Code	Description	Qty.	Material	Dimensions
A	Table support	2	$^3/_4$" plywood	29"x35$^1/_4$"

Constructing the Table

1 The two-piece stand fits together by means of a slot system (see *figure 1*). First cut two 29"x35$^1/_4$" table supports (A) from $^3/_4$"-thick plywood. Then carefully cut the slot in the center of each table support (A). Be certain that you make these cuts very carefully, or the table supports will not fit together correctly.

2 Apply glue to the inner edges of the cut slots. Then fit the slots in the two table supports (A) together so that the supports form an X shape when viewed from above.

3 The quarter-circles are fastened in the openings between the table supports (A), with their upper surfaces flush with the upper edges of the supports,

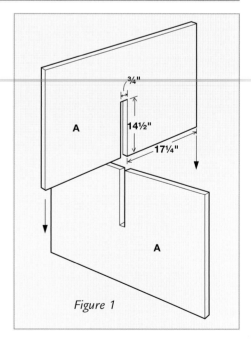

Figure 1

as shown in *figure 2*. Apply glue to both straight edges of one quarter-circle and position it between two adjacent table supports (A). Fasten the quarter-circle in place by inserting three 1¹/₄" screws through the table support (A) and into the gingerbread; place one screw as close as possible to each end of the support and one in the middle. Repeat to fasten the other edge of the quarter-circle to the other support.

4 Repeat Step 3 to attach another quarter-circle opposite to the one you attached in the last step. Then attach the remaining two quarter-circles. You'll need to angle the screws into these last two quarter-circles from underneath the previously attached quarter-circles next to them.

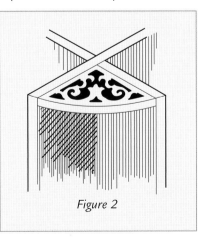

Figure 2

Finishing

1 Fill any holes, cracks, or crevices with wood filler.

2 Paint or stain the table the color of your choice.

3 Affix the five small felt or plastic pads to the upper edges of the table support, as shown in the photo of the table without glass. These will protect the lower surface of the glass and will prevent the glass from sliding out of place.

4 Place the circular glass on top of the table.

Cedar Keepsake Box

Who can't use this pretty box around the house? It's the ideal container for treasured family heirlooms—tiny baby shoes, cherished letters, and old photographs—and is the perfect size for storing cigars. The addition of a tray makes it an ideal jewelry box.

Materials

- 4 linear feet of 1x6 cedar
- 2 linear feet of 1x10 cedar
- 3 linear feet of 1x3 cedar
- 1 linear feet of 1x8 cedar

Note: Pine may be substituted for cedar

Hardware

- Approximately 40 $1\frac{1}{2}$" (4d) finish nails
- 2 2" hinges

Cutting List

Code	Description	Qty.	Material	Dimensions
A	Box Side	2	1x6 cedar	$7\frac{3}{4}$" long
B	Box Front/Back	2	1x6 cedar	10" long
C	Box Top/Bottom	2	1x10 cedar	10" long
D	Tray Side	2	1x3 cedar	6" long
E	Tray Front/Back	2	1x3 cedar	$7\frac{3}{4}$" long
F	Tray Bottom	1	1x8 cedar	6"x$6\frac{1}{4}$"

Making the Box

1 Cut two Box Sides (A) from 1x6 cedar, each measuring $7\frac{3}{4}$ inches.

2 Cut two Box Front/Backs (B) from 1x6 cedar, each measuring 10 inches.

3 Place two Box Front/Backs (B) on edge parallel to each other and 7 inches apart. Place the ends of the two Box Sides (A) between the Box Front/Backs (B), as shown in *figure 1*. Apply glue to the meeting surfaces. Nail through the Box Front/Backs (B) into the ends of the Box Sides (A), using three $1\frac{1}{2}$-inch nails on each joint.

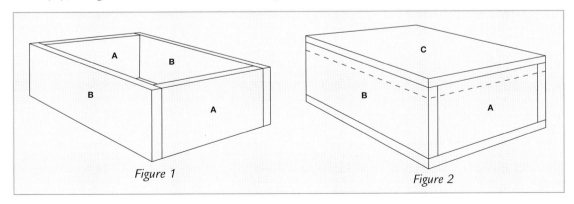

Figure 1

Figure 2

4 Cut two Box Top/Bottoms (C) from 1x10 cedar, each measuring 10 inches.

5 Place one Top/Bottom (C) over the edges of the Box Sides (A) and Box Front/Backs (B), as shown in *figure 2* on page 97. Apply glue to the meeting surfaces. Nail through the Top/Bottom (C) into the edges of the Box Sides (A) and Box Front/Backs (B), using 1¹/₂-inch nails.

6 Turn the Box assembly upside down, and repeat step 5 to attach the remaining Box Top/Bottom (C).

7 Carefully mark around the perimeter of the box, 1¹/₂ inches from one Box Top/Bottom (C), as shown in *figure 2* on page 97. Cut carefully along the marked lines through the box to create two pieces.

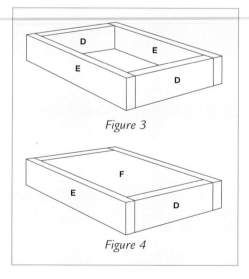

Figure 3

Figure 4

Making the Tray

1 Cut two Tray Sides (D) from 1x3 cedar, each measuring 6 inches.

2 Cut two Tray Front/Backs (E) from 1x3 cedar, each measuring $7^3/_4$ inches.

3 Place two Tray Front/Backs (E) on edge parallel to each other and 7 inches apart. Place the ends of the two Tray Sides (D) between the Tray Front Backs (E), as shown in *figure 3* on page 98. Apply glue to the meeting surfaces, and nail through the Tray Front/Backs (E) into the ends of the Tray Sides (D), using two $1^1/_2$-inch nails on each joint.

4 Cut one Tray Bottom (F) from 1x8 cedar, measuring $6x6^1/_4$ inches. This piece will fit inside the Tray Sides and Front/Backs (D and E), as shown in *figure 4* on page 98. Apply glue to the meeting surfaces, and nail through the Tray Sides (D) and Tray Front/Backs (E) into the ends and edges of the Tray Bottom (F), using $1^1/_2$-inch nails spaced 2 inches apart.

Finishing

1 Fill any cracks, crevices, or screw holes with wood filler.

2 Thoroughly sand all surfaces of the completed cedar box.

3 Seal and paint or stain your completed cedar box the color of your choice.

4 Attach 2-inch hinges to the lid and box.

Chaise Lounge

Do you want a comfortable retreat in your bedroom where you can read quietly or watch television? Anyone who has priced chaise lounges in furniture stores knows how expensive they can be. We made our very own chaise, and here's the result! You can now have your own little corner of the world—at a reasonable price.

Special Tools & Techniques

- Beveling

Materials

- 65 linear feet of 2x4 pine
- 1 sheet of 3/4"-thick plywood, 4'x8'
- 15 yards of 36"-wide fabric
- 8 bags of polyester fiberfill
- 1 piece 2"-thick foam, 14"x50"
- 1 piece 2"-thick foam, 28"x45 1/2"

Hardware

- Approximately 20 #6x2" flathead wood screws
- Approximately 200 #6x2 1/2" flathead wood screws
- Approximately 10 3d finishing nails

Cutting List

Code	Description	Qty.	Material	Dimensions
A	Long Frame	4	2x4 pine	54"-long
B	Short Frame	4	2x4 pine	25" long
C	Short Connector	2	2x4 pine	19" long
D	Long Connector	4	2x4 pine	31" long
E	Top Side	2	2x4 pine	20" long
F	Top Back	1	2x4 pine	28" long
G	Arm Connector	2	2x4 pine	8 1/2" long
H	Side Connector	4	2x4 pine	13" long
I	Short Seat Support	2	2x4 pine	22" long
J	Long Seat Support	2	2x4 pine	25" long
K	Back	1	3/4" plywood	13 7/8"x22"
L	Seat	1	3/4" plywood	See *figure 9*

Making the Lower Frame

1 The lower portion of the inner frame consists of an upper and lower support and is constructed entirely of 2x4 pine. To make the lower support, begin by cutting two long frames (A), each measuring 54" long, and two short frames (B), each measuring 25" long.

2 Place the two long frames (A) on a level surface, parallel to each other, on edge, and 25" apart. Fit the two short frames (B) between the ends of the long frames (A) to form a rectangle measuring 28"x54", as shown in *figure 1* on page 101. Glue the pieces together and insert two 2 1/2" screws through each long frame (A) and into the end of each short frame (B) at each joint.

3 Repeat Steps 1 and 2 to make a 28"x54" upper support.

4 The upper and lower supports are joined by 2x4 pine connectors (C and D). Cut two short connectors (C), each 19" long, and four long connectors (D), each 31" long.

5 Place the lower support on a level surface and glue the two short connectors (C) inside adjacent corners of the lower support, as shown in *figure 2* on page 102. Insert two 2¹/₂" screws, one through each long frame (A) and one through each short frame (B) into each short connector (C).

6 Glue two of the long connectors (D) in the opposite corners of the lower support, as shown in *figure 2* on page 102. Insert two 2¹/₂" screws, one through each long frame (A) and one through each short frame (B) at each joint.

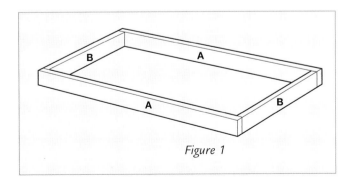

Figure 1

7 Glue the remaining two long connectors (D) in the lower support, placing each one 13" from the long connector (D) on that side, as shown in *figure 2*. Secure with two 2¹/₂" screws driven through each long connector (D) and into the lower support at each joint.

8 The next step is to add the upper support to the assembly, as shown in *figure 3*. Carefully fit the upper support over the long and short connectors (C and D). The upper support should be flush with the ends of the short connectors (C) and should be perfectly level. Glue the upper support in place and secure it with two 2¹/₂" screws driven through the long or short support (A or B) at each joint.

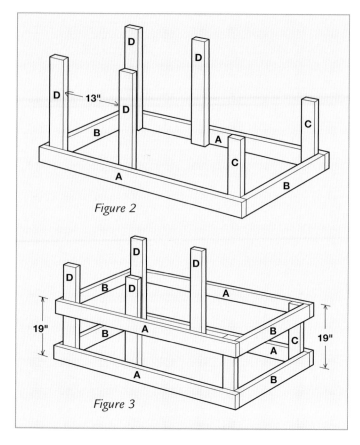

Figure 2

Figure 3

Adding the Top Frame Pieces

1 Cut two 20"-long top sides (E) from 2x4 pine.

2 Glue the top sides (E) to the outer surfaces of the long connectors (D), as shown in *figure 4*. Insert two 2¹/₂" screws at each joint.

3 Cut one 28"-long top back (F) from 2x4 pine.

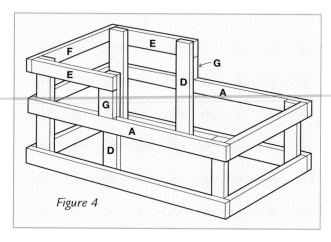

Figure 4

4 Glue the top back (F) to the ends of the top sides (E) and edges of the long connectors (D), as shown in *figure 4*. Insert two 2¹/₂" screws at each joint.

5 Cut two 8¹/₂"-long arm connectors (G) from 2x4 pine.

6 Glue the arm connectors (G) between the top sides (E) and the long frames (A) in the upper supports, as shown in *figure 4*. Insert two 2¹/₂" screws at each end of each arm connector (G).

7 Cut four 13"-long side connectors (H) from 2x4 pine.

8 Cut two short seat supports (I), each measuring 22" long, from 2x4 pine.

9 Place two of the side connectors (H) on a level surface, parallel, on edge, and 22" apart. Place the two short seat supports (I) face down, at opposite ends of the two side connectors (H), as shown in *figure 5*.

10 Glue the side connectors (H) to the short seat supports (I) and secure with 2½" screws inserted through the side connectors (H) and into the ends of the short seat supports (I).

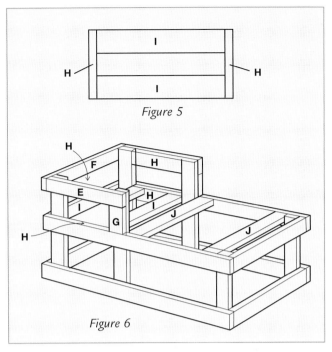

Figure 5

Figure 6

11 Fit the assembly (H and I) inside the upper support, as shown in *figure 6*, so that the two side connectors (H) are flush against the inner faces of the upper support between the two long connectors (D). Glue the assembly in place and insert three 2½" screws through each side of the upper support and into each side connector (H).

12 Glue the remaining two side connectors (H) to the inner faces of the top sides (E), between the two long supports (D), as shown in *figure 6*. Insert three 2½" screws through each side connector (H) and into each top side (E).

13 Cut two long seat supports (J) from 2x4 pine, each 25" long.

14 Attach one long seat support (J), face up, inside the upper support, next to the two short connectors (C), as shown in *figure 6*. Glue the long seat support (J) in place and insert two 2½" screws through each side of the upper support at each joint.

    Repeat to attach the second long seat support (J) inside the upper support, flush with the edges of the two long connectors (D), as shown in *figure 6*.

Constructing the Back & Seat

1 Cut a 13⅞"x22" back piece (K) from ¾"-thick plywood. Bevel one 22" edge at a 30-degree angle and the other at a 60- degree angle, as shown in *figure 7* on page 104.

2 Glue the beveled edges of the back (K) to the top back (F) and the front of the short seat support (I) closest to the top back (F), as shown in *figure 8* on page 104. Secure the back (K) with four evenly spaced finishing nails driven through the 22"-long edge.

3 Cut a 14"x50" piece of 2"-thick foam. Center the 53" length across the front face of the back (K), so that approximately 14" of foam extends outward from each side of the back (K).

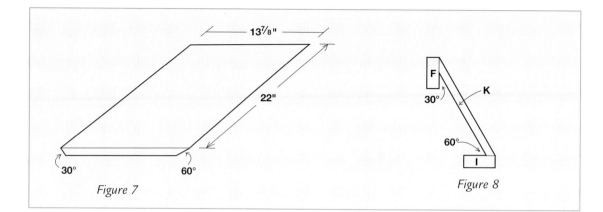

Figure 7

Figure 8

Staple the foam to the front face of the back, placing just one staple in each of the corners to hold the foam temporarily. Fill the resulting depressions in the foam with a small amount of polyester fiberfill. Push the foam that extends from the sides of the back (K) into the cavities formed by the two long connectors (D) behind the back.

4 Using *figure 9* as a guide, cut a seat (L) from ³/₄"-thick plywood.

5 Cut a piece of 2"-thick foam to match the dimensions of the plywood seat (L).

6 Staple the matching foam to the plywood seat (L) in three or four places to hold it in place temporarily. Fill the resulting depressions with a small amount of polyester fiberfill.

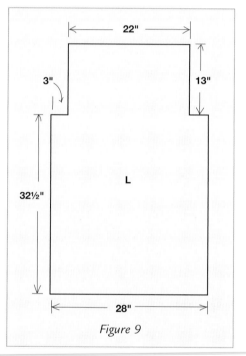

Figure 9

7 Cut a piece of fabric that is 4" larger than the seat (L) on all sides.

8 Place the fabric on a smooth surface, right side down. Center the seat (L), foam side down, on top of the fabric. Wrap the fabric over the edges of the seat (L) and staple it to the plywood. To minimize wrinkles, first staple the center of one side, then the center of the opposite side, and then work your way out to the corners, smoothing the fabric as you go. Staple the centers of the remaining sides and again work your way to the corners. Be generous with the staples; use enough to keep the fabric taut and to eliminate puckering.

Adding the Fabric to the Frame

1 Cut six 24"-long pieces of fabric, each 36" wide, and seam them together at the sides to form a long rectangle, approximately 6 yards wide and 24" long, as shown in *figure 10* on page 105.

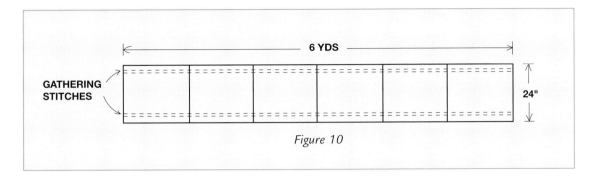

6 YDS

GATHERING STITCHES

24"

Figure 10

2 Sew two lines of gathering stitches on each of the 6-yard-long edges, as shown in *figure 10*. Pull the gathers until the fabric measures 98" long on both the top and bottom edges.

3 This gathered piece of fabric will be used to cover the area between the upper and lower supports at the end of the chaise where you place your feet. Beginning just behind one of the middle long connectors (D), staple the fabric to the top of the long frame (A). Pull it down tightly and staple the other gathered edge to the bottom edge of the lower support. Continue working around the side, across the front, and down the other side, alternately stapling at the top and bottom. End just behind the opposite long connector (D).

4 Cut four 35"-long pieces of fabric, each 36" wide, and seam them together at the sides to form a rectangle about 4 yards long and 35" wide.

5 Sew two lines of gathering stitches on each of the 4-yard-long edges. Pull the gathers until the fabric measures 72" long on both the top and bottom edges.

6 This second gathered piece of fabric will be used to cover the area between the top frame and the lower support on the back and sides of the chaise lounge. Fold under a 1"-edge and begin just at the front edge of the long connector (D). Staple the fabric to the top of the top side (E). Pull the fabric down tightly and staple the other gathered edge to the bottom edge of the lower support. Continue working around the side, across the back, and along the other side, alternately stapling at the top and bottom. End just at the front edge of the opposite long connector (D), folding over the final raw edge of the fabric at the end.

7 Cut two 20"-long pieces of fabric, each 36" wide. These will be used to cover the fronts of the arms.

8 On one fabric width, sew two lines of gathering stitches on each of the 36" edges. Pull the gathers until the fabric measures 16" long on both the top and bottom edges.

9 Fold under a 1" edge on one 20" side of the fabric. Then staple the 16" gathered fabric edge, with the fabric's right side facing the chaise, along the inner edge of the arm connector (G), starting at the bottom rear, where the arm connector (G) meets the upper support. Fold over the final raw edge at the end.

10 The next step is to pad the arm (D and G). This is easy to do, but may require a few trial-and-error efforts to find out just how much fiberfill to use and to distribute it evenly over the arm. Cover the arm with a generous amount of fiberfill. Then pull the fabric, with its right side up, over the fiberfill to cover the opposite side and the top front of the arm. Finding a helper to hold the fabric in place while you evaluate your work will make your life easier. Adjust the amount of fiberfill, if necessary. When you're satisfied with the way the arm looks, staple the other gathered edge of the fabric to the inner edge of the arm connector (G) and the side connector (H). Adjust the gathers evenly along the arm.

11 Repeat Steps 9 and 10 to pad the remaining arm and cover it with fabric.

12 Now you're on the home stretch! Cut four 34"-long fabric widths. Seam them together to form a rectangle 4 yards long x 34" wide. This will be used to cover the rest of the arms and the back (E, F, and H).

13 Sew two lines of gathering stitches on each of the 4-yard-long edges. Pull the gathers until the fabric measures 72" long on both the top and bottom edges.

14 Fold under a 1" edge and begin at the lower edge of the top side (E) where it meets the back edge of the arm connector (G). Place the fabric right side up against the chaise, so that the gathering stitches are along the lower edge of the top side (E). Staple the fabric to the lower edge of the top side (E) and then work your way around, stapling the fabric along the lower edge of the top back (F) and the lower edge of the opposite top side (E), ending directly opposite to where you started. Fold over the final raw edge at the end.

15 The next step is to pad the arms and back (E, F, and H). Follow the same procedure outlined in Step 10, covering the arms and back with a generous amount of fiberfill, pulling the fabric over the fiberfill to cover the arms and back, and stapling the gathered edge to the bottom edges of the side connectors (H) and to the bottom edge of the plywood back (K). Adjust the gathers evenly along the arms and back.

Finishing

1 Install the padded seat (L) over the upper support. Insert three 2" screws through each seat support (I and J) into the padded seat (L).

2 Find your favorite book or magazine, throw a couple of pillows and a quilt on your chaise, and take a breather.

Footstool

Who says a footstool has to be boring? This perky upholstered stool can hold its own anywhere in your home. Placed in front of a favorite easy chair, it's a great place to prop your feet—with enough room left over to hold a cup of tea. It also works well tucked underneath our Wall Table (see page 60).

Special Tools & Techniques

- Miter
- Staple gun

Materials

- 5 linear feet of 2x4 pine
- 3 linear feet of 1x12 pine
- 11"x17" piece of 4" thick foam padding
- 4 fence post finials, approx. 7³⁄₄" long and 5" in diameter, with screws in ends
- 1¹⁄₂" yards of 45" upholstery fabric
- 37"x30" piece of quilt batting

Hardware

- 4 corrugated metal fasteners
- 50 1¹⁄₂" finish nails.

Cutting List

Code	Description	Qty.	Material	Dimensions
A	Long Inner Sides	2	2x4 pine	17" long
B	Short Inner Sides	2	2x4 pine	11¹⁄₄" long
C	Top/Bottom	2	1x12 pine	17" long
D	Legs	4	fence post finials	7³⁄₄" long and 5" dia. at top

Building the Footstool

1 Cut two Long Inner Sides (A) from 2x4 pine, each measuring 17 inches.

2 Miter each end of both Long Inner Sides (A) at opposing 45° angles.

3 Cut two Short Inner Sides (B) from 2x4 pine, each measuring 11¹⁄₄ inches.

4 Miter each end of both Short Inner Sides (B) at opposing 45° angles.

5 Place the two Long Inner Sides (A) on a level surface, parallel to each other and 4 inches apart. The 10-inch edges should be facing each other, as shown in *figure 1*. Place the two Short Inner Sides (B) between the ends of the Long Inner Sides (A), matching miters. Secure the joints temporarily with a corrugated metal fastener across each joint.

6 Cut two Top/Bottoms (C) from 1x12 pine, each measuring 17 inches. Designate one piece as Top (C) and one as Bottom (C).

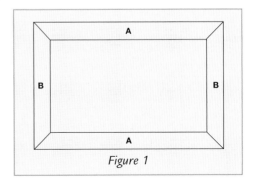

Figure 1

7 Place the Top (C) over the Long and Short Inner Sides (A and B), as shown in *figure 2*. Nail through the Top (C) into the Long and Short Inner Sides (A and B), using 1¹/₂-inch nails spaced every 4 inches.

Upholstering the Footstool

1 Apply glue on the Top (C), and place the 11x17-inch piece of 4-inch-thick foam on the Top (C).

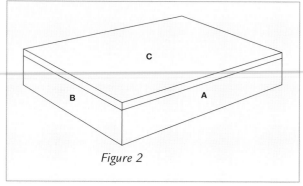

Figure 2

2 Wrap the top and sides of the entire assembly with a thin layer of quilt batting. Staple it in place through the batting into the Long and Short Inner Sides (A and B).

3 Cut a rectangle from upholstery fabric measuring 37x30 inches.

4 Center the upholstery fabric over the batting, wrap the fabric over the edge of the footstool bottom, and staple it to the underside. You can minimize the number of wrinkles if you first staple the center of one side, then the center of the opposite side, then work your way out to the corners. Smooth the fabric as you go. Staple the centers of the remaining sides, and again work your way to the corners. Be generous with the staples; use enough to keep the fabric from puckering along the sides. Finish the corners as you would the sheets on a hospital bed, then staple the fabric in place.

5 Wrap the top and sides of the Bottom (C) with a thin layer of quilt batting. Staple the batting in place through the batting into the underside of the Bottom (C).

6 Cut a rectangle from upholstery fabric measuring 21x17 inches.

7 Center the upholstery fabric over the batting, wrap the fabric over the edge of the footstool bottom, and staple it to the underside.

Finishing

1 The fence post finials will be used as legs for the footstool. Fill any cracks or crevices in the finials with wood filler then sand them smooth.

2 Paint or stain the finials with the color of your choice. We chose a bright white paint.

3 Place the top assembly (with foam and upholstery) upside down on a flat surface. Place the upholstered Bottom (C) on top of it, matching sides. Nail through the fabric-covered Bottom (C) into the Long and Short Sides (A and B), using 1$\frac{1}{2}$-inch nails every 4 inches around the edges.

4 Measure 2$\frac{3}{4}$ inches in both directions from each corner, as shown in *figure 3*. Mark the measurement, and screw in the four finial legs at the marked points.

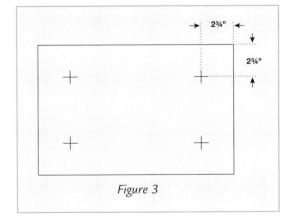

Figure 3

Wooden Window Valance

Looking for unique and easy-to-make window treatments? This valance can be adjusted to fit any window, or painted to coordinate with your new or existing curtains. We added some sponge-painted trim to create extra visual interest.

Materials

- 7 linear feet of 1x12 pine
- 7 linear feet of 1x4 pine

Hardware

- 30 1½" (4d) finish nails
- 4 metal shelf brackets

*Notes on Materials

This valance can be adjusted to fit any window, by either subtracting or adding 5¾-inch cutout squares. Keep in mind, however, that to make the valance look symmetrical, you must always have an even number of cutouts. An alternate method is to change the width of the cutouts.

Cutting List

Code	Description	Qty.	Material	Dimensions
A	Front	1	1x12 pine	74¾" long
B	Sides	2	1x12 pine	2¾" long
C	Top	1	1x4 pine	74¾" long

Cutting the Pieces

1 Cut one Front (A) from 1x12 plywood, measuring 74¾ inches.

2 Referring to *figure 1*, transfer the dimensions for the cutouts to the Front (A). To make certain that you cut out the properly sized squares, we suggest that you mark a large "X" on the areas to be cut out.

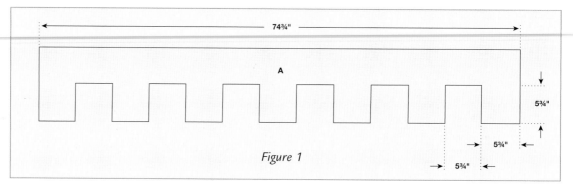

Figure 1

3 Cut out the squares marked with an "X" on the Front (A).

4 Cut two Sides (B) from 1x12 pine, each measuring 2¾ inches.

5 Cut one Top (C) from 1x4 pine, measuring 74¾ inches.

Assembly

1 Place the two Sides (B) on end on a flat surface, parallel to each other, and 73^1/$_2$ inches apart. Apply glue to the meeting surfaces, and place the Front (A) over the ends of the Sides (B), as shown in *figure 2* on page 112. Nail through the Front (A) into the ends of the Sides (B), using four evenly spaced 1^1/$_2$-inch nails.

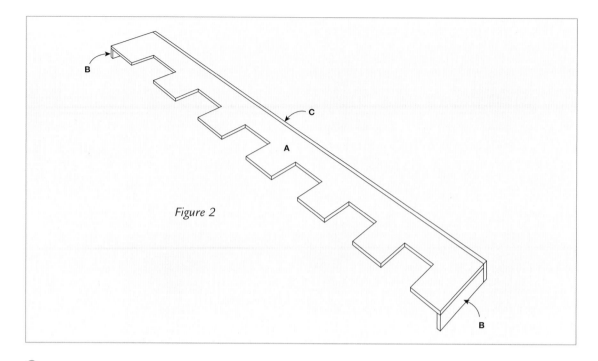

Figure 2

2 Stand the assembly upright and place the Top (C) over the edges of the Front (A) and Sides (B), as shown in *figure 2*. Apply glue to the meeting surfaces, and nail through the Top (C) into the edges of the Front (A) and Sides (B), using 1¹/₂-inch nails spaced every 5 inches.

Finishing

1 Fill any holes, cracks, or crevices with wood filler.

2 Thoroughly sand all areas of the completed valance.

3 Paint or stain the valance with the color of your choice. We painted our valance pale green, then added sponged squares in a checkerboard pattern using pale pink paint.

4 Install four evenly spaced metal shelf brackets to the inside top of the valance. To hang, screw through the metal shelf brackets into the wall.

Faux Poster Bed

Although it looks as if it came from an expensive furniture store, it's really just a plywood headboard and footboard between four posts connected to an existing metal bed frame. Add ordinary curtain rods and holders, and voilà—a charming four-poster bed!

Materials

- 115 linear feet of 1x6 pine
- 6 linear feet of 1x8 pine
- 7 linear feet of 2x10 pine
- 2 4-x-8-foot sheets of $3/4$" plywood
- 14 linear feet of $2^1/4$" handrail
- 22 linear feet of 3"–wide beaded molding
- 8 $3^3/4$" decorative squares
- 7 linear feet of 1x4 pine
- 6 linear feet of 2x2 pine
- 2 closet rod holders
- 6 curtain rod holders
- 4 8-foot beaded curtain rods
- 6 curtain rod finials

Hardware

- 300 $1^1/2$"(4d) finish nails
- 100 2" (6d) finish nails
- 60 $1^1/4$" (3d) finish nails
- 75 1" (2d) finish nails
- 20 $2^1/2$" wood screws
- 20 $1^5/8$" wood screws

Cutting List

Code	Description	Qty.	Material	Dimensions
A	Poster Side	16	1x6 pine	84" long
B	Small Base	8	1x8 pine	$7^1/4$" long
C	Large Base	8	2x10 pine	$9^1/4$" long
D	Headboard	1	$3/4$" plywood	79"x34"
E	Top Rail	2	$2^1/4$" handrail	79" long
F	Long Molding	2	3"-wide beaded molding	57" long
G	Short Molding	2	3"-wide beaded molding	5" long
H	Decorative Squares	8	pine decorative squares	$3^3/4$" square
I	Footboard	1	$3/4$" plywood	79"x28"
J	Long Footboard	2	3"-wide beaded molding	57" long
K	Short Footboard	2	3"-wide beaded molding	$9^1/2$" long
L	Base Rail	1	1x4 pine	79" long
M	Supports	4	2x2 pine	15" long

Making the Poster Columns

1 Cut 16 Poster Sides (A) from 1x6 pine, each measuring 84 inches.

2 Assemble four Poster Sides (A), overlapping each piece in rotation as shown in *figure 1* on page 115. With the four Sides (A) in position, the leg should measure $6^1/4$ inches wide on all sides. Apply glue to the meeting surfaces, and nail together the four sides (A). Use $1^1/2$-inch nails, spacing nails about 6 inches apart.

3 Repeat Step 2 three times to create the other three poster columns.

4 Cut eight Small Bases (B) from 1x8 pine, each measuring 7¼ inches.

5 Cut eight Large Bases (C) from 2x10 pine, each measuring 9¼ inches.

6 Center one Small Base (B) over one end of an assembled column, as shown in *figure 2* on page 115. Apply glue to the meeting surfaces, and nail through the Small Base (B) into the assembled column, using eight 1½-inch nails.

7 Repeat Step 6 to attach a second Small Base (B) to the opposite end of the same column.

8 Repeat Steps 6 and 7 three times to attach the remaining seven Small Bases (B) on both ends of each of the remaining columns.

9 Place one Large Base (C) on a flat, level surface (preferably the floor, due to the height of the columns). Center one assembled column with the Small Bases (B) attached, over the Large Base (C) as shown in *figure 3*. Apply glue to the meeting surfaces, and nail through the edge of the Small Base (B) into the Large Base (C), using eight 2-inch nails.

10 Turn the same column upside down, and repeat Step 9 to attach a second Large Base (C).

11 Repeat Steps 9 and 10 three times to attach the remaining Large Bases (C) to the ends of the remaining columns.

Making the Headboard

1 Cut one Headboard (D) from ³/₄-inch plywood, measuring 79x34 inches.

2 Cut two Top Rails (E) from 2¹/₄-inch handrail, each measuring 79 inches.

3 Center one Top Rail (E) over the one 79-inch inch edge of the Headboard (D). Apply glue to the meeting surfaces, and nail through the Top Rail (E) into the edge of the Headboard (D), using 2-inch nails spaced every 6 inches. Set the remaining Top Rail (E) aside; it will be used later on the footboard.

4 Cut two Long Moldings (F) from 3-inch-wide beaded molding, each measuring 57 inches.

5 Cut two Short Moldings (G) from 3-inch-wide beaded molding, each measuring 5 inches.

6 Referring to *figure 4* on page 116, position the Long and Short Moldings (F and G) and four Decorative Squares (H) on the Headboard (D). Note that the 3-inch moldings must be centered widthwise on the 3³/₄-inch Decorative Squares (H). Nail through each corner of the four Decorative Squares (H) using 1¹/₄-inch nails. Nail through the molding, using 1-inch nails. Use two nails on each of the Short Moldings (G), and 11 nails on each of the Long Moldings (F).

Making the Footboard

1 Cut one Footboard (I) from ³/₄-inch plywood, measuring 79x28 inches.

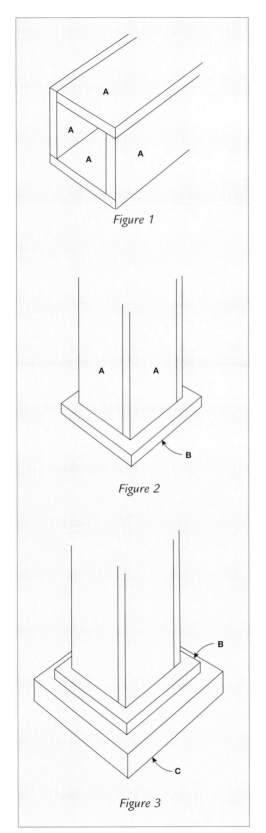

Figure 1

Figure 2

Figure 3

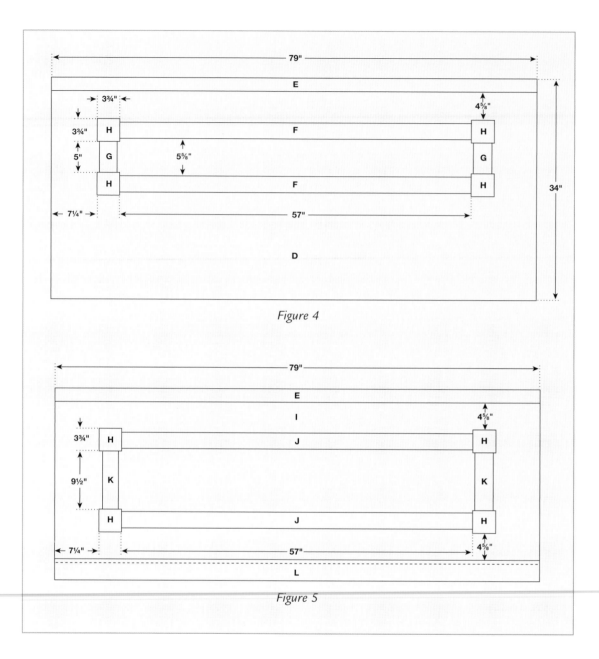

Figure 4

Figure 5

2 Locate the Top Rail (E) that you set aside earlier, and center the Top Rail (E) over the one 79-inch edge of the Footboard (I). Apply glue to the meeting surfaces, and nail through the Top Rail (E) into the edge of the Footboard (I), using 2-inch nails spaced every 6 inches.

3 Cut two Long Footboard Moldings (J) from 3-inch-wide beaded molding, each measuring 57 inches.

4 Cut two Short Footboard Moldings (K) from 3-inch-wide beaded molding, each measuring 9½ inches.

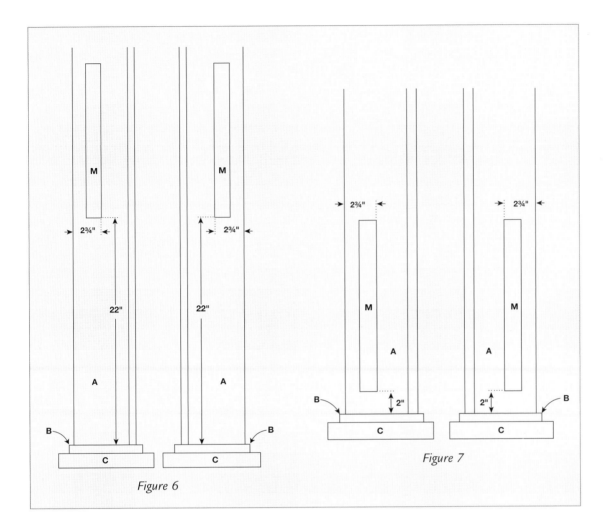

Figure 6

Figure 7

5 Referring to *figure 5* on page 116, position the Long and Short Footboard Moldings (J and K) and four Decorative Squares (H) on the Footboard (I). Note that the 3-inch moldings must be centered widthwise on the Decorative Squares (H). Nail through each corner of the four Decorative Squares (H) using 1¼-inch nails. Nail through the molding, using 1-inch nails. Use two nails on each of the Short Footboard Moldings (K), and 11 nails on each of the Long Footboard Moldings (J).

6 Cut one Base Rail (L) from 1x4 pine, measuring 79 inches.

7 Apply glue to the meeting surfaces, and attach the Base Rail (L) to the bottom of the Footboard (I). The top of the Base Rail (L) should overlap the bottom of the Footboard (I) 1 inch. Use 1¼-inch nails spaced every 5 inches.

Assembling the Headboard & Footboard

1 Cut four Supports (M) from 2x2 pine, each measuring 15 inches.

2 Attach two Supports (M) 22 inches above the bottom of two of the assembled columns into Side (A), as shown in *figure 6* on page 117. Apply glue to the meeting surfaces, and screw through the Support. (M) into the Side (A), using four 2¹/₂-inch wood screws on each joint. Note: These two columns will support the headboard.

3 Attach two Supports (M) 2 inches above the bottom of the remaining assembled columns, as shown in *figure 7* on page 117. Apply glue to the meeting surfaces, and screw through the Support (M) into the Side (A), using four 2¹/₂ inch wood screws. Note: These two columns will support the footboard.

4 Place the two headboard columns on a flat surface, with the two attached Supports (M) facing each other. Place the Headboard (D) over the two Supports (M) between the two headboard columns. The bottom of the Rail (L) should be flush against the top of Supports (M). Screw through the Headboard (D) into the Supports (M), using four 1⁵/₈-inch wood screws on each joint.

5 Repeat step 4 to attach the footboard to the footboard columns.

Finishing

1 Fill any holes, cracks, or crevices with wood filler.

2 Thoroughly sand all areas of the completed headboard and footboard assemblies.

3 Attach two closet rod holders on the inner sides of the two headboard columns, centered widthwise and 1¹/₂ inches from the top of the column.

4 Attach one curtain rod holder on the outside of each of the headboard columns.

5 Attach one curtain rod holder on the two outer sides of each of the footboard columns.

6 Paint or stain the project the color of your choice. We painted the entire bed assembly white. After the white paint dried, we applied a coat of light moss green paint, then ragged off the second coat. Remember to paint the curtain rods and the finials. The curtain rods will be cut to length during the final assembly.

7 Depending on the type of metal frame on your bed, the installation of the headboard and footboard may vary. We had a metal frame with brackets for both a headboard and footboard, and screwed through the metal brackets into both the headboard and footboard. If your frame has only one bracket, you can turn the frame around and attach that bracket to the footboard. Then you can either attach the headboard to the wall or simply place the headboard against the wall and push the bed against it to hold it in place (assuming your bed is in no danger of moving across the floor).

8 Cut one beaded curtain rod to a length of 79 inches. Install the rod in the curtain rod holders above the headboard.

9 Screw a finial on one of the remaining curtain rods. Place the end with the finial on the curtain rod holder on the headboard column, and the other end on the curtain rod holder on the footboard column. Mark the desired length on the rod (ours extended past the holder about 1 inch), remove the curtain rod, and cut the rod at the mark. Screw a second finial into the cut end, and reinstall the curtain rod.

10 Repeat Step 9 to install another curtain rod on the opposite side of the headboard/footboard.

11 Repeat the procedure one more time to cut and install the remaining curtain rod on the curtain rod holders over the footboard.

Birdhouse Floor Lamp

Place this cheerful floor lamp beside a comfortable chair in a corner of any room, and it will surely become your favorite spot to curl up with a good book. It's also a terrific addition to a garden room or a little girl's bedroom.

Special Tools & Techniques

- Miter
- Bar clamps

Materials

- 18 linear feet of 1x8 pine
- 10 linear feet of 1x1 pine
- 4 linear feet of 2x4 pine

Hardware

- 50 1½" (4d) finish nails
- 30 1¼" (3d) finish nails
- 20 2½" (8d) finish nails
- Lamp kit (available at most hardware stores)
- Lampshade of your choice

Cutting List

Code	Description	Qty.	Material	Dimensions
A	Back/Front	2	1x8 pine	46¼" long
B	Side	2	1x8 pine	43⅝" long
C	Roof	2	1x8 pine	10½" long
D	Side Trim	8	1x1 pine	8¾" long
E	Front Trim	4	1x1 pine	8¾" long
F	Base	4	2x4 pine	10½" long

Constructing the Base

1 Cut two Back/Front pieces (A) from 1x8 pine, each measuring 46¼ inches.

2 Referring to *figure 1*, remove the shaded area on one end of a Back/Front (A).

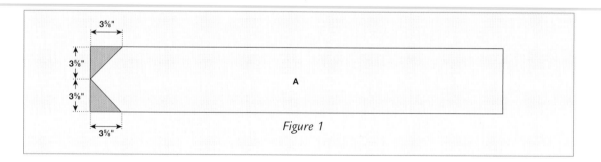

Figure 1

3 Repeat Step 2 to remove the shaded area on one end of the remaining Back/Front (A).

4 Cut two Sides (B) from 1x8 pine, each measuring 43⅛ inches.

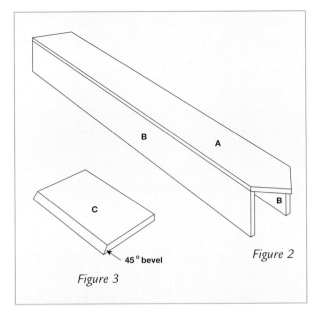

Figure 2

Figure 3

45° bevel

5 Place the two Sides (B) on a level surface, parallel to each other and 5³/₄ inches apart. Apply glue to the meeting edges, and place one Back/Front (A) over the two Sides (B), as shown in *figure 2*. Note that the square end of the Back/Front (A) is even with the ends of the Sides (B), and that the pointed end of the Back/Front (A) extends beyond the Sides (B). Nail through the Back/Front (A) into the edges of the two Sides (B), using 1¹/₂-inch nails spaced approximately every 5 inches.

6 Turn the assembly upside down, and repeat Step 4 to attach the remaining Back/Front (A).

Constructing the Roof

1 Cut two Roofs (C) from 1x8 pine, each measuring 10¹/₂ inches.

2 Bevel one 10¹/₂-inch edge of one Roof (C) at a 45° angle, as shown in *figure 3*.

3 Repeat Step 2 to bevel one edge of the remaining Roof (C).

4 Apply glue to the beveled edges, and place the two Roofs (C), beveled edges together, on top of

the base assembly, and nail pieces together. Nail through each of the Roofs (C) into the beveled edge of the other Roof (C), using four 1¹/₂ inch nails on each side. Do not nail into the base structure yet, as the roof-will have to be removed to wire the lamp.

5 Drill a ¹/₂-inch-diameter hole through the center of the roof peak to accommodate the later addition of the lamp parts.

6 Remove the completed roof, and set it aside.

Adding the Trim

1 Referring to *figure 4*, mark the trim placement lines on the two Sides (B) and one Back/Front (A) with a soft pencil.

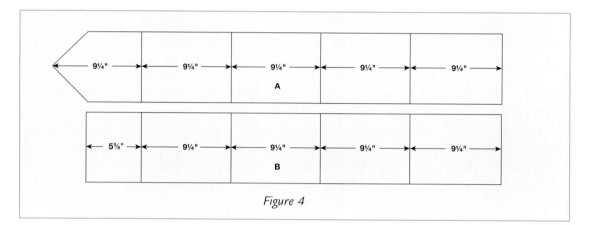

Figure 4

2 Cut eight Side Trims (D) from 1x1 pine, each measuring 8³/₄ inches.

3 Apply glue to the meeting surfaces, and place one Side Trim (D) on the base assembly, under the penciled placement line. Nail through the Side Trim (D) into the Side (B), using two ¹/₄-inch nails.

4 Repeat Step 3 seven times to attach the remaining Side Trims (D) to the base assembly.

5 Cut four Front Trims (E) from 1x1 pine, each measuring 8³/₄ inches.

6 Apply glue to the meeting surfaces, and attach one Front Trim (E) to the front of the base assembly (choose the best-looking peaked Back/Front [A]), under the placement line, and over the ends of the Side Trims (D). Nail through the Front Trim (E) into the Back/Front (A) and Side Trims (D), using three 1¹/₄-inch nails.

7 Repeat Step 6 three times to attach the remaining three Front Trims (E) to the front of the base assembly.

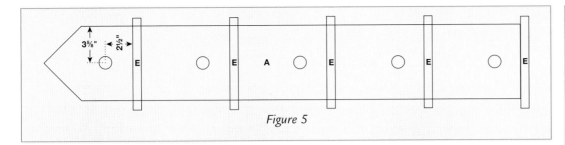

Figure 5

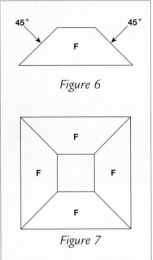

Figure 6

Figure 7

Completing the Base Assembly

1 Referring to *figure 5*, mark the placement of five holes in the front of the base assembly.

2 Drill five 1¼-inch-diameter holes through the front of the base assembly, using the marks as a guide.

3 Cut four Bases (F) from 2x4 pine, each measuring 10½ inches.

4 Miter the ends of each of the four Bases (F) at opposing 45° angles, as shown in *figure 6*.

5 Apply glue to the meeting surfaces, and position the four Bases (F), with the mitered ends together, to form a square, as shown in *figure 7*.

6 Clamp the four Bases (F) together, and toenail through both sides of each joint to hold the assembly together. Use two 2½-inch nails on each joint.

7 Center the four Bases (F) over the bottom of the base assembly. Nail through the Bases (F) into the bottom edges of the two Back/Fronts (A) and the two Sides (B). Use two 2½-inch nails through each Base (F).

Finishing

1 Fill all cracks and crevices with wood filler.

2 Sand the completed floor lamp thoroughly.

3 Paint the floor lamp the color of your choice. We painted the roof and the trim hunter green, and the rest of the lamp bright white.

4 Install the lamp kit following the manufacturer's instructions.

5 Center the assembled roof (with lamp kit installed) over the top of the base assembly, threading the wire through the center of the assembly. Apply glue to the meeting surfaces, and nail through each side of the roof into the Back/Fronts (A) and the Sides (B). Use two 1½-inch nails on each of the roof sections.

Breakfast Tray

If you're a pushover for lazy weekend mornings in bed, you'll love this generously sized breakfast tray. It's large enough for a newspaper, a pot of coffee, and a plate of delectable goodies.

Materials

- 2-x-4-foot sheet of ³/₄" plywood
- 7 linear feet of 1x3 pine
- 1 linear feet of ³/₄"-wide rope molding

Hardware

- 20 2" finish nails
- 6 1⁵/₈" wood screws
- 4 1" finish nails

Cutting List

Code	Description	Qty.	Material	Dimensions
A	Tray Stands	2	³/₄" plywood	12"x13"
B	Tray Top	1	³/₄" plywood	24"x 13"
C	Long Tray Sides	2	1x3 pine	24" long
D	Short Tray Sides	2	1x3 pine	14¹/₂" long
E	Stand Trims	4	³/₄"-wide rope molding	11¹/₄" long

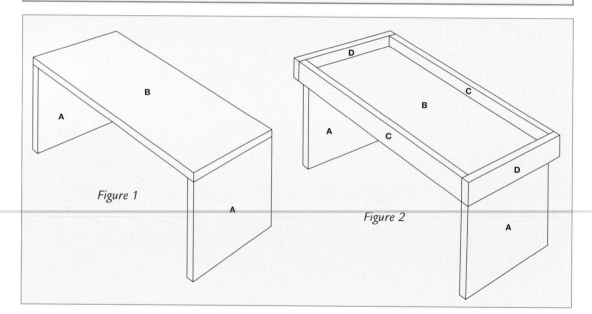

Figure 1

Figure 2

Making the Tray

1 Cut two Tray Stands (A) from ³/₄" plywood, each measuring 12x13 inches.

2 Cut one Tray Top (B) from ³/₄" plywood, measuring 24x13 inches.

3 Using *figure 1* as a guide, place the two Tray Stands (A) on edge 22¹/₂ inches apart with the 13-inch edge at the top. Place the Tray Top (B) over the ends of the Tray Stands (A). Apply

glue to the meeting surfaces, and nail through the face of the Tray Top (B) into the edges of the Tray Stands (A) using four 2-inch nails.

4 Cut two Long Tray Sides (C) from 1x3 pine, each measuring 24 inches.

5 Place the Long Tray Sides (C) over the 24-inch edges of the Tray Top (B). The Long Tray Sides (C) will extend 1 inch above and $^{3}/_{4}$ inch below the Tray Top (B), as shown in *figure 2* on page 124. Apply glue to the meeting surfaces, and nail through the Long Tray Sides (C) into the edge of the Tray Top (B), using 2-inch nails spaced 5 inches apart.

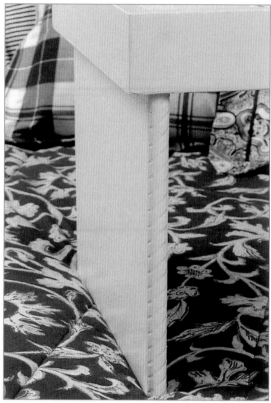

6 Cut two Short Tray Sides (D) from 1x3 pine, each measuring 14¹/₂ inches.

7 Place the two Short Tray Sides (D) over the ends of the Tray Top (B), as shown in *figure 2* on page 124. Apply glue to the meeting surfaces, and nail through the Short Tray Sides (D) into the edges of the Tray Top (B) using four 2-inch nails.

8 Using three 1⁵/₈-inch screws on each side, screw through the Short Tray Sides (D) into the Tray Stands (A). This will give added support to the Tray Stands (A).

Adding the Trim

1 Cut four Stand Trims (E) from ³/₄-inch-wide rope molding, each measuring 11¹/₄ inches.

2 Place the Stand Trims (E) over the exposed plywood edges of the Tray Stands (A). Apply glue to the meeting surfaces. Nail through the Stand Trims (E) into the Tray Stands (A) using four 1-inch nails.

Finishing

1 Fill all cracks, crevices, and nail holes with wood filler.

2 Thoroughly sand the completed breakfast tray.

3 Paint or stain the tray the color of your choice.

4 After our paint dried, we added a little whimsy to our breakfast tray. We went to a color copy store and copied a plate, butter knife, napkin, and cup and saucer; then we cut out the copies and decoupaged newsprint and the color copies to the top of the tray. The finished project was then sealed with a coat of polyurethane.

Planter for Cuttings

When plants overproduce, you can clip off the new growth and put it in water until it roots—a procedure which pays off in new plants, but which is also somewhat unsightly. This planter is just large enough to contain the glasses and plastic cups of water used for rooting and shows off the green parts of the plants without displaying the unattractive containers.

Special Tools & Techniques

- Bar clamps
- Mitering

Materials

- 6 linear feet of ³/₄"x³/₄" pine
- 10 linear feet of 1x6 pine
- 6 linear feet of 1"x1" corner molding

Hardware

- Approximately 25 #6x1¹/₄" flathead wood screws
- Approximately 50 3d finishing nails

Cutting List

Code	Description	Qty.	Material	Dimensions
A	Side	8	1x6 pine	8¹/₂" long
B	End	2	1x6 pine	8¹/₂" long
C	Bottom	1	1x6 pine	23¹/₂" long
D	Long Trim	2	³/₄"x³/₄" pine	23¹/₂" long
E	Short Trim	2	³/₄"x³/₄" pine	7" long
F	Molding	4	1"x1" corner molding	Cut to fit (approx. 62" total)

Constructing the Planter Box

1 Cut ten 8¹/₂"-long A and B pieces from 1x6 pine. For ease of instruction, we'll refer to eight of these pieces as sides (A) and two as ends (B).

2 Cut a 23¹/₂"-long bottom (C) from 1x6 pine.

3 Position four sides (A) next to each other on a level surface, as shown in *figure 1*. Also place two ends (B) on edge at each end. Glue the pieces together, making certain that the assembly is perfectly-square, and clamp the six pieces in place. Leave the clamp on for several hours.

4 Glue together the four remaining sides (A), as you did the previous four. Clamp these four sides together and leave the clamp in place for several hours.

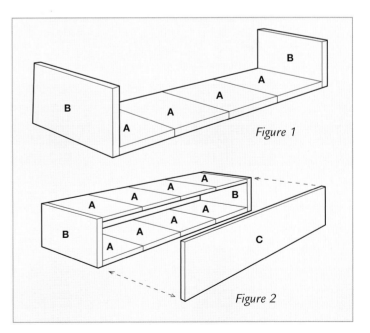

Figure 1

Figure 2

5 To create the long box shown in *figure 2* on page 127, glue the four sides (A) that you assembled in Step 4 between the two ends (B) on the assembly that you constructed in Step 3.

6 Glue the bottom (C) over the exposed edges of the long box assembly, as shown in *figure 2*. Insert two 1¼" screws through the bottom (C) into each of the eight sides (A) and two ends (B).

Adding the Trim

1 Cut two long trim pieces (D) from ¾"x¾" pine, each measuring 23½" long.

2 Cut two short trim pieces (E) from ¾"x¾" pine, each measuring 7" long.

3 Glue one long trim piece (D) along the bottom of the box, placing its bottom edge ⅝" from the bottom of the planter box (see *figure 3*). Secure the long trim piece (D) in place with 3d finishing nails spaced 4" apart.

4 Repeat Step 3 to attach the other long trim piece (D) to the opposite side of the planter box.

5 Glue one short trim piece (E) to the end of the planter box so that it overlaps the ends of the long trim pieces (see *figure 3*). Secure the short trim piece (E) with three 3d finishing nails.

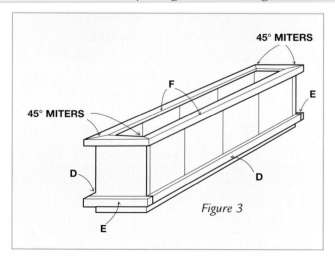

Figure 3

6 Repeat Step 5 to attach the remaining short trim piece (E) to the opposite end of the planter box.

Adding the Corner Molding

1 The top edges of the planter box are concealed by mitered lengths of corner molding (F). Measure and cut four pieces of molding to fit over the top of the planter box mitering the ends to fit together exactly.

2 Glue the four mitered molding pieces (F) onto the top edges of the planter box. Then secure them with 3d finishing nails spaced about 3" apart on the longer pieces and about 2" apart on the shorter pieces.

Finishing

1 Fill all holes, cracks, and crevices with wood filler.

2 Sand all surfaces of the planter box thoroughly.

3 Stain or paint the planter box the color of your choice. We've decorated our planter with 4"x4" tiles. If you'd like to ad tiles to yours, just turn to the instructions provided with the Tiled Lamp project on page 163.

Dressing Table

Most girls have lots of very important "stuff" that can't be accommodated in their dressers, and they never have enough room for displaying perfume bottles, pictures, knickknacks, and jewelry. This fabric-covered dressing table (see page 131) solves the problem. It's even large enough to double as a study desk!

Materials

- 22 linear feet of 1x8 pine
- 19 linear feet of 1x12 pine
- 1 piece of $\frac{1}{4}$"-thick plywood, 30"x48"
- 1 piece of $\frac{3}{4}$"-thick plywood, 22"x48"
- 1 piece of $\frac{1}{8}$"-thick glass, 22"x48"
- 1 double-layered piece of quilt batting, 26"x52"
- 5$\frac{1}{2}$ yards of $\frac{3}{4}$"-diameter cording
- 2 coordinating fabrics, each 36"-wide:
  - Fabric #1, 1$\frac{1}{2}$ yards for table top
  - Fabric #1, $\frac{1}{2}$ yard for cording
  - Fabric #2, 5$\frac{1}{2}$ yards for skirt
  - Fabric #2, $\frac{1}{2}$ yard for cording

Optional extra fabric for covering back of assembly:

- Fabric #1, $\frac{1}{4}$ yard for cording
- Fabric #2, 2$\frac{3}{4}$ yards for skirt
- Fabric #2, $\frac{1}{4}$ yard for cording

Hardware

- Approximately 50 #6x1$\frac{1}{4}$" flathead wood screws
- Approximately 40 #6x2" flathead wood screws
- Approximately 25 3d finishing nails

*Notes on Materials

Because we wanted to place the finished dressing table against a wall, we bought only enough fabric to cover its front and sides. If you'd like to skirt the back of the dressing table, too, add the extra fabric and cording listed in the "Materials List."

Unless you want to make your own cording, purchase it from a fabric shop, coordinating it with your selected fabrics.

Cutting List

Code	Description	Qty.	Material	Dimensions
A	Side	4	1x12 pine	28$\frac{1}{2}$" long
B	Top/Bottom	4	1x12 pine	13$\frac{1}{2}$" long
C	Shelf	4	1x12 pine	12" long
D	Back	2	$\frac{1}{4}$" plywood	13$\frac{1}{2}$"x30"
E	Bin Front/Back	12	1x8 pine	11$\frac{3}{4}$" long
F	Bin Side	12	1x8 pine	9" long
G	Bin Bottom	6	$\frac{1}{4}$" plywood	9$\frac{3}{8}$"x10$\frac{5}{8}$"
H	Table Top	1	$\frac{3}{4}$" plywood	22"x48"

Making the Base Units

1 Underneath the skirt, the dressing table is supported by two identical units, each of which contains three drawers. To make the first unit, start by cutting the following pieces from 1x12 pine: two 28$\frac{1}{2}$"-long sides (A); two 13$\frac{1}{2}$"-long top/bottom pieces (B); and two 12"-long shelf pieces (C).

2 Glue the two top/bottom pieces (B) over the raw ends of the two sides (A) to form a rectangular box as shown in *figure 1* on page 132. Insert three 1$\frac{1}{4}$" screws at each joint.

3 Fit the two shelves (C) into the rectangular box, spacing them evenly, so that each of the three openings is exactly 9" high (see *figure 1* on page 132).

4 Glue the shelves (C) to the sides (A) and insert four 2" screws along the length of each joint.

5 Cut one 13¹/₂"x30" back (D) from ¹/₄"-thick plywood. Glue the back (D) onto the back edges of the assembled unit, as shown in *figure 1* on page 132, and secure it with 3d finishing nails spaced 4" apart.

6 Repeat Steps 1 through 5 to construct a second base unit that is identical to the first.

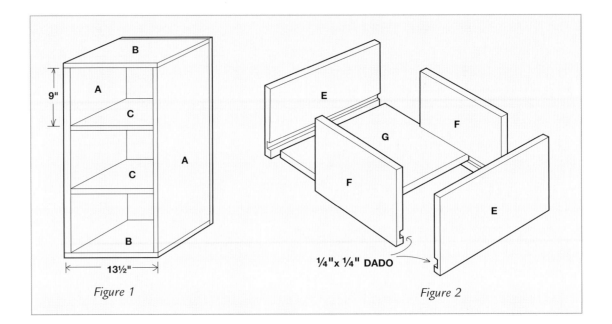

Figure 1

¼"x ¼" DADO

Figure 2

Making the Drawer/Bins

1 There are a total of six bins, three in each of the dressing-table units. These aren't actually drawers, as they simply sit inside the units, but they can be pulled out if desired. Each bin is identical in size and in the method of construction (see *figure 2*). To make them, start by cutting twelve 11¾"-long bin front/back pieces (E) and twelve 9"-long bin sides (F) from 1x8 pine.

2 Cut a ¼"x¼" dado on the inside of each bin piece (E and F), ⅜" from its lower edge, to accommodate the plywood bottom.

3 From ¼"-thick plywood, cut six 9⅜"x10⅝" bin bottoms (G).

4 Assemble and glue together one bin as shown in *figure 2*. Note that the bin front/back pieces (E) overlap the ends of the bin sides (F). Use three 1¼" screws at each joint.

5 Repeat the bin-assembly process in Step 4 five more times to construct the remaining five bins.

Constructing the Top

1 The dressing table top is constructed of ¾"-thick plywood covered with quilt batting and fabric # 1. The skirt—made from fabric #2—is then attached to the table top (H). Start by cutting a 22"x48" table top (H) from ¾"-thick plywood.

2 Cut a 26"x52" double layer of quilt batting.

3 Cut a 26"x52" piece of fabric # 1.

4 Place the piece of fabric # 1 on a smooth surface, right side down. Place the double layer of quilt batting over the fabric. Center the top (H) over the quilt batting. Then bring the edges of the fabric up and over the edges of the table top (H) and staple them to the plywood. To minimize wrinkling, first staple the center of one side, then the center of the opposite side, and work your way out to the corners, smoothing the fabric as you go. Staple the centers of the remaining sides and again work your way out to the corners. Be generous with the staples; use enough to keep the fabric taut and eliminate puckering along the sides.

5 To attach the fabric-covered top to the two base units, place the top upside down on a flat surface. Place the two-base units upside down on top of it, spacing them as shown in *figure 3*. Attach the base units to the top by inserting 1¼" screws through all four corners of each of the units. Turn the entire assembly right side up when you're finished.

Making the Skirt

1 If you intend to skirt all four sides of the assembly, skip to Step 7. To skirt the two sides and front, first cut the 5½-yard-long piece of fabric #2 in half to get two pieces, each 2¾ yards long.

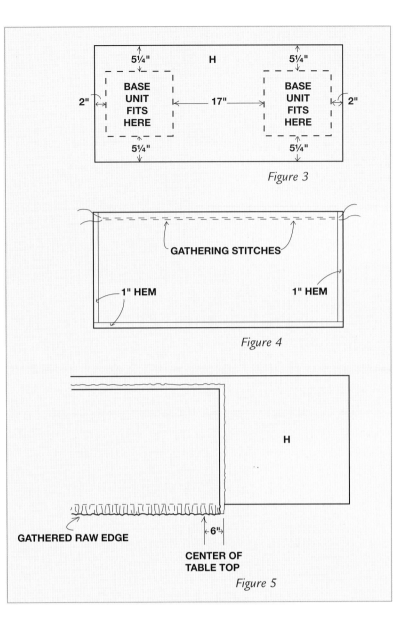

Figure 3

Figure 4

Figure 5

2 Sew a 1" hem along the 2¾-yard edge of one of these two pieces and along both of the sides, as shown in *figure 4*.

3 Sew a double row of gathering stitches 1" from the remaining raw edge (see *figure 4*). Pull the gathers until the gathered edge measures 56".

4 Repeat Steps 2 and 3 to hem and gather the remaining 2¾-yard long piece of fabric #2.

5 Now you'll attach the gathered edges of these two pieces onto the edge of the padded table top (H). Place the first fabric piece right side down on the left side of the table top (H), with the gathered edge overhanging the edge of the table top and the hem 6" right of center, as shown in *figure 5* on page 133. Adjust the overhang so that when the gathered skirt piece is stapled and pulled down, the skirt will just touch the floor. Staple the skirt to the top edge of

the table top. Don't be stingy with the staples; you want a perfectly straight edge after you turn the skirt down. Work your way from 6" left of center, left across the front, across the side, and 4" around on the back.

6 Repeat Step 5 to attach the remaining piece of gathered fabric to the right side of the padded table top. The two pieces should overlap by 6" in the center of the dressing table.

7 To skirt all four sides of the entire assembly, hem and attach the entire 8$\frac{1}{4}$ yards of fabric #2 as a single piece, beginning and ending with a 6" overlap in the front.

Adding the Cording

1 Now you'll cover the edge of the skirt cording with fabric # 1. Because the fabric will be gathered, it must be twice as long as the cording itself. Start by cutting the 5$\frac{1}{2}$ yards of cording in half so that you have two equal pieces, each 2$\frac{3}{4}$ yards long.

2 Using the $\frac{1}{2}$ yard of fabric #1, cut and seam together enough 3"-wide x 36"-long strips to produce a strip 3" wide and 5$\frac{1}{2}$ yards long.

3 Fold the fabric strip lengthwise and sew a $\frac{1}{2}$" seam along the raw edges.

4 Turn the fabric strip right side out to form a tube.

5 Pull one piece of the cording through the tube and adjust the gathers evenly along the length.

6 Repeat Steps 2 through 5 to cover the remaining cording with the $\frac{1}{2}$ yard of fabric #2.

7 Glue the cording covered with fabric # 1 to the top edge of the padded table top (H), over the gathered skirt. Begin at the back, work across one side, across the front, across the other side, and end at the back.

8 Repeat Step 7 to glue the cording covered with fabric #2 just below the previously glued cording.

9 Set the piece of $\frac{1}{4}$" glass on top of your finished dressing table and await the rave reviews!

Bathroom Wall Rack

Does anyone ever have enough shelf space in the bathroom? This project is one solution to the problem of where to store towels, magazines, perfume bottles, and other items you need within reach. It's easy to build, and you can paint the finished project to pick up the colors of your bathroom.

Special Tools & Techniques

- Ripping

Materials

- 4 linear feet of 1x2 pine
- 13 linear feet of 1x6 pine
- 5 linear feet of 1x8 pine

Hardware

- Approximately 20 #6x1¼" flathead wood screws
- Approximately 25 #6x1½" flathead wood screws

Cutting List

Code	Description	Qty.	Material	Dimensions
A	Shelf	4	1x6 pine	20¾" long
B	Divider	1	1x6 pine	8½" long
C	Side	2	1x6 pine	29½" long
D	Rail	2	1x2 pine	20¾" long
E	Top/Bottom	2	1x8 pine, ripped	24¼" long

Making the Basic Frame

1 Cut four 20¾"-long shelves (A) from 1x6 pine.

2 Cut one 8½"-long divider (B) from 1x6 pine.

3 Position two of the shelves (A) on a level surface, parallel to each other and 8½" apart. Position the divider (B) between the two shelves (A), locating its ends in the exact center of each shelf (see *figure 1*). Glue the divider (B) in place and insert two 1½" screws through each of the shelves (A) end into the divider (B).

4 Cut two sides (C) from 1x6 pine, each 29½" long.

5 Place the divider/shelf assembly (see Step 3) on a level surface. Place a third shelf (A) parallel to the divider/shelf assembly and 8" above it, as shown in *figure 2*. Position the remaining shelf (A) parallel to the divider/shelf assembly and 10" below it. Position the two sides (C) along the sides of the assembly and the third and fourth shelves (A). Glue the sides (C) to the edges of the shelves (A) and insert two 1½" screws through each side (C) and into the ends of each shelf (A).

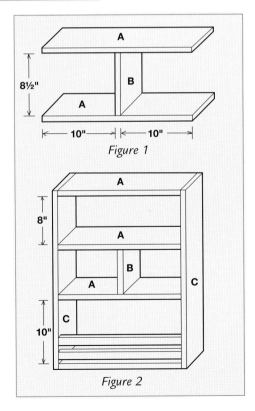

Figure 1

Figure 2

Adding the Rails

1 Cut two 20³/₄"-long rails (D) from 1x2 pine.

2 Glue one rail (D) between the two sides (C), ¹/₂" above the bottom shelf (A), as shown in *figure 3* on page 137. Secure the rail by inserting a 1¹/₄" screw through each side (C) and into each end of the rail (D).

3 Repeat Step 2 to attach the second rail (D), leaving ³/₄" between its lower edge and the upper edge of the first rail (see *figure 3*).

Adding the Top & Bottom

1 Rip 5 linear feet of 1x8 pine to a width of 6¹/₄".

2 Cut two 24¹/₄"-long top/bottom pieces (E) from the ripped pine.

3 To attach one top/bottom piece (E) to the top of the shelf assembly, first center the top/bottom piece over the assembly so that there is a 1" overhang at each end (see *figure 3*). Because the completed rack must hang on the wall, the back of the top/bottom piece (E) should be flush with the back of the shelf assembly and should overhang by ³/₄" in front. Glue top/bottom piece (E) in place arid use four 1¹/₄" screws to attach it to the top shelf (A), centering the screws along the length of the board and spacing them evenly.

4 Repeat Step 3 to attach the remaining top/bottom piece (E) to the bottom of the shelf assembly.

Finishing

1 Fill all holes, cracks, and crevices with wood filler.

2 Sand all surfaces of the completed shelf thoroughly.

3 Paint or stain the shelf with colors of your choice.

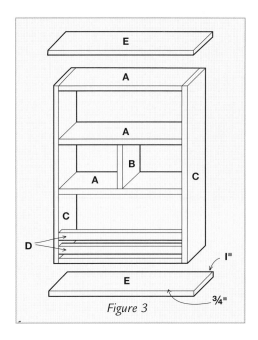

Figure 3

Wastebasket

Here's an easy (and handsome) alternative to those unattractive plastic wastebaskets. It can be built from just a few feet of pine, rope molding, and some drawer pulls. Paint and a little imagination will transform the wastebasket into a one-of-kind decorative accent.

Special Tools & Techniques

- Miter

Materials

- 6 linear feet of 1x12 pine
- 5 linear feet of ³/₄"-wide rope molding
- 4 1½"-diameter round drawer pulls

Hardware

- 30 1½"(4d) finish nails
- 20 1" (2d) finish nails

Cutting List

Code	Description	Qty.	Material	Dimensions
A	Sides	4	1x12 pine	14" long
B	Bottom	1	1x12 pine	9³/₄" long
C	Long Trims	2	³/₄"-wide rope molding	12³/₄" long
D	Short Trims	2	³/₄"-wide rope molding	11¹/₄" long

Constructing the Wastebasket

1 Cut four Sides (A) from 1x12 pine, each measuring 14 inches.

2 Place two Sides (A) on a level surface, parallel to each other and 9³/₄ inches apart. Apply glue to the meeting surfaces, and place a third Side (A) over the edges of the first two Sides (A), as shown in *figure 1*. Nail through the third Side (A) into the edges of the first two Sides (A). Use four 1¹/₂-inch nails evenly spaced along each joint.

3 Turn the assembly upside down and repeat Step 2 to attach the fourth Side (A) to the assembly.

4 Cut one Bottom (B) from 1x12 pine, measuring 9³/₄ inches.

5 Fit the Bottom (B) inside the assembled Sides (A), flush with the ends of the Sides (A), as shown in *figure 2* on page 140. Apply glue to the meeting surfaces, and nail through the face of the four Sides (A) into the edge of the Bottom (B), using 1¹/₂-inch nails on each Side (A).

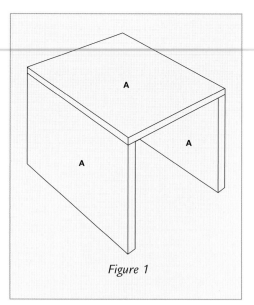

Figure 1

Adding the Top Trim

1 Cut two Long Trims (C) from ³/₄-inch-wide rope molding, each measuring 12³/₄ inches. Miter each end at opposing 45° angles.

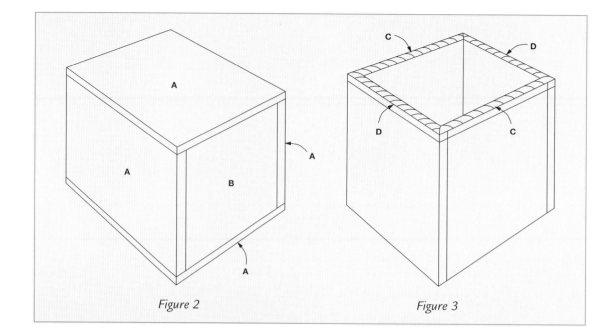

Figure 2

Figure 3

Figure 4

2 Place the Sides/Bottom assembly so that the Bottom (B) is down on the working surface. Place the Long Trims (C) on the 12³/₄-inch top edge of the Sides (A), as shown in *figure 3*. Apply glue to the meeting surfaces, and nail through the Long Trims (C) into the edge of the Sides (A), using four 1-inch nails.

3 Cut two Short Trims (D) from ³/₄-inch-wide rope molding, each measuring 11¹/₄ inches. Miter each end at opposing 45° angles.

4 Place the Short Trims (D) on the 11¼-inch top edge of the Sides (A), as shown in *figure 3* on page 140. Apply glue to the meeting surfaces, and nail through the Short Trims (D) into the edge of the Sides (A), using four 1-inch nails.

Adding the Feet

1 Place the assembled Sides/Bottom upside down so that the trims are on the working surface.

2 Using *figure 4* on page 140 as a guide, mark the holes for the foot screws. Drill holes through the Bottom (B) large enough to accommodate the drawer pull screws. Place the screws through the drilled holes from inside the assembly Bottom (B) and screw onto the round drawer pulls.

Finishing the Wastebasket

1 Fill any holes, cracks, or crevices with wood filler.

2 Thoroughly sand all areas of the completed wastebasket.

3 Paint or stain the wastebasket with the color of your choice. We chose a honey maple stain. We purchased a decorative stamp and gold paint, then stamped random designs over the stained wastebasket. See page 24 for more information on decorative painting.

Upholstered Ottoman

This ottoman is an extremely versatile piece of furniture. As well as using it as a regular ottoman, you can place a tray on top of it and use it as a table between two chairs and it also can be used as extra seating. The project is fairly easy to make and inexpensive to build.

Special Tools & Techniques

- Mitering

Materials

- 5 linear feet of ³/₄"x³/₄" pine
- 22 linear feet of 1x4 pine
- 1 piece of ³/₄"-thick plywood, 16¹/₂"x16¹/₂"
- 1 piece of 2"-thick foam rubber, 17"x17"
- 3 yards of decorative fabric, 36" wide

Hardware

- Approximately 150 #6x1¹/₄" flathead wood screws
- Approximately 10 #6x2¹/₂" flathead wood screws

Cutting List

Code	Description	Qty.	Material	Dimensions
A	Leg	8	1x4 pine	16" long
B	Front/Back Connector	2	1x4 pine	14" long
C	Side Connector	2	1x4 pine	15¹/₂" long
D	Front/Back Spacer	2	1x4 pine	8¹/₂" long
E	Side Spacer	2	1x4 pine	10" long
F	Corner Support	4	1x4 pine	8¹/₂" long
G	Leg Support	4	³/₄"x³/₄" pine	12¹/₂" long
H	Seat Bottom	1	³/₄" plywood	16¹/₂"x16¹/₂"

Cutting & Assembly

1 Cut all the wooden parts in the "Cutting List," and label each one with its code letter.

2 The seat frame consists of two side assemblies, a front assembly, and a back assembly. All of the components should be fastened together with both wood glue and screws, and each assembly should be checked carefully to make sure that the joints are perfectly square.

The construction of these assemblies is shown in *figure 1.* Start by positioning one side connector (C) on two legs (A), spacing the pieces as shown in the illustration. The upper edge of the side connector (C) should be flush with the ends of the legs (A), and there should be a ³/₄" offset at each end of the side connector (C). Fasten the parts together using glue and two 1¹/₄" screws at each end of the side connector (C) to attach it to the legs (A).

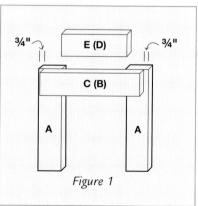

Figure 1

3 Glue the side spacer (E) between the legs (A), as shown in *figure 1* on page 143. Drive three 1¹/₄" screws through the side connector (C) and into the side spacer (E).

4 Repeat Steps 2 and 3 to construct the second side assembly.

5 The front assembly is assembled in the same fashion (see *figure 1* on page 143). Assemble two legs (A) and one front/back connector (B), spacing the parts as shown. Again, the pieces should be flush at the top, and there should be a ³/₄" offset at the ends of the connector (B). To secure the legs (A), use glue and two 1¹/₄" screws at each end of the front/back connector (B). Attach the front/back spacer (D) between the legs (A), using three 1¹/₄" screws driven through the front/back connector (B) and into the front/back spacer (D).

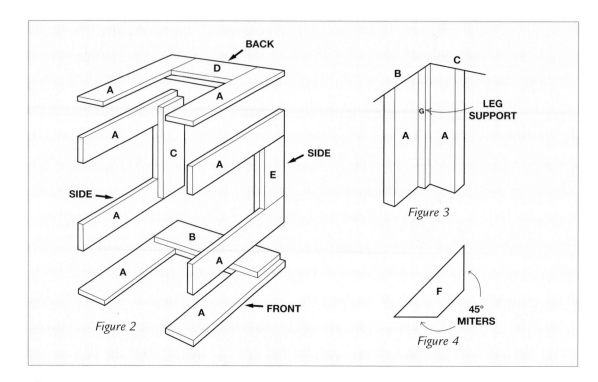

BACK

D

A

A

A

SIDE →

C

A

SIDE →

E

B

A

A

A

A ← FRONT

Figure 2

B

C

LEG SUPPORT

G

A

A

Figure 3

F

45° MITERS

Figure 4

6 Repeat Step 5 to make the identical back assembly.

7 Attach the two side assemblies to the front and back assemblies as shown in *figure 2*, making certain that the legs (A) are flush at both the top and bottom. Note that the side assemblies overlap the exposed ends of the front and back assemblies. Apply glue to the meeting edges and insert $1^{1}/_{4}$" screws, spacing them about 5" apart along the joints at the legs (A).

8 Cut four $12^{1}/_{2}$"-long leg supports (G) from $^{3}/_{4}$"x$^{3}/_{4}$" pine. Glue one leg support (G) to the inside corner of each of the four leg assemblies (see *figure 3*) and insert three or four $1^{1}/_{4}$" screws through each of the exposed sides of the leg supports (G) and into the legs (A) behind them.

9 Set each corner support (F) on its face and miter each end at a 45-degree angle, as shown in *figure 4*.

10 Using *figure 5* as a placement guide, position the mitered corner supports (F), making certain that their faces are flush with the top edges of the assembled frame. Glue the corner supports (F) in place and insert $2^{1}/_{2}$" screws through the edges of each one, driving the screws at an angle into the front, back, and side connectors (B and C).

11 Patch any crevices or gaps in the completed frame with wood putty; then sand the frame thoroughly.

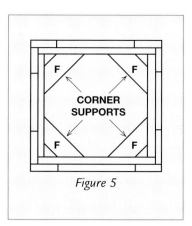

F   F

CORNER SUPPORTS

F   F

Figure 5

12 Because the entire ottoman will be covered with fabric, you needn't stain or paint the wooden portions. If you'd like to, however, now is the time.

Adding the Skirt

1 Cut four 19" lengths of 36"-wide fabric. Seam the four widths together along their 19"-long edges to form a long rectangular piece of fabric, as shown in *figure 6*.

2 Sew a 1"-wide hem along one long edge of the seamed fabric and along both 19"-long ends.

3 Fold the long fabric strip in half across its 19" width to find its center. Mark the center point with a pin. Fold the fabric in half across its width again and mark each of the half-points with a pin. Unfold the fabric and hold the center point of the raw edge onto the top surface of the ottoman assembly at the center front (see *figure 7*). This is the time to decide how long you want the fabric skirt to be. I let mine drape on the floor, but you can attach the raw edge to allow for whatever skirt length you prefer. Just be sure to keep the length equal on all sides of the ottoman. Staple the fabric at the center front to the top of the ottoman assembly. Then staple each of the half-points to the top of the ottoman assembly at the center sides. Overlap the two hemmed ends and staple them to the center back.

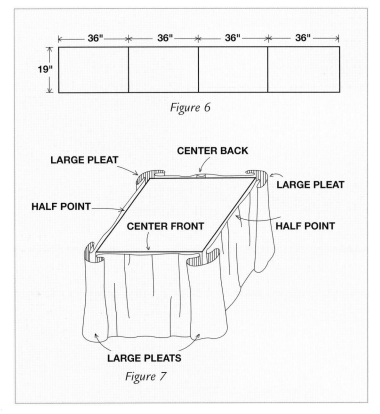

Figure 6

Figure 7

4 Working from the center back out to the two nearest corners, smooth and staple the fabric to the top of the ottoman assembly. Repeat this procedure, working from each of the stapled center and half-points out to the corners. You will now have excess fabric at each corner.

5 Form the excess fabric into a giant pleat at each corner (see *figure 7*) and staple the pleat to the top of the ottoman frame.

Making the Seat Cushion

1 Center the 17"-square piece of foam rubber over the 16$\frac{1}{2}$"-square plywood seat bottom (H) and glue it in place.

2 Center the remaining 32"x36" piece of fabric over the foam rubber and wrap the fabric over the edges of the seat bottom (H). To minimize wrinkles as you staple the fabric to the underside of the seat bottom (H), first staple the center of one side, then the center of the

opposite side, and then work your way out to the corners, smoothing the fabric as you go. Staple the centers of the remaining sides and again work your way out to the corners. Be generous with the staples; use enough to keep the fabric from puckering along the sides.

3 To attach the upholstered seat cushion to the frame, place the seat cushion upside down on a flat surface and place the frame upside down on top of it. Insert two or three 1¹/₄" screws through each of the corner supports (F) and into the seat bottom (H).

4 Place the completed ottoman right side up and have a seat!

Kitchen
& Dining Room

Kitchen Island Topper

We love this great island topper. It keeps everyday china accessible—plates for sandwiches or bowls for morning cereal—and it frees up lots of kitchen cabinet space.

Special Tools & Techniques

- Router and a round-over bit (optional)
- Bar clamps
- Miter

Materials

- 8 linear feet of 1x1 pine
- 22 linear feet of $^3/_8$"-diameter wooden dowel rod
- 12 linear feet of 2x2 pine
- 5 linear feet of 2x2 pine
- 9 linear feet of 1x12 pine
- 8 linear feet of $^3/_4$"-wide cove molding

Hardware

- 30 1$^5/_8$" wood screws
- 20 1$^1/_4$" (3d) finish nails
- 50 1" (2d) finish nails

Cutting List

Code	Description	Qty.	Material	Dimensions
A	Rack Support	4	1x1 pine	22$^1/_2$" long
B	Rack Rod	18	$^3/_8$"dia dowel	14" long
C	Inner Vertical	2	1x10 pine	14" long
D	Shelf	2	1x10 pine	11$^1/_2$" long
E	Shelf Support	4	2x2 pine	14" long
F	Inner Top/Bottom	2	1x10 pine	47$^3/_4$" long
G	Top/Bottom	2	1x12 pine	49$^1/_2$" long
H	Cove Molding	8	$^3/_4$"- wide cove molding	cut to fit

Making the Plate Rack

1 Cut four Rack Supports (A) from 1x1 pine, each measuring 22$^1/_2$ inches.

2 Holes must be drilled in each of the four Rack Supports (A) to accommodate the dowel rods that hold the plates. It is very important that the holes are accurate and straight, or your finished plate rack will be crooked. Referring to the measurements in *figure 1*, drill nine $^3/_8$-inch-diameter holes in one Rack Support (A). Note that the holes are centered widthwise on the Rack Support (A), and 2$^1/_4$ inches apart on center.

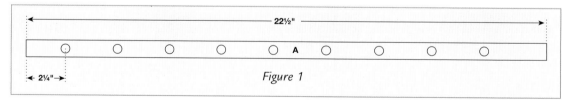

Figure 1

3 Use the drilled Rack Support (A) as a template to drill holes in each of the remaining three Rack Supports (A).

4 Cut 18 Rack Rods (B) from ³/₈-inch-diameter dowel rod, each measuring 14 inches.

5 Place one Rack Support (A), with the holes facing up, on a flat surface. Apply glue to the end of one Rack Rod (B), and insert it in the first hole in the Rack Support (A). Make certain that the Rack Rod (B) is completely through the hole and flush with the bottom surface of the Rack Support (A).

6 Repeat Step 5 eight times to insert eight additional Rack Rods (B) in the first Rack Support (A). Let the glue set up for several hours.

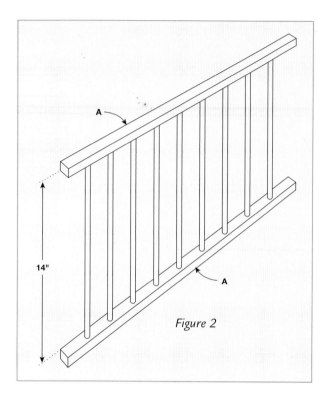

Figure 2

A

14"

A

7 Place a second Rack Support (A) on a level surface. Turn the Rack Rod/Support assembly upside down, apply glue to the exposed ends of each of the Rack Rods (B), and insert each Rack Rod (B) into the corresponding holes in the second Rack Support (A) to form a ladder arrangement, as shown in *figure 2*.

8 Repeat Steps 5 through 7 to assemble the second rack assembly, using the remaining nine Rack Rods (B), and remaining two Rack Supports (A).

Assembling the Shelf Sections

1 Cut two Inner Verticals (C) from 1x10 pine, each measuring 14 inches.

2 Cut two Shelves (D) from 1x10 pine, each measuring 11³/₄ inches.

3 Cut four Shelf Supports (E) from 2x2 pine, each measuring 14 inches.

4 An optional step is to cut two ¹/₈-x¹/₈-inch grooves on all four sides of each Shelf Support (E). (This is for decorative purposes only.)

5 Place one Shelf (D) on a flat surface. Referring to *figure 3*, mark the cutout to accommodate a Shelf Support (E) in the two outer corners of the Shelf (D). Place the end of one Shelf Support (E) exactly in place, and trace around it. Remove the Shelf Support (E), and cut out the marked corners from the Shelf (D).

6 Repeat Step 5 to cut out the corners on the remaining Shelf (D).

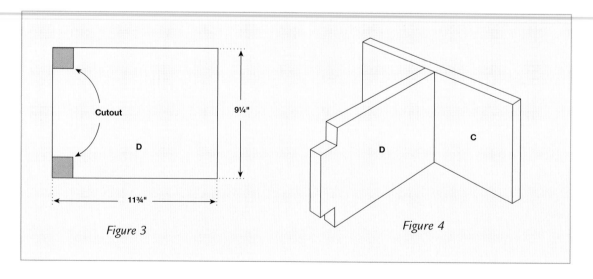

Cutout

D

9¼"

11¾"

Figure 3

D

C

Figure 4

7 Place one Inner Vertical (C) on edge on a flat surface. Center the Shelf (D) over the Inner Vertical (C), with the cutouts facing up, as shown in *figure 4* on page 150. Apply glue to the meeting surfaces and screw through the Inner Vertical (C) into the edge of the Shelf (D), using four 1⅝-inch wood screws.

Cutting the Top/Bottoms

1 Cut two Inner Top/Bottoms (F) from 1x10 pine, each measuring 47½ inches.

2 Cut two Top/Bottoms (G) from 1x12 pine, each measuring 49½ inches.

3 An optional step at this point is to use a router and a round-over bit to finish the edges of each of the two Top/Bottoms (G).

Assembly

1 Place the two Inner Top/Bottoms (F) on edge on a level surface, parallel to each other and 14 inches apart. Fit one rack/rod assembly (centered lengthwise) between the two Inner Top/Bottoms (F), as shown in *figure 5*. Place one shelf assembly on each end of the centered rack/rod assembly. Apply glue to the meeting surfaces, clamp the assembly together to hold it in position, and screw through the Inner Verticals (C) into the ends of the rack/rod assemblies, using a 1⅝-inch screw on each joint.

2 Apply glue on the meeting surfaces, and screw through the Inner Top/Bottoms (F) into the edge of each Inner Vertical (C), using three 1⅝-inch screws on each joint.

3 Apply glue to the meeting surfaces, and fit the Shelf Supports (E) between the Inner Top/Bottoms (F), and into the cut-out corners of the Shelves (D). Screw through the Inner Top/Bottoms (F) into the ends of each Shelf Support (E), using a 1⅝-inch screw on each joint.

4 Apply glue to the meeting surfaces, and center one Top/Bottom (G) on one Inner Top/Bottom (F). There should be a 1-inch-wide

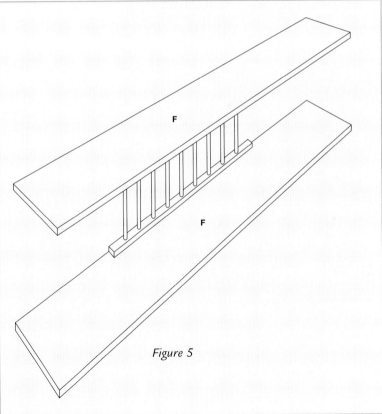

Figure 5

meeting surfaces, and screw through the face of the Rack Sides (A) into the ends of the Rack Top/Bottoms (B), using three 1⁵/₈-inch screws on each side.

6 Cut one Rack Middle (C) from 1x4 pine, measuring 24¹/₂ inches.

7 Place the Rack Middle (C) perpendicular between the Rack Sides (A) 13 inches above the cut ends of the Rack Sides (A), and screw in place.

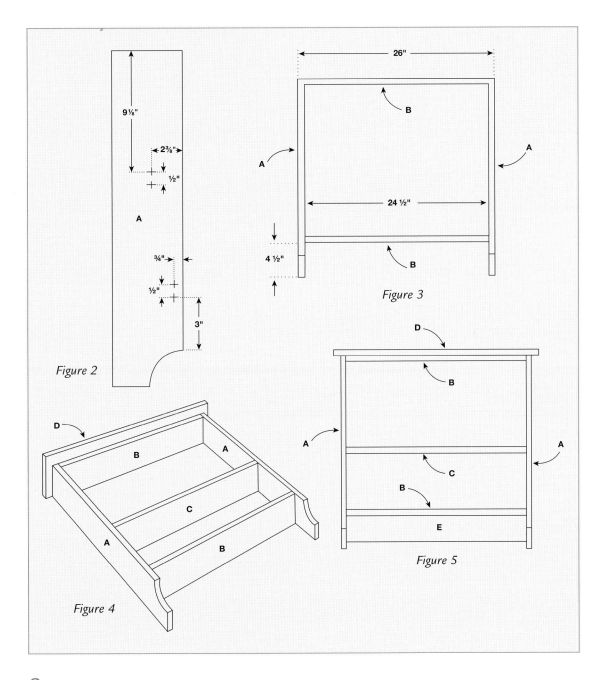

Figure 2

Figure 3

Figure 4

Figure 5

8 Cut one Rack Ledge (D) from 1x8 pine, measuring 28 inches.

9 Place the Rack Ledge (D) over the ends of the Rack Sides (A) as shown in *figure 4*. Apply glue to the meeting surfaces. Screw through the face of the Rack Ledge (D) into the ends of the Rack Sides (A) using three $1^5/_8$-inch screws on both ends.

10 Cut one Rack Base (E) from 1x4 pine, measuring $24^1/_2$ inches.

11 Place the Rack Base (E) below the Rack Bottom (B) between the Rack Sides (A), as shown in *figure 5* (page 155). Apply glue to the meeting surfaces. Screw through the face of the Rack Sides (A) into the end of the Rack Base (E); also screw through the face of the Rack Bottom (B) into the edge of the Rack Base (E) using three 1⁵⁄₈-inch screws on both sides.

Adding the Dowel Rods

1 Cut four Dowels (F) from ³⁄₈-inch-diameter dowel rod, each measuring 25 inches.

2 Wipe a small amount of glue in the holes drilled in the Rack Sides (A). Place one end of the dowel rod into one Rack Side (A) and, slightly bending the rod, place the other end into the opposing hole on the other Rack Side (A).

Finishing

1 Fill any cracks, crevices, or screw holes with wood filler.

2 Thoroughly sand all surfaces of the completed plate rack.

3 Seal and paint or stain the completed plate rack the color of your choice.

4 Attach the hooks to the Rack Base (E).

Tiled Kitchen Table

If your kitchen is small, the table shown on page 159 may be the answer to the problem of limited space. Although its top measures only 29"x46", the table is large enough to hold a hearty breakfast for two and can also serve as an additional work surface. Select tile colors—and paint colors if you choose to paint the table—to match your kitchen decor.

Special Tools & Techniques

- 3 or 4 bar clamps
- Saber saw or large chisel
- Trowel for spreading mastic
- Rubber-surfaced trowel for applying grout
- Tile cutter (if necessary)
- Mitering

Materials

- $9^1/_2$ linear feet of 1x3 pine
- 12 linear feet of 1x4 pine
- 22 linear feet of 1x6 pine
- 2 linear feet of 2x6 pine
- 1 piece of $^1/_2$"-thick plywood, 22"x40"
- $9^1/_2$ linear feet of $2^1/_2$"-wide baseboard molding
- 4 decorative table legs, each $3^1/_2$"x$3^1/_2$" at the top
- 40 tiles, each 4"x4" (or enough tiles of a different size to cover an area $21^3/_4$"x39")
- Small containers of tile grout, mastic, and sealer

Hardware

- Approximately 50 #6x$1^1/_4$" flathead wood screws
- Approximately 50 #6x2" flathead wood screws
- Approximately 30 # 10x3" flathead wood screws
- Approximately 50 3d finishing nails

*Notes on Materials

If you don't own a lathe or don't want to turn the table legs yourself, simply follow our lead by purchasing four newel posts from a building-supply store and cutting them to length. When they're turned upside down, the posts make extremely attractive table legs—and who would guess?

Be sure to purchase exterior-grade plywood for the center top (C). Also buy a few extra tiles; they're breakable, and "stuff happens."

Most tiles sold at building-supply stores are now "self-spacing"; they come with small projections on their edges so that when you lay the tiles out, the grout lines between them will be even. Because the spacing is determined by individual tile manufacturers and because the actual size of a so-called 4" tile can vary slightly from manufacturer to manufacture, we recommend that you check your tile design. Slight variations in tile size and spacing can increase or decrease the finished table-top dimensions significantly, so before you cut any wood, make certain that your tiles will fit the dimensions we've provided. Here's how:

Arrange your tiles on the uncut piece of $^1/_2$"-thick plywood. We arranged five rows of nine tiles each, as shown in *figure 1* on page 158. Draw a rectangle around the length and width of your tile arrangement, allowing for a border of grout around the outer edges that is the same width as the grout between the tiles. Then measure the rectangle. Compare the dimensions of this rectangle to the size specified in the instructions for the center top (C) —$21^3/_4$"x39". If your measurements deviate from these, adjust the size of the center top (C) and the lengths of the other table-top pieces (A, B, H, and I)—or cut your tiles to fit.

To ensure that the finished table top will be flat, check to see that the thickness of the plywood plus the combined thickness of the tiles you plan to use and the mastic you place under it will equal the thickness of the 1x4 pine pieces (A and B) that will border the table top (see *figure 2* on page 158). You can alter the thickness of the mastic underneath the tiles by a very small amount, but to make sig-nificant alternations, you'll need to alter the thickness of either the plywood or the tile.

Cutting List

Code	Description	Qty.	Material	Dimensions
A	Long Top Frame	2	1x4 pine	46" long
B	Short Top Frame	2	1x4 pine	21³/₄" long
C	Center Top	1	¹/₂" plywood	21³/₄"x39"
D	Table Leg	4	3¹/₂"x3¹/₂"	27" long newel post
E	Long Side Rail	2	1x6 pine	38" long
F	Short Side Rail	2	1x6 pine	20³/₄" long
G	Corner Support	4	2x6 pine	5¹/₂" on short sides
H	Short Bottom Frame	2	1x6 pine	28³/₄" long
I	Long Bottom Frame	2	1x6 pine	35" long
J	Long Trim	2	1x3 pine	34¹/₂" long
K	Short Trim	2	1x3 pine	17¹/₄" long
L	Long Molding	2	2¹/₂"-wide molding	34¹/₂" long
M	Short Molding	2	2¹/₂"-wide molding	17¹/₄" long

Constructing the Table Top

1 The table top is composed of a top and bottom layer. The top layer consists of two long top frames (A) and two short top frames (B), which surround the center top (C), as shown in *figure 2*. The bottom layer will be attached to the table base later. To make the top layer, start by cutting two 46" lengths of 1x4 pine and labeling each one as a long top frame (A). Cut two 21³/₄" lengths of 1x4 pine and label them as short top frames (B).

2 Cut a 21³/₄"x39" piece of ¹/₂"-thick plywood and label it as the center top (C).

3 Place the center top (C) on a level surface. Position the short and long top frames (A and B) along the outer edges of the center top (C), as shown in *figure 2*. Glue the frame pieces (A and B) to the center top (C), checking to make certain that the assembly is perfectly square. Clamp the five pieces of wood together with bar clamps for at least 24 hours.

Constructing the Table Base

1 The newel posts will serve as the table legs (D). Cut each one to 27" in length, being careful to not to cut off the decorative ends.

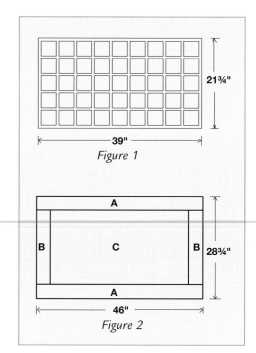

Figure 1

Figure 2

2 In order to support the long and short side rails (E and F) of the kitchen table, you must remove a 1³/₄"x1³/₄"x5¹/₂" corner section from the inside of the square top of each leg. Set the depth of your saber saw to 1³/₄" and make three cuts in the order shown in *figure 3*. (The blade edges in the illustration indicate the direction in which these cuts should be made.) These cuts may be made with a chisel rather than a saber saw.

3 Take a good look at *figure 4* on page 160. The long and short side rails (E and F) that connect the table legs (D) are cut from 1x6 pine. Cut two 38"-long boards from 1x6 pine and label them as long side rails (E). Cut two 20³/₄"-long boards from 1x6 pine and label them as short side rails (F). Set each of the four pieces (E and F) on edge and miter each end of each board at a 45-degree angle, as shown in *figure 4* on page 160.

4 This step probably requires the assistance of a willing helper (or an unwilling helper and substantial financial remuneration) and should be performed on a level surface. Each of the legs (D) must be connected to the long and short side rails (E and F), and the entire assembly must be

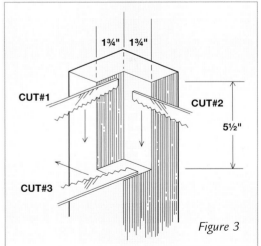

CUT#1

CUT#2

CUT#3

1³/₄" 1³/₄"

5¹/₂"

Figure 3

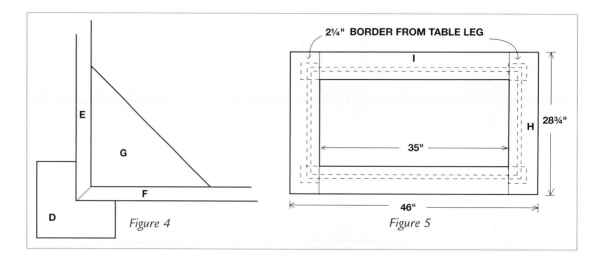

Figure 4

Figure 5

perfectly level. This is easiest to accomplish if you work with the legs upside down. (For help in making sure your project is level, see page 17.)

Carefully fit the end of one long side rail (E) and one short side rail (F) inside the opening that you previously cut in one leg (D), matching the miters as you do (see *figure 4*). Glue the rails to the leg and to each other, then insert two 2" screws through each of the rails (E and F) and into the leg. Repeat the process to attach the remaining three legs (D) to the remaining two side rails (E and F). A word of caution: It's easy to get so involved in what you're doing that you forget you're constructing a rectangular base. Don't forget that the two short side rails (F) must be opposite each other on the base; the two long side rails (E) must also be opposite each other.

5 Cut four triangular corner supports (G) from 2x6 pine. These should measure 5½" on each of their two short sides. To attach one in each of the four corners, as shown in *figure 6* on page 161, glue them flush with the top of the legs and rails. Then insert two 3" screws through each corner support (G) and into each set of side rails (E and F).

Adding the Bottom Layer of the Table Top

1 The bottom layer of the table top, which consists of four lengths of 1x6 pine, adds visual thickness and also supports the center plywood. In order to avoid creating screw holes in the table top, the bottom layer is connected first to the table base assembly. Start by cutting two 28¾" lengths from 1x6 pine and labeling them as short bottom frames (H). Also cut two 35" lengths from 1x6 pine and label them as long bottom frames (I).

2 Place the short bottom frames (H) and long bottom frames (I) on a flat surface, positioning the long bottom frames (I) inside the short bottom frames (H), as shown in *figure 5*. The resulting rectangle should measure 28¾"x46".

3 Turn the assembled table base upside down and center it over the four bottom pieces (H and I). You should have a 2¼"-wide border outside each of the four table legs (D). This dimension may vary slightly if you've altered the dimensions of your table top.

4 Apply glue to the upper edges of the long and short side rails (E and F), the exposed ends of the table legs (D), and the upper faces of the corner supports (G). To hold the assembly together, insert 2" screws diagonally through the inner faces of the long and short side rails (E and F) and into the bottom frame pieces (H and I), spacing the screws about 6" apart.

5 Turn the assembly right side up. To further stabilize the table, insert two 3" screws through the bottom frame pieces (H and I) and into each table leg (D). Also insert 1¼" screws through the bottom frame pieces (H and I) and into the upper edges of the long and short side rails (E and F).

Joining the Table Top to the Base

1 Turn the top assembly (pieces A, B, and C) upside down on a flat surface. Make certain that the side which will accommodate the tiles is face down. Place the base assembly upside-down over the top assembly, as shown in *figure 6*. The two short bottom frame pieces (H) and the two long bottom frame pieces (I) should be flush with the outer edges of the top assembly. The inner edges of the bottom frame pieces (H and I) will overlap the center top (C) by 2".

2 Glue the four bottom frame pieces (H and I) to the top assembly. Then drive four 1¼" screws through each short bottom frame piece (H) and five 1¼" screws through each long bottom piece (I) into the long and short top frames (A and B). Space the screws evenly along the length of each board. Allow the glue to dry and then turn the assembled table right side up.

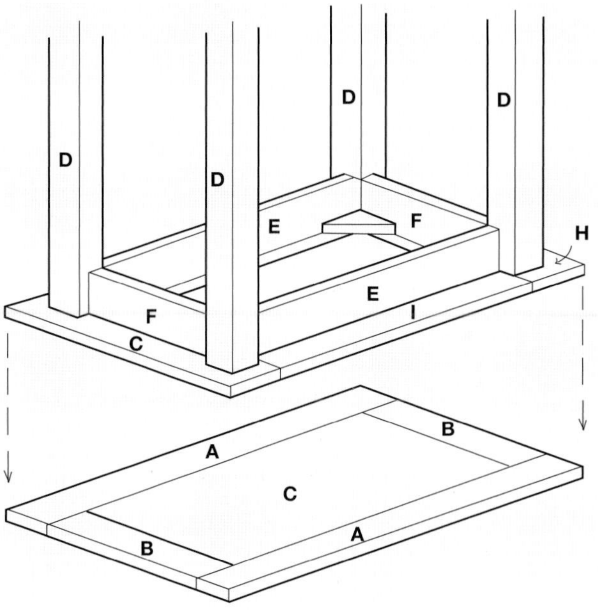

Figure 6

Adding the Trim

1 Next, you'll add the trim to the outside faces of the side rails (E and F). We added a length of 1x3 pine just under the table top and a length of 2½"-wide baseboard molding below that. Although our measurements should be very close to the cutting size for the trim, we suggest that you measure between your table legs before cutting the trim pieces, since your assembly may vary slightly. Even a ¹/₃₂" error on a trim piece will make your project look less than professional.

   Cut two long trim pieces (J) from 1x3 pine, each measuring 34½" in length. Cut two short trim pieces (K) from 1x3 pine, each measuring 17¼" in length.

2 Glue the first long trim piece (J) onto one long side rail (E) between the table legs (D). The upper edge of the long trim (J) should be flush against the bottom of the table top. Insert 3d finishing nails to attach the long trim piece (J) in place, spacing the nails about 6" apart and countersinking each one. Repeat to attach the remaining long trim piece (J) to the opposite side of the table.

3 Glue the first short trim piece (K) onto one short side rail (F) between the table legs (D), with its top edge flush against the bottom of the table top. Insert 3d finishing nails to attach the short trim piece (K) in place, spacing the nails about 6" apart and countersinking each one. Repeat to attach the remaining short trim piece (K) to the opposite side of the table.

4 Cut two 34$\frac{1}{2}$"-long pieces of 2$\frac{1}{2}$"- wide baseboard molding (L). Cut two 17$\frac{1}{4}$"-long pieces of 2$\frac{1}{2}$"-wide baseboard molding (M).

5 Glue the two long molding pieces (L) beneath the long trim pieces (J) and between the two table legs (D) and secure with 3d finishing nails spaced about 6" apart. Countersink these nails as before.

6 Glue the two short molding pieces (M) beneath the short trim pieces (K) in the same way that you attached the long molding pieces (L) in Step 5.

Adding the Tile

1 Following the manufacturer's directions carefully and using a mastic trowel, spread an even coat of tile mastic over the surface of the plywood center top (C).

2 Place the tiles on the mastic one at a time, making sure that they are absolutely straight. Do not slide them, or the mastic will be forced up onto the sides of the tiles. Let the mastic dry overnight.

3 Mix the tile grout according to the manufacturer's directions (or use pre-mixed grout).

4 Using a rubber-surfaced grout trowel, spread the grout over the tiles with arcing motions. Hold the trowel at an angle so that the grout is forced evenly into the spaces between the tiles.

5 When the grout begins to set up, use a damp rag to wipe the excess from the tiles and joints. If you let the grout harden too long, it will be very difficult to remove. Use as little water as possible when removing the excess so that you don't thin the grout that remains. Let the grout dry overnight.

6 Use a damp rag to wipe the remaining film from the tile.

7 Apply grout sealer, following the manufacturer's directions, which may tell you to wait several days before applying the sealer to the project.

Finishing

1 Fill any screw holes with wood filler.

2 Thoroughly sand all wood portions of the completed table.

3 Stain or paint the wood portions of the table the color of your choice.

Tiled Lamp

This project was made as a present to our neighbor Patti, who needed a lamp for her kitchen desk but who couldn't find an attractive one that was short enough to fit under her cabinets. Because Patti had several kitchen tiles left over from a decorating project, we decided to use them on the lamp.

Special Tools & Techniques

- Beveling

Materials

- 4 linear feet of 1x6 pine
- 2 linear feet of 1x8 pine
- 1 small tube of paneling-and-construction adhesive
- 8 ceramic tiles, each 4"x4"
- 1 lamp shade
- 4 small felt or plastic pads for the bottom of the lamp base

Hardware

- Approximately 10 3d finishing nails
- Approximately 40 wire brads
- Lamp kit (See "Notes on Materials")

*Notes on Materials

Lamp kits, consisting of all the hardware necessary to wire a lamp, are carried by most building-supply stores. Purchase the shade, which is not included with the kit, after your project is finished. When you shop for the shade, take the completed project with you and try several different shades while you're at the store.

Cutting List

Code	Description	Qty.	Material	Dimensions
A	Side	4	1x6 pine	9$\frac{1}{2}$"long
B	Top/Bottom	2	1x8 pine	7$\frac{1}{4}$"long

Constructing the Base

1 The lamp base has four identical 9$\frac{1}{2}$"-long sides (A), which are cut from a single length of beveled 1x6 pine. To make the sides/first cut a 40" length of 1x6 and bevel both its long edges at a 45-degree angle, as shown in *figure 1* on page 164.

2 Cut four 9$\frac{1}{2}$"-long sides (A) from the beveled 1x6.

3 Glue together the beveled edges of the four sides (A) to form a hollow rectangle measuring 5$\frac{1}{2}$"x9$\frac{1}{2}$", as shown in *figure 2* on page 164. Secure the four sides by driving four wire brads through the beveled edges along each side of each joint.

4 Cut two top/bottom pieces (B) from 1x8 pine, each 7$\frac{1}{4}$" long.

5 Center one top/bottom piece (B) over one open end of the hollow rectangular base and glue it in place. Insert one 3d finishing nail through the top/bottom and into the end of each side (A).

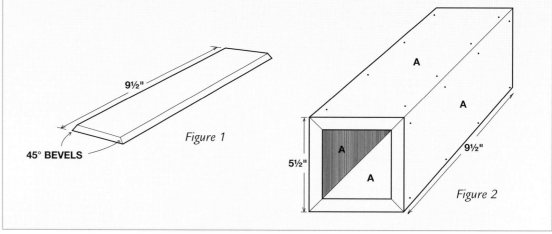

9½"

45° BEVELS

Figure 1

A

A

A

A

5½"

9½"

Figure 2

6 Repeat Step 5 to attach the other top/bottom piece (B) to the other end of the hollow rectangular base.

7 Fill any holes or crevices with wood filler, sand the lamp base thoroughly, and paint or stain as desired.

8 To wire the lamp, follow the manufacturer's directions in your lamp kit. The kit will contain a threaded hollow pipe that you'll guide through holes (you'll need to drill these) in each top/bottom piece (B). Next, you'll secure the tube in place with nuts. Then you'll thread the lamp wire, with a plug at one end, through the pipe and connect it to a switch. The kit will also include spacers so that you can adjust the kit to the size of your lamp base.

Laying the Tiles

1 After the base is assembled and the wiring is in place, use paneling-and-construction adhesive to glue two ceramic tiles in place on one side (A).

2 Allow the adhesive to set up for about an hour. (You'll know the glue has set when you're unable to move the tiles with your hands.) Then repeat Step 1 three times to attach the remaining six tiles to the remaining three sides (A).

3 To raise the completed lamp from the desk surface and provide clearance for the electrical cord running from beneath the base, affix small felt or clear plastic pads to all four corners of the bottom (B) of the lamp.

Multiple Planter

If you're looking for a really attractive way to screen a portion of your window or deck, turn to page 167. You can't beat this multiple planter. It holds eight pots filled with your favorite sun-loving plants on its top, as well as shade-loving plants—or your favorite knickknacks—on the shelf beneath.

Special Tools & Techniques

- Ripping

Materials

- 19 linear feet of 1x3 pine
- 70 linear feet of 1x4 pine
- 10 linear feet of 1x6 pine
- 12 linear feet of 1x10 pine
- 8 clay pots, 8" in diameter

Hardware

- Approximately 100 #6x1¼" flathead wood screws
- Approximately 250 #6x1½" flathead wood screws

Notes on Materials

Check the diameters of the pots that you intend to place in the 7¼"-square planter openings. You can alter the planter dimensions if you wish, but you may find that it's easier to buy pots the right size. As you can see in the photo on page 167, the wider lips of the pots rest on the shelf spacers, while the narrower portions fit into the openings between the spacers.

If you plan to use your planter outdoors, buy galvanized screws and weather-resistant lumber and finish the completed project with outdoor paint or stain.

Cutting List

Code	Description	Qty.	Material	Dimensions
A	Long Inner Frame	2	1x4 pine	70" long
B	Short Inner Frame	16	1x4 pine	7¼" long
C	Leg	14	1x4 pine	31" long
D	Leg Spacer	8	1x6 pine	13⅛" long
E	Short Spacer	2	1x6 pine	3¼" long
F	Shelf	2	1x10 pine, ripped	70" long
G	Shelf Spacer	8	1x4 pine	13⅛" long
H	Short Shelf Spacer	2	1x4 pine	3¼" long
I	Long Trim	2	1x3 pine	75" long
J	Short Trim	2	1x3 pine	7¼" long
K	Inner Trim	7	1x3 pine, ripped	7¼" long

Making the Inner Frame

1 Cut two long inner frames (A) from 1x4 pine; each should be 70" long.

2 Cut 16 short inner frames (B) from 1x4 pine; each should be 7¼" long.

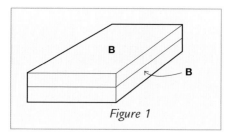

Figure 1

3 Glue two short inner frames (B) together to form a double thickness, as shown in *figure 1* on page 166, and secure them by inserting four 1¼" screws, one near each corner.

4 Repeat Step 3 six more times to create a total of seven double-thick short inner frames (B). You'll have two single short inner frames (B) left over.

5 Place the two long inner frames (A) on edge, parallel to each other and 7¼" apart. Fit the double and single short inner frames (B) between the two long inner frames (A), as shown in *figure 2* on page 168. Note that the single short inner frames (B) are on the ends of the assembly and that each of the openings measures 7¼" square. Glue the long inner frames (A) to the short inner frames (B) and insert two 1½" screws through the long inner frames (A) and into the ends of the short inner frames (B) at each joint.

Adding the Legs

1 Cut fourteen 31"-long legs (C) from 1x4 pine.

2 Cut eight leg spacers (D) from 1x6 pine, each measuring 13⅛" long.

3 To attach five legs (C) and four leg spacers (D) to one side of the inner frame, first refer to *figure 3* on page 168. Note that the top ends of the legs (C) and the upper edges of the leg spacers (D) should be flush with the top edges of the inner frame. Glue the legs (C) and spacers (D) in place and insert two 1¼" screws through each leg (C) and four 1¼" screws through each leg spacer (D) into the inner frame.

4 Turn the assembly over and repeat Step 3 to attach five legs (C) and four leg spacers (D) to the other side of the inner frame.

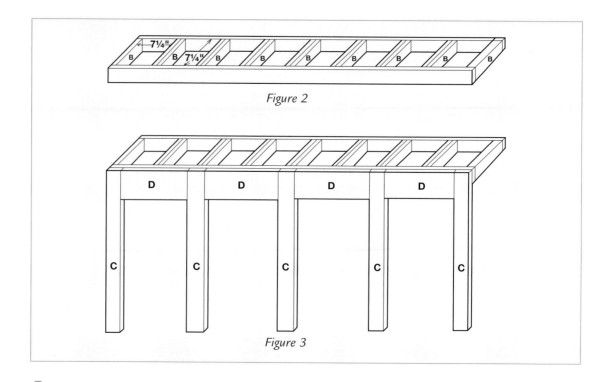

Figure 2

Figure 3

5 Cut two short spacers (E) from 1x6 pine, each measuring 3¹/₄" long.

6 To attach two legs (C) and one short spacer (E) to one end of the inner frame, first refer to *figure 4* on page 169. Note that the legs (C) to be attached will overlap the edges of the legs (C) already in place. Glue the two legs (C) and short spacer (E) in place and insert two 1¹/₄" screws at each joint. Also insert 1¹/₂" screws to join the overlapped legs (C) together, spacing the screws about 6" apart down the length of the legs (C) you've just added.

7 Repeat Step 6 to attach the remaining two legs (C) and short spacer (E) to the 5 opposite end of the assembly.

Adding the Shelves

1 Rip the 12 linear feet of 1x10 pine to a width of 8³/₄". Then cut two 70"-long shelves (F) from the ripped boards.

2 Glue the first shelf (F) in place inside the legs (C), positioning its bottom surface flush with the lower edges of the leg spacers (D) and short spacers (E), as shown in *figure 5* on page 169. Secure the shelf in position by inserting two 1¹/₂" screws through each leg (C), each leg spacer (D), and each short spacer (E) into the edges of the shelf (F).

3 Repeat Step 2 to attach the second shelf (F), positioning it 9³/₄" from the bottoms of the legs (C).

4 Cut eight shelf spacers (G) from 1x4 pine, each measuring 13¹/₈".

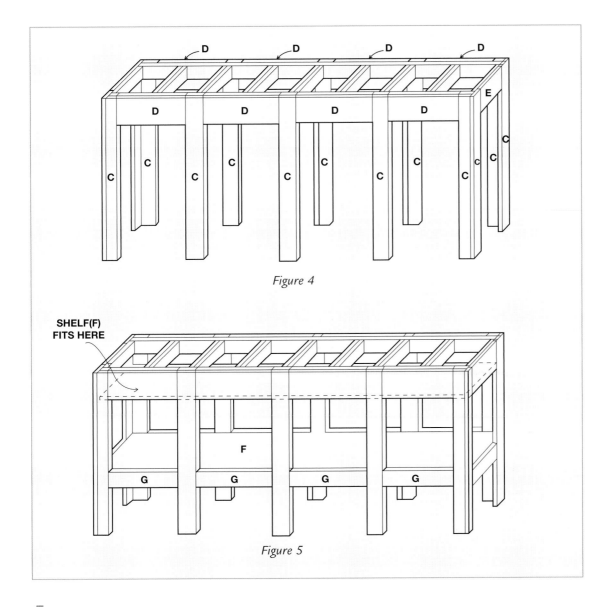

Figure 4

SHELF(F) FITS HERE

Figure 5

5 Position four of the shelf spacers (G) between the legs on one side of the planter, as shown in *figure 5*, placing their upper edges flush with the top face of the lower shelf (F). Glue the shelf spacers (G) in place and secure each one with two 1¹/₂" screws driven through the spacer and into the edge of the shelf (F).

6 Repeat Step 5 to attach the remaining four shelf spacers (G) to the opposite side of the planter.

7 Cut two short shelf spacers (H) from 1x4 pine, each measuring 3¹/₄" long.

8 Glue the short shelf spacers (H) in place between the legs (C) at both ends of the planter, positioning them so that their upper edges are flush with the top of the lower shelf (F). Secure each short shelf spacer (H) to the shelf (F) with two 1¹/₂" screws.

Adding the Top Trim

1 Cut two long trim pieces (I) from 1x3 pine, each measuring 75" long.

2 Cut two short trim pieces (J) from 1x3 pine, each measuring 7¼" long.

3 Rip a 52" length of 1x3 to a width of 1½".

4 Cut seven 7¼"-long inner trim pieces (K) from the 1½"-wide ripped pine.

5 Glue the seven inner trim pieces (K) to the top edges of the seven double-thick short inner frames (B), as shown in *figure 6*. Insert four 1½" screws through each inner trim piece (K) and into the paired short inner frames (B) beneath.

6 Glue the two short trim pieces (J) and the two long trim pieces (I) to the top edges of the planter, so that their inner edges are flush with the inner faces of the long and short inner frames (A and B). Secure the trim pieces (J and I) with 1½" screws spaced about 6" apart.

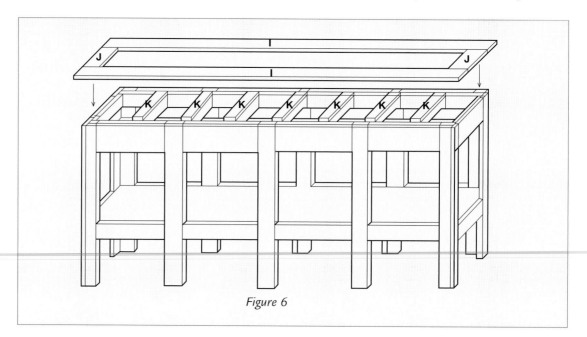

Figure 6

Finishing

1 Fill all screw holes and crevices with wood filler.

2 Sand the entire planter thoroughly.

3 Paint or stain the completed planter the color of your choice.

Buffet Table

This project, shown on page 172, is a versatile piece of furniture that several friends have admired. It works well in an entry hall, as a sofa table, or as a buffet in the dining room.

Materials

- 30 linear feet of 1x3 pine
- 54 linear feet of 1x4 pine
- 4 linear feet of 1x6 pine
- 5 linear feet of 1x10 pine
- 1 piece of laminated pine, 26"x54"
- 1 piece of ¼"-thick plywood, 9"x15"
- Iron-on bonding material

Hardware

- Approximately 300 #6x1¼" flathead wood screws
- Approximately 35 3d finishing nails

*Notes on Materials

The buffet table top and shelf are constructed of laminated 1x4 pine boards. Most building-supply stores sell sections of pine that have already been laminated. You can laminate the boards yourself, of course, but we don't recommend doing so unless you're a very experienced woodworker and own the necessary tools.

Before you decide whether to add fabric cutouts to your finished project, read over the instructions in the "Finishing" section; they'll explain how to add these cutouts and how to estimate the amount of bonding material (available at most fabric stores) you'll need to buy for the fabric you choose.

Cutting List

Code	Description	Qty.	Material	Dimensions
A	Shelf	1	Laminated pine	11½"x50½"
B	Long Shelf Support	2	1x4 pine	50½" long
C	Short Shelf Support	2	1x4 pine	10" long
D	Long Top Support	4	1x3 pine	50½" long
E	Short Top Support	4	1x3 pine	10" long
F	Long Guide	6	1x4 pine	11½" long
G	Short Guide	6	1x4 pine	10" long
H	Leg	8	1x4 pine	30" long
I	Back Trim	1	1x10 pine	45" long
J	Side Trim	2	1x10 pine	4½" long
K	Top/Bottom Trim	2	1x3 pine	45" long
L	Vertical Trim	2	1x3 pine	4¼" long
M	Drawer Front/Back	4	1x4 pine	15¼" long
N	Drawer Side	4	1x4 pine	8" long
O	Drawer Bottom	2	¼" plywood	8¼"x14"
P	Small Drawer Front/Back	2	1x4 pine	8¾" long
O	Small Drawer Side	2	1x4 pine	8" long
R	Small Drawer Bottom	1	1/4" plywood	7½"x8¼"
S	Long Drawer Front	2	1x6 pine	16½" long
T	Short Drawer Front	1	1x6 pine	10" long
U	Table Top	1	Laminated pine	13½"x54"

Making the Shelf

1 Cut one 11½"x50½" shelf (A) from laminated pine.

2 Cut two long shelf supports (B) from 1x4 pine, each measuring 50$\frac{1}{2}$" long. Cut two short shelf supports (C) from 1x4 pine, each measuring 10" long.

3 Place the two long shelf supports (B) on a level surface, parallel to each other, on edge, and 10" apart. Place the two short shelf supports (C) between the two long shelf supports (B) as shown in *figure 1* on page 173. Glue the supports together and drive two 1$\frac{1}{4}$" screws through the long shelf supports (B) into the short shelf supports (C) at each joint.

4 Glue the shelf (A) onto the shelf support assembly, as shown in *figure 1* on page 173. Drive 1$\frac{1}{4}$" screws through the top of the shelf (A) into the edges of the shelf-support assembly, spacing the screws about 6" apart.

Making the Support Assemblies

1 Cut four long top supports (D) from 1x3 pine, each measuring 50½" long.

2 Cut four short top supports (E) from 1x3 pine, each measuring 10" long.

3 Place two of the long top supports (D) on a level surface, parallel to each other, on edge, and 10" apart. Place two short top supports (E) between the two long top supports (D), as shown in *figure 2*. Glue the supports together and insert two 1¼" screws through the long top supports (D) into the short top supports (E) at each joint.

4 Repeat Step 3, using the remaining two long top supports (D) and two short top supports (E) to form a second support assembly. Set the second assembly aside.

5 The support assembly that you built in Step 3 will support the drawers. The next step is to construct the drawer-guide assemblies and add them to the support assembly. Start by cutting six long guides (F) from 1x4 pine, each measuring 11½" long. Also cut six short guides (G) from 1x4 pine, each measuring 10" long.

6 Glue one short guide (G) to the edge of one long guide (F), as shown in *figure 3*, leaving, a ¾" space at each end of the long guide (F). Note that the back face of the long guide (F) should be flush with the back edge of the short guide (G). Fasten the pieces with three 1¼" screws, spacing them evenly along the joint.

7 Repeat Step 6 five more times, using the remaining five short guides (G) and five long guides (F).

8 Now you'll attach the guide assemblies to the first support assembly, as shown in *figure 4*. Begin on the left side, placing the first guide assembly with its short guide (G) portion inside the first support assembly and with the outer face of its long guide portion (F) 1¼" from the inside edge of the support assembly.

9 Position the second guide assembly so that the two short guide (G) portions of the first and second assemblies are 10" apart.

10 Position the third assembly so that the long guide (F) portions of the second and third assemblies are 1" apart.

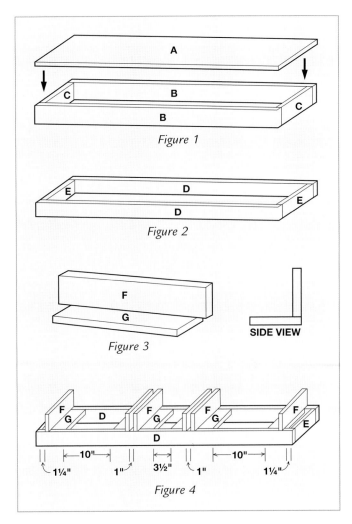

Figure 1

Figure 2

SIDE VIEW

Figure 3

Figure 4

11 Repeat Steps 8 through 10, working from the right side of the support assembly to attach the remaining guide assemblies, as shown in *figure 4* on page 173.

Adding the Legs

1 Cut eight 30"-long legs (H) from 1x4 pine. Before assembling the legs, study *figures 5* and *6* to see how they're attached to both the inner support assemblies and the shelf assembly. The tops of the legs (H) will be flush with the upper edges of the inner support assembly (the one without the drawer guides attached). The inner support assembly with the drawer guides attached will be positioned 4$\frac{1}{4}$" below the bottom edge of the first inner support assembly, and the bottom edge of the shelf assembly will be positioned 4" from the bottom of the legs. The front and back legs (H) will overlap the edges of the side legs (H).

Start by gluing two legs (H) together at a 90-degree angle, as shown in *figure 7*. Secure with 1$\frac{1}{4}$" screws spaced about 6" apart along the joint.

2 Repeat the leg-gluing procedure in Step 1 three more times to form the remaining three leg assemblies.

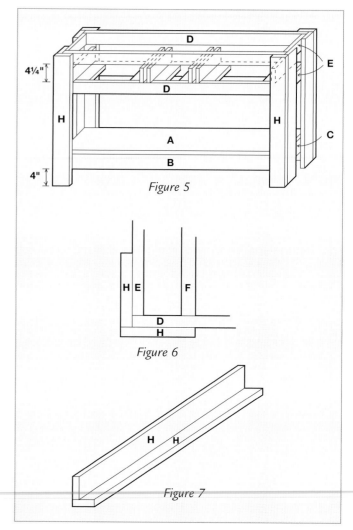

Figure 5

Figure 6

Figure 7

3 Position the assembled legs as shown in *figures 5* and *6*; then glue them to each of the three center assemblies. Secure with two 1$\frac{1}{4}$" screws at each joint.

Adding the Back and Side Trim

1 Cut one 45"-long back trim (I) from 1x10 pine.

2 Glue the back trim (I) between the two back legs (H). Insert 1$\frac{1}{4}$" screws through the back trim (I) into the inner support assemblies, spacing the screws about 6" apart.

3 Cut two 4$\frac{1}{2}$"-long side trim pieces (J) from 1x10 pine.

4 Glue a side trim piece (J) between each set of legs (H) on the sides of the buffet. Insert four 1¼" screws through each side trim piece (J) into the inner support assemblies, locating two screws at the top and two at the bottom.

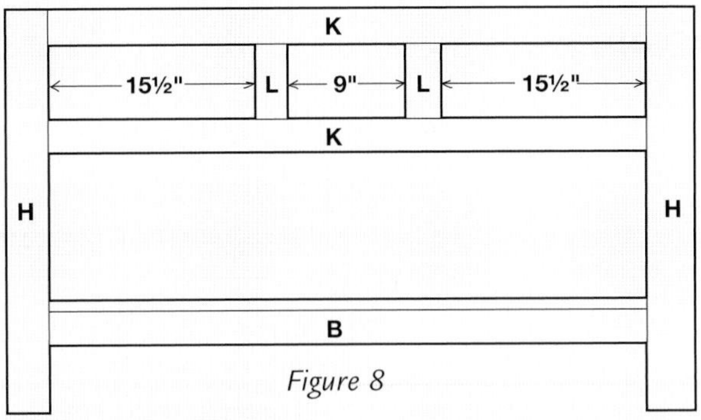

Adding the Front Trim

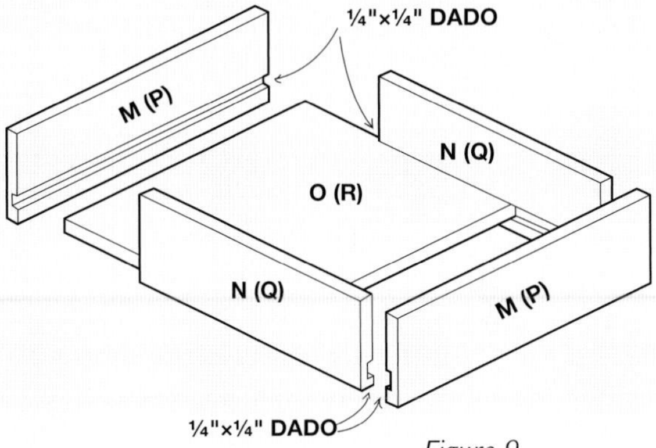

1 Cut two top/bottom trim pieces (K) from 1x3 pine, each measuring 45" long.

2 Glue one top/bottom trim (K) to the top front of the assembly, over the long top support (D), as shown in *figure 8*. Secure the trim with 1¼" screws spaced about 6" apart.

3 Repeat Step 2 to attach the remaining top/bottom trim (K) to the assembly, over the lower long top support (D).

4 Cut two 4¼"-long vertical trim pieces (L) from 1x3 pine.

5 Using *figure 8* as a guide, glue one vertical trim (L) between the two top/bottom pieces (K), 15½" from the left leg (H). Insert two 1¼" screws through the vertical trim (L) into the ends of the long drawer guides (F).

6 Repeat Step 5 to attach the remaining vertical trim (L) on the right side, as shown in *figure 8*. This will leave a 9"-wide opening between the two vertical trim pieces (L).

Making the Drawers

1 The two outermost drawers in the buffet are identical in size; the center drawer is smaller. All three are constructed as shown in the assembly diagram in *figure 9*. Start by cutting the following parts for the two larger drawers from 1x4 pine: four drawer front/back pieces (M), each 15¼" long, and four drawer sides (N), each 8" long.

2 To accommodate the plywood drawer bottoms, cut a ¼"x¼" dado on the inside of each drawer piece (M and N), ³⁄₈" from the lower edge.

3 Cut two 8¼"x14" drawer bottoms (O) from ¼"-thick plywood. Assemble one drawer as shown in *figure 9*. Note that the drawer front/back pieces (M) overlap the ends of the drawer sides (N). Use glue and 3d finishing nails at each end of the overlapping boards. The long drawer front (S) will be added later.

4 Repeat the drawer assembly using the remaining two drawer front/back pieces (M), two drawer sides (N), and drawer bottom (O).

Figure 8

Figure 9

Wall Cabinet

We built this cabinet (see page 179) for our kitchen to provide both storage and visual interest on a very blank wall. We saved space—and materials—by allowing the wall to serve as the cabinet's back. The project is built in sections and then attached to the wall. The center shelves can be altered in length to fit just about any space you wish. If you have a smaller wall (perhaps in a bathroom), build only one of the end cabinets.

Materials

- 24 linear feet of 1x3 pine
- 63 linear feet of 1x4 pine
- 50 linear feet of 1x6 pine
- 4 shutter doors, each measuring 15¼"x23"

Hardware

- Approximately 150 #6x1¼" screws
- Approximately 50 3d finishing nails
- 4 door latches
- 4 decorative door pulls
- 8 flush-mounted hinges
- 18 molly bolts (or other appropriate hardware to attach the project to the wall)

*Notes on Materials

To save time and to avoid having to build cabinet doors, we purchased pre-made shutter doors, which are available at most building-supply stores. If you can't find shutters in the specified size, it's usually possible to cut them down to fit. If all else fails, simply alter the dimensions of the cabinet to accommodate the shutters you find.

Cutting List

Code	Description	Qty.	Material	Dimensions
A	Top/Bottom	4	1x6 pine	37½" long
B	Side	4	1x6 pine	28½" long
C	Shelf	4	1x6 pine	36" long
D	Vertical Trim	4	1x4 pine	30" long
E	Center Vertical Support	2	1x4 pine	28½" long
F	Horizontal Trim	4	1x4 pine	30½" long
G	Long Base	4	1x4 pine	30" long
H	Short Base	4	1x4 pine	3½" long
I	Base Top	2	1x4 pine	31½" long
J	Center Shelf	3	1x6 pine	58" long
K	Center Shelf Trim	3	1x4 pine	58" long
L	Side Support	6	1x3 pine	5½" long
M	Back Support	3	1x3 pine	56½" long
N	Wall Support	2	1x3 pine	32" long

Making the Cabinet Frame

1 Cut four 37½"-long top/bottom pieces (A) from 1x6 pine.

2 Cut four 28½"-long side pieces (B) from 1x6 pine.

3 Place two of the top/bottom pieces (A) on a level surface, on edge, parallel to each other, and 28½" apart. Fit two of the side pieces (B) between the ends of the top/bottom pieces (A),

as shown in *figure 1*. Glue the pieces together and insert three 1¼" screws through the top/bottom pieces (A) into the ends of the sides (B) at each joint.

4 Cut four 36"-long shelves (C) from 1x6 pine.

5 A slot must be cut into each of the four shelves (C) at the center front to accommodate the center vertical support (E). Using *figure 2* on page 180 as a guide, cut a slot 3½" wide and ¾" deep in the center front of each shelf (C).

6 Use 1¼" screws and glue to attach two of the shelves (C) inside the assembly, spacing shelves as desired. *Figure 1* shows the spacing that I chose for mine.

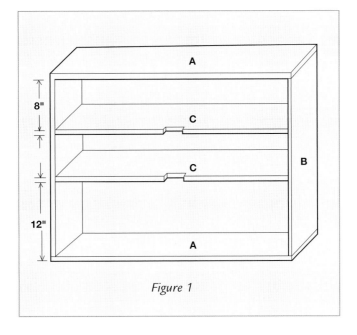

Figure 1

7 Repeat Steps 3 through 6 to construct a second cabinet frame using the remaining two top/bottom pieces (A), two sides (B), and two shelves (C).

Adding the Trim

1 Cut four vertical trim pieces (D) from 1x4 pine, each measuring 30" long.

2 Glue one vertical trim piece (D) to the left side of the cabinet, as shown in *figure 3*, and secure it with 1¹⁄₄" screws inserted through the vertical trim piece (D) and into the edge of the side (B). Space the screws about 6" apart.

3 Repeat Step 2 to attach a second vertical trim piece (D) to the right side of the cabinet, as shown in *figure 3*.

4 Cut two 28¹⁄₂"-long center vertical supports (E) from 1x4 pine.

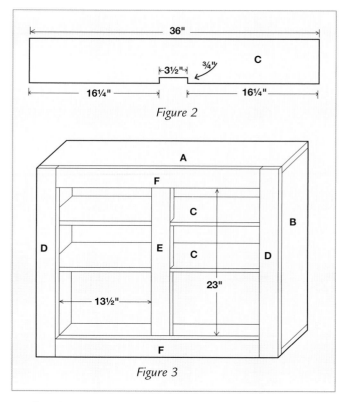

Figure 2

Figure 3

5 Fit one center vertical support (E) into the slots in the center front of the shelves (C), as shown in *figure 3*. Glue the support in place and insert two 1¹⁄₄" screws through the top/bottom (A) and into the end of the center vertical support (E) at each joint. Then drive two 3d finishing nails through the center vertical support (E) and into the slot in the center front of each shelf (C). Note that the spacing between the vertical pieces (D and E) should be exactly 13¹⁄₂".

6 Cut four 30¹⁄₂"-long horizontal trim pieces (F) from 1x4 pine.

7 Glue two of the horizontal trim pieces (F) flush with the top and bottom of the cabinet, between the vertical trim pieces (D), as shown in *figure 3*. Then insert three 1¹⁄₄" screws along each horizontal trim piece (F) to secure it to the edge of the top/bottom piece (A). Note that the opening between the top and bottom horizontal trim pieces (F) should be exactly 23".

8 Repeat Steps 1 through 7 to attach two vertical trim pieces (D), one center vertical support (E) and two horizontal trim pieces (F) to the remaining cabinet frame.

Constructing the Cabinet Base

1 To stabilize the cabinet and lift it off of the floor, we built very simple base units and attached them to the bottoms of the two assembled cabinets. Cut two long bases (G) from 1x4 pine, each measuring 30" long.

2 Cut two short bases (H) from 1x4 pine, each measuring 3½" long.

3 Cut one 31½" long base top (I) from 1x4 pine.

4 Place the two long bases (G) on a level surface, parallel to each other, on edge, and 2" apart. Glue the two short bases (H) to the ends of the two long bases (G), as shown in *figure 4*, and insert two 1¼" screws through the short bases (H) and into the ends of the long bases (G) at each joint. You should end up with a rectangular base frame measuring 31½"x3½".

5 Glue the base top (I) to the top edges of the base frame, as shown in *figure 4*. Then drive 3d finishing nails through the base top (I) and into the edges of the base frame, spacing the nails about 4" apart.

6 Turn the cabinet upside down and place the completed base on its bottom, with the base top (I) against the cabinet bottom. Position the base so that the cabinet overlaps it by 2¾" in the front and by 3" on each side. Note that the rear of the base should be flush with the back edge of the cabinet bottom.

7 Repeat Steps 1 through 6 to build and attach a second cabinet base to the remaining cabinet.

Constructing the Center Shelves

1 The center shelves are constructed separately and then attached to the wall between the assembled cabinets. Each shelf unit is constructed in an identical manner. Our completed shelf units measure 58" long, but you can adjust them to the exact length that you require between your two cabinets. Cut three 58"-long center shelves (J) from 1x6 pine.

2 Cut three 58"-long center shelf trim pieces (K) from 1x4 pine.

3 Cut six 5½"-long side support pieces (L) from 1x3 pine.

4 Cut three 56½"-long back support pieces (M) from 1x3 pine.

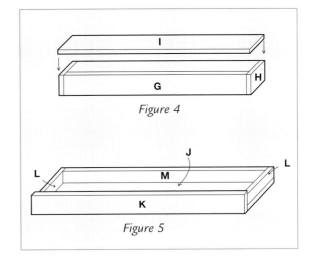

Figure 4

Figure 5

5 Place one center shelf piece (J) on a level surface and glue one shelf trim piece (K) onto it, flush with one long edge, as shown in *figure 5* on page 181. Insert $1^{1}/_{4}$" screws, spaced approximately 6" apart, through the center shelf trim (K) and into the edge of the center shelf (J).

6 Glue the side support pieces (L) so that their outer faces are flush with the ends of the center shelf (J), as shown in *figure 5* on page 181. Note that the center shelf trim (K) overlaps the ends of the side supports (L) and that the side supports (L) are narrower than the center shelf trim (K). Insert two $1^{1}/_{4}$" screws through the center shelf (J) into the edge of each side support (L).

7 Glue one back support (M) to the remaining long edge of the center shelf (J) between the two side supports (L), as shown in *figure 5* on page 181. Insert $1^{1}/_{4}$" screws through the center shelf (J) and into the edge of the back support (M), spacing them about 6" apart.

8 Repeat Steps 5 through 7 twice to construct two more shelf units.

Finishing

1 Fill any holes or crevices with wood filler.

2 Pre-fit the shutter doors in their openings, and plane or sand any surface that doesn't permit smooth opening of the doors. Then sand all surfaces of the cabinet, shutter doors, and center shelf units thoroughly.

3 Paint and/or stain each of the pieces the color of your choice. I chose an off-white to match the color of my wall.

4 Follow the manufacturer's instructions to attach the hinges to the painted shutter doors, spacing them exactly the same on all four doors. Then attach the hinges to the cabinet.

5 Attach a door pull to the front of each shutter door. Make certain that the pulls are positioned in exactly the same place on each door.

6 Attach the door latches to the inside of each of the four doors, following the manufacturer's instructions.

Final Assembly

1 The final assembly will probably require the assistance of a helper or two. Measure the length of the two cabinets and the helves and mark their positions on the wall.

2 The cabinets are mounted by attaching wood strips to the wall and positioning the cabinets so that the undersides of their tops rest on the strips. Start by cutting one 32"-long wall support (N) from 1x3 pine. Position the wall support (N) on the wall, $^{3}/_{4}$" lower than

where the upper surface of the cabinet will be. Note that the wall support (N) is shorter than the cabinet top; this will allow you to shift the cabinet back and forth to center it over the support. Level the wall support (N) carefully and attach it to the wall using molly bolts or other secure methods.

3 Lift the cabinet and place it on top of the wall support (N) that is now attached to the wall. To secure the cabinet, drive four or five evenly spaced 3d finishing nails through its top (A) and into the wall support (N). Recess the nail heads, carefully fill the nail holes, sand gently, and touch up the spot with paint or stain.

4 Position one shelf unit flush with the top of the mounted cabinet. Level it carefully and attach it to the adjoining cabinet side by inserting two $1^{1}/_{4}$" screws through the side support (L) and into the cabinet side (B). Attach the shelf to the wall using four evenly-spaced molly bolts, or other secure methods, bolting through the back support (M) into the wall.

5 Position the second shelf unit as desired and attach it to the cabinet and wall as before. Then attach the third shelf unit, making sure that it will be flush with the bottom of the adjoining cabinet.

6 Position the remaining cabinet on the opposite end of the shelf units. Repeat Steps 2 and 3 to attach the cabinet to the wall, and then attach the shelf units to the cabinet side (B) by following the procedure outlined in Step 4.

Bench with Planters

The combination planter and bench shown on page 185 makes an attractive addition to any kitchen, dining area, indoor patio, or deck. A standard chaise-lounge cushion—available almost anywhere—fits the bench easily, and the planters on both ends are large enough to hold a wealth of cheerful flowers or greenery.

Special Tools & Techniques

- Mitering

Materials

- 52 linear feet of 1x3 pine
- 85 linear feet of 1x4 pine
- 1 sheet of ³/₄"-thick plywood, 4'x8'

Hardware

- Approximately 500 #6x1¼" flathead wood screws
- Approximately 30 #6x2½" flathead wood screws
- Approximately 60 3d finishing nails
- Eight ³/₈"-diameter bolts, at least 3" long, with matching wing nuts

*Notes on Materials

If the finished project will be exposed to the elements, choose materials, hardware, glue, and a wood finish that are suited for exterior use. We used pressure-treated pine to build our sun lounge, but redwood, western cedar, or other exterior-grade woods make good substitutes. Depending upon the type of wood you buy (each is likely to have a different finish cut), you may need to trim the plywood base and bottom of the planter to fit properly.

Cutting List

Code	Description	Qty.	Material	Dimensions
A	Side	34	1x4 pine	23" long
B	Long Support	4	1x3 pine	21" long
C	Medium Support	4	1x3 pine	10" long
D	Short Support	16	1x3 pine	6" long
E	Base	2	³/₄" plywood	See *figure 2*
F	Bottom	2	³/₄" plywood	See *figure 2*
G	Trim	12	1x3 pine	Cut to fit (approx. 128" total)
H	Long Frame	2	1x4 pine	72" long
I	Short Frame	2	1x4 pine	21" long
J	Long Lounge Support	2	1x3 pine	70½" long
K	Short Lounge Support	6	1x3 pine	19½" long
L	Lounge Platform	1	³/₄" plywood	19½"x70½"

Making the Planter Sides

1 The six sides (one long, one medium, and four short) of each planter are different widths and contain different numbers of 1x4s. The long side has six 1x4s, the medium side has three, and the four short sides have two each. To start building the twelve sides for both planters, first cut thirty-four 23"-long sides (A) from 1x4 pine.

2 Cut four long supports (B) from 1x3 pine, each measuring 21" long.

3 Lay six of the side pieces (A) on a level surface, positioning them parallel to each other as shown in *figure 1*. Adjust the spacing between the side pieces (A) so that the total width is exactly 22¹/₂". Glue one long support (B) flush with the ends of all six side pieces (A). Note that there is a ³/₄" inset at each end of this long support (B). Secure the long support (B) to the side pieces (A) by inserting two 1¹/₄" screws through the long support (B) and into each side piece (A).

4 Attach the remaining long support (B), 7³/₄" from the other ends of the six side pieces (A), as shown in *figure 1* and described in Step 3.

5 Repeat Steps 3 and 4 to construct another long side for the second planter.

6 Cut four 10"-long medium supports (C) from 1x4 pine.

7 The medium sides, one for each planter, are constructed in the same manner as the long sides—but each one contains only three side pieces (A) and these are spaced differently. Lay three side pieces (A) parallel to each other on a level surface. Adjust the spacing between them so that

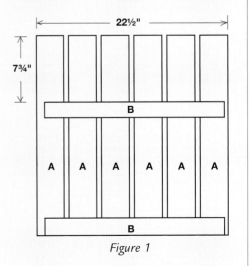

Figure 1

the total width is exactly 11½". Glue and attach the medium supports (C) as explained in Steps 3 and 4, leaving a ³/₄" overlap at each end of each medium support (C).

8 Repeat Step 7 to make another medium side for the second planter.

9 Cut sixteen 6"-long short supports (D) from 1x4 pine.

10 Lay two side pieces (A) parallel to each other on a level surface. Adjust the spacing between the side pieces (A) so that the total width is exactly 7½". Attach two short supports (D) to the two side pieces (A), following the instructions in Steps 3 and 4.

11 Repeat Step 10 seven more times to build all the short sides for both planters.

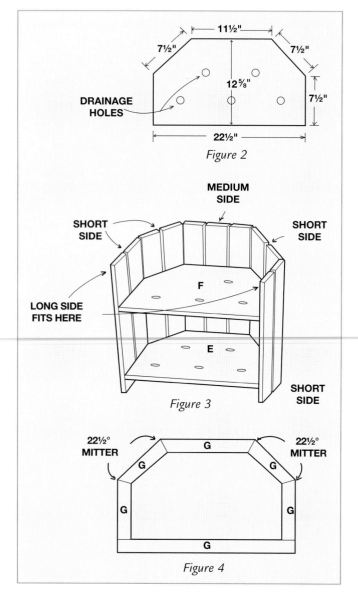

Figure 2

Figure 3

Figure 4

Adding the Bottoms and Bases

1 Using *figure 2* as a guide, cut four identical pieces from ³/₄"-thick exterior-grade plywood. Two pieces will be bases (E) and two will be bottoms (F) for the planters.

2 To allow for drainage, drill five 1"-diameter holes in each base (E) and bottom (F), as shown in *figure 2*. The exact placement of these holes is not important.

3 To attach each base (E) to each side assembly, first position the base over the lower supports (B, C, and D), as shown in *figure 3*. If necessary, trim the base to fit. Give the base (E) in place and insert 1¼" screws through it and into the edges of the supports (B, C, and D), using two screws at each joint. Also insert two 1¼" screws through each of the side pieces (A) and into the edges of each base (E).

4 Fit a planter bottom (F) into each assembly, as shown in *figure 3*, making certain that the bottom rests evenly on its supports (B, C, and D) and is level inside the assembly. Glue the bottom (F) in place and insert two 1¼" screws through it and into each of the supports (B, C, and D). Also insert two screws through each of the side pieces (A) and into the edges of each bottom.

Completing the Planter

1 Measure carefully and cut lengths of trim (G) from 1x3 pine to cover the exposed top edges of the planters, as shown in *figure 4*. Note that some of the trim pieces (G) must be mitered at a 22½-degree angle on one or both ends.

2 Glue the trim pieces (G) to the exposed upper ends of the planter side pieces (A). Secure the trim in place with 3d finishing nails spaced about 2" apart.

Constructing the Sun Lounge Frame

1 Cut two long frames (H) from 1x4 pine, each 72" long.

2 Cut two short frames (I) from 1x4 pine, each 21" long.

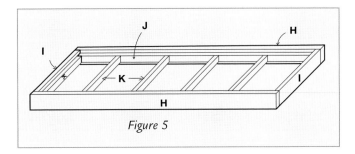

Figure 5

3 Place the two long frames (H) on a level surface, parallel to each other, on edge, and 21" apart. Glue the two short frames (I) between the ends of the long frames, as shown in *figure 5*. Then insert 1¼" screws through the long frames (H) and into the ends of the short frames (I), using two screws at each joint.

4 Cut two long lounge support (J), each 70½", from 1x3 pine.

5 Glue each long lounge support (J) to the inside of each long frame (H), ¾" from the top edge of the long frame. Secure the parts by inserting 1¼" screws spaced 6" apart.

6 Cut six short lounge supports (K), each 19½" long, from 1x3 pine.

7 Glue one short lounge support (K) to the inside of each short frame (I), ¾" from the top edge of the short frame. Use 1¼" screws spaced 6" apart to secure the two short lounge supports in place.

8 Glue the remaining four short lounge supports (K) between the two long lounge supports (J), spacing them approximately 13" apart. Insert two 2½" screws through the long frames (H) and the long lounge supports (J) into each end of each short lounge support (K).

9 Cut one 19½"x70½" lounge platform (L) from ¾"-thick plywood.

10 Glue the lounge platform (L) to the top edges of the lounge supports (J and K). Insert 1¼" screws, spacing them 6" apart, through the lounge platform and into the lounge supports.

Final Assembly and Finishing

1 The two planters must now be connected to the lounge. In order to determine the correct placement, first take a look at the project photo. Note that we attached our lounge so that the cushion would rise slightly above the planters. Place your cushion on top of the lounge and measure the distance from the bottom of the lounge frame to the top of the cushion. Using this measurement as a guide, mark across the long side of each planter to indicate where you'd like to locate the bottom of the lounge. Make sure that the mark you've just made is no more than 9" down from the upper face of the planter trim, or the bolts you insert to attach the lounge to the planters will end up being below the base (F), and you won't be able to reach them in order to tighten the wing nuts onto them.

2 Drill four equally-spaced holes, slightly larger in diameter than the bolts, through each short lounge support (K) and the short frame (I) to which it's attached.

3 Enlist the services of a helper and, holding the lounge at the marked location on each planter, mark the corresponding hole locations on one long side of each planter. Then drill bolt holes in the planter side at the marked locations.

4 Fit the $3/8$" bolts through the drilled holes in the lounge and through the long side of each planter. Add the wing nuts, tightening the nuts firmly to connect the lounge securely.

5 You may have noticed that the lounge in the photo has additional lounge supports underneath it. These really aren't necessary. We added them because we have groups of very large teenage boys involved in horseplay around our pool. If you'd like to add the supports, just attach a length of 1x2 to each planter side, $3/4$" below the lower edges of the lounge. Then slip two or three 70" lengths of 1x4 between these supports and the bottom of the lounge.

6 Sand the completed project thoroughly.

7 Stain or paint the sun lounge and planters the color of your choice.

Wine Cabinet

Our wine rack doubles as a serving bar; it has storage for bottles below, and accommodates lots of glasses above. The bottom opens for extra storage, and the tile surface serves as an instant bar, saving those constant treks to the kitchen for mixing drinks.

Special Tools & Techniques

- Bar clamps
- Miters
- Trowel (for applying tile adhesive)
- Rubber tile float

Materials

- 2 4- x8-foot sheets of $^3/_4$" plywood
- 42 linear feet of 1x4 pine
- 1 4- x4-foot sheet of $^3/_8$" plywood
- 22 linear feet of 1x3 pine
- 5 linear feet of 1x1 pine
- 8 linear feet of $3^1/_4$"-wide crown molding
- 8 linear feet of $^3/_4$"-wide cove molding
- Ceramic tile, enough to cover $3^1/_2$ square feet
- Small container of ceramic tile adhesive
- 7-lb. bag of sanded tile grout in the color of your choice
- Grout sealer

Hardware

- 120 $1^5/_8$" wood screws
- 6 $1^1/_2$" (4d) finish nails
- 55 1" drywall screws
- 15 $1^1/_4$" drywall screws
- 30 1" (2d) finish nails
- 8 cabinet door hinges
- 4 magnetic door catches
- 4 drawer pulls

*Notes on Materials

Most tiles sold at building-supply stores are now "self-spacing"; that is, they come with small projections on their edges so that when you lay the tiles out, the grout lines between them will be even. Because the spacing is determined by individual tile manufacturers, we recommend that you buy enough tile to cover the square foot area specified. If the tiles do not fit exactly, you will also need to purchase a tile cutter to cut the necessary tiles at the back and one side of the shelf.

Cutting List

Code	Description	Qty.	Material	Dimensions
A	Side	2	$^3/_4$" plywood	$63^1/_4$"x$15^1/_4$"
B	Top/Bottom	2	$^3/_4$" plywood	$33^3/_8$"x$15^1/_4$"
C	Shelf	3	$^3/_4$" plywood	$31^7/_8$"x$15^1/_4$"
D	Vertical Trim	2	1x4 pine	$64^3/_4$" long
E	Horizontal Trim	3	1x4 pine	$26^3/_4$" long
F	Horizontal Wine Trim	2	1x4 pine	$26^3/_8$" long
G	Ledge	1	1x4 pine	$31^7/_8$" long
H	Upper Panel	2	$^3/_8$" plywood	$19^3/_4$"x$11^3/_8$"
I	Upper Vertical Trim	4	1x3 pine	$21^3/_4$" long
J	Upper Horizontal Trim	4	1x3 pine	$8^3/_4$" long
K	Lower Panel	2	$^3/_8$" plywood	$15^1/_4$"x$11^3/_8$"
L	Lower Vertical Trim	4	1x3 pine	$17^1/_4$" long
M	Lower Horizontal Trim	4	1x3 pine	$8^3/_4$" long
N	Wine Bottle Support	2	1x4 pine	$31^7/_8$" long
O	Side Base Support	2	1x4 pine	$17^5/_8$" long
P	Front Base Support	1	1x4 pine	$35^1/_4$" long
Q	Stem Supports	5	1x4 pine	10" long
R	Connectors	5	1x1 pine	10" long
S	Frame Supports	2	1x4 pine	31" long
T	Top Molding		$3^1/_4$"-wide crown molding	cut to fit
U	Base Molding		$^3/_4$"-wide crown molding	cut to fit

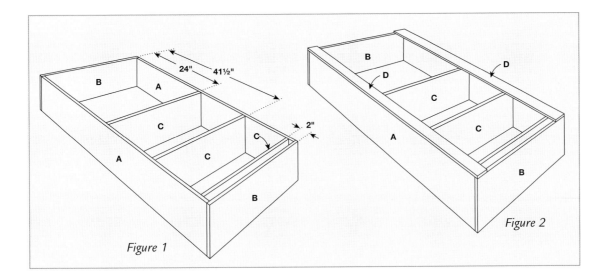

Figure 1

Figure 2

Constructing the Cabinet

1 Cut two Sides (A) from $^3/_4$-inch plywood, each measuring $63^1/_4$x$15^1/_4$ inches.

2 Cut two Top/Bottoms (B) from $^3/_4$-inch plywood, each measuring $33^3/_8$x$15^1/_4$ inches.

3 Place the two Sides (A) on edge on a level surface parallel to each other $31^7/_8$ inches apart. Fit the Top/Bottoms (B) over the ends of the Sides (A) to form a rectangle measuring $64^3/_4$x$33^3/_8$ inches, as shown in *figure 1*. Apply glue to the meeting surfaces, and screw through the Top/Bottoms (B) into the edge of the Sides (A). Use $1^5/_8$-inch wood screws spaced about every 5 inches.

4 Cut three Shelves (C) from $^3/_4$-inch plywood, each measuring $31^7/_8$x$15^1/_4$ inches. Place the first Shelf (C) 24 inches below the Top (B), as shown in *figure 1*. Screw through the Sides (A) into the edges of the Shelf (C). Use $1^5/_8$-inch wood screws spaced every 5 inches.

5 Repeat Step 4 to attach the second Shelf (C) $41^1/_2$ inches below the Top (B).

6 Repeat Step 4 to attach the third Shelf (C) 2 inches above the Bottom (B).

Adding the Front Trim & Ledge

1 Cut two Vertical Trims (D) from 1x4 pine, each measuring $64^3/_4$ inches. Apply glue to the meeting surfaces, and place one Vertical Trim (D) over the edge of one Side (A). Screw through the Vertical Trim (D) into the edge of Side (A), as shown in *figure 2*. Use $1^5/_8$-inch wood screws about every 5 inches.

2 Repeat Step 1 to attach the remaining Vertical Trim (D) to the opposing Side (A).

3 Cut three Horizontal Trims (E) from 1x4 pine, each measuring $26^3/_8$ inches.

4 Apply glue to the meeting surfaces, and attach one Horizontal Trim (E) over the edge of the Top (B), as shown in *figure 3*. Screw through the Horizontal Trim (E) into the edge of the Top (B). Use 1⅝-inch wood screws spaced every 5 inches.

5 Repeat Step 4 to attach the remaining two Horizontal Trims (E) flush with the upper edge of the Shelf (C) and flush with the lower edge of the Bottom (B). See *figure 3*.

6 Cut two Horizontal Wine Trims (F) from 1x4 pine, each measuring 26⅜ inches.

7 Referring to *figure 4*, mark and cut the semi circular cuts that will hold the tops of the wine bottles. Apply glue to the meeting surfaces, and attach one of the Horizontal Wine Trims (F) on die edge of the lower Shelf (C), as shown in *figure 3*. Use 1⅝-inch wood screws spaced every 5 inches.

8 Repeat Step 7 to attach the second Horizontal Wine Trim (F) 5½ inches above the first Horizontal Wine Trim (F). Apply glue to the meeting surfaces, and fit the second Horizontal Wine Trim (F) between the two Vertical Trims (D). Toenail through the Horizontal Wine Trim (F) into each of the Vertical Trims (D). Use 1½-inch nails.

9 Cut one Ledge (G) from 1x4 pine, measuring 31½ inches. Place the Ledge (G) between the two Sides (A) 18½ inches below the Top (B), as shown in *figure 5*. Use 1⅝-inch wood screws to attach.

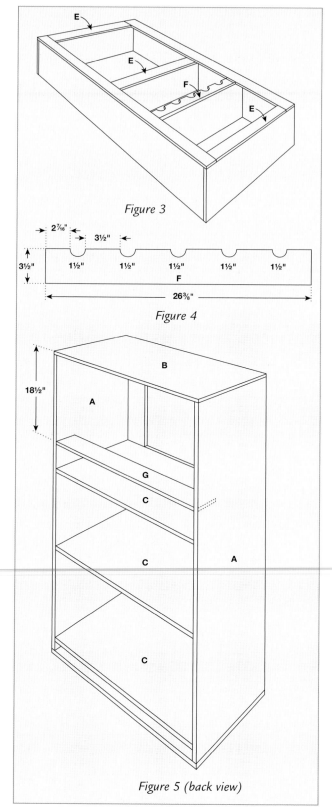

Figure 3

Figure 4

Figure 5 (back view)

Making the Door Panels

1 Cut two Upper Panels (H) from $^3/_8$-inch plywood, each measuring $19^3/_4$x$11^3/_8$ inches.

2 Cut four Upper Vertical Trims (I) for the door from 1x3 pine, each measuring $21^3/_4$ inches.

3 Cut four Upper Horizontal Trims (J) for the door from 1x3 pine, each measuring $8^3/_4$ inches.

4 Position two of the Upper Vertical Trims (I) face down on a level surface, parallel to each other and $8^3/_4$ inches apart. Position two of the Upper Horizontal Trims (J) between the Upper Vertical Trims (I), as shown in *figure 6*. Apply glue to the meeting surfaces. Hold the trims in place temporarily using bar clamps.

5 Center one Upper Panel (H) over the Trims (I and J), as shown in *figure 7*. Apply glue to the meeting surfaces, and screw through the Upper Panel (H) into Horizontal and Vertical Trims (I and J) using 1-inch drywall screws spaced every 5 inches.

6 Repeat Steps 4 and 5 to create the second door panel.

7 Cut two Lower Panels (K) for the door from $^3/_8$-inch plywood, each measuring $15^1/_4$x$11^3/_8$

8 Cut four Lower Vertical Trims (L) for the door from 1x3 pine, each measuring $17^1/_4$ inches.

9 Cut four Lower Horizontal Trims (M) for the door from 1x3 pine, each measuring $8^3/_4$ inches.

10 Position two of the Lower Vertical Trims (L) face down on a level surface parallel to each other and $8^3/_4$ inches apart. Position two of the Lower Horizontal Trims (M) between the Lower Vertical Trims (L) $12^1/_4$ inches apart, as you did for the Upper Trims (I and J) (see *figure 6*). Apply glue to the meeting surfaces, and use bar clamps to hold the Horizontal and Vertical Trims (L and M) in place temporarily.

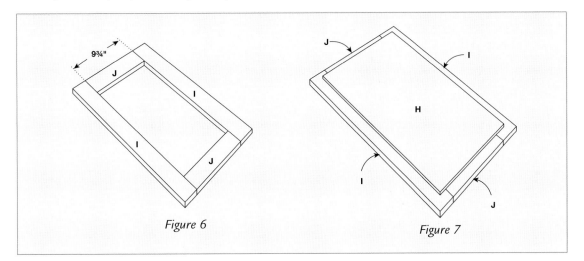

Figure 6

Figure 7

11 Center one Lower Panel (K) face down over the Lower Trims (L and M), as you did for the Upper Trims (I and J) (see *figure 7* on page 193). Apply glue to the meeting surfaces, and screw through the edges of the Lower Panel (K) into the Lower Vertical and Horizontal Trims (L and M), using 1-inch drywall screws spaced every 5 inches.

12 Repeat Steps 10 and 11 to construct another lower door.

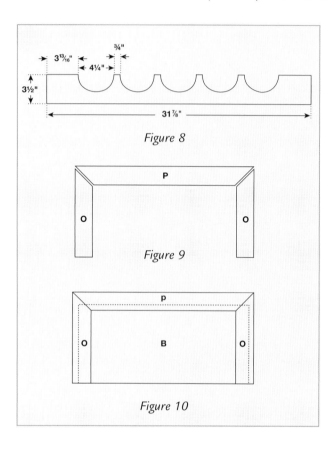

Figure 8

Figure 9

Figure 10

Adding the Bottle Supports

1 Cut two Wine Bottle Supports (N) from 1x4 pine, each measuring 31⅞ inches. Referring to *figure 8*, cut five semicircular cutouts to hold the bottom of the wine bottles. Each cutout has a radius of 4¼ inches. (The cutout is the same diameter as one-quarter of a paint can.) Use 1⅝-inch wood screws to attach the Wine Bottle Supports (N) level with and 6 inches behind the Horizontal Wine Trims (F). Screw through the Sides (A) into the end of the Wine Bottle Supports (N), using two screws for each end.

2 Cut two Side Base Supports (O) from 1x4 pine, each measuring 17⅝ inches. Miter one end of each of the Side Base Supports (O) at a 45° angle, as shown in *figure 9*.

3 Cut one Front Base Support (P) from 1x4 pine, measuring 35¼ inches. Miter the ends of the Front Base Support (P) at opposing 45° angles, as shown in *figure 9*.

4 Apply glue to the meeting surfaces, and attach the Base Supports (O and P) to the Bottom (B), as shown in *figure 10*. Use 1⅝-inch wood screws spaced 5 inches apart.

Adding the Glass Holders

1 Cut five Stem Supports (Q) from 1x4 pine, each measuring 10 inches.

2 Cut five Connectors (R) from 1x1 pine, each measuring 10 inches.

3 Cut two Frame Supports (S) from 1x4 pine, each measuring 31 inches.

4 Apply glue to the meeting surfaces and center one Connector (R) lengthwise over one Stem Support (Q), as shown in *figure 11* on page 195. Nail through the Connector (R) into the Stem Support (Q), using four evenly spaced 1⅝-inch wood screws.

5 Repeat Step 4 four times to attach the remaining Connectors (R) to the remaining Stem Supports (Q).

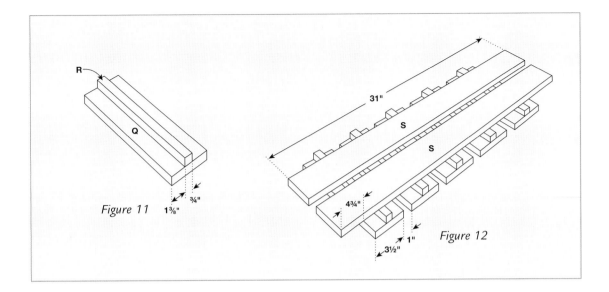

Figure 11   1⅜"   ¾"

31"   S   S   4¾"

3½"   1"   Figure 12

6 Place the five connector/support assemblies on a level surface, parallel to each other and 1 inch apart. Center the two Frame Supports (S) over the five connector/support assemblies as shown in *figure 12*. Note that the Frame Supports (S) will overhang the connector/support assemblies by 4³/₄ inches on each side.

7 Center the entire glass holder assembly inside the cabinet under the Top (B), flush with the back edge of the cabinet. Apply glue to the meeting surfaces and screw through the two Frame Supports (S) into the Top (B). Use 1¹/₄-inch drywall screws spaced 5 inches apart.

Installing the Doors

1 Place the completed cabinet on its back, and fit the four cabinet doors over the front openings in the cabinet. Allow about ¹/₈ inch between the doors. Check to make certain that the doors are level and fit evenly over the openings in the cabinet.

2 Attach the doors to the cabinet using two hinges on each door. Attach door catches on each of the doors to make certain that they stay closed when shut.

3 Install a drawer pull on each of the cabinets, following the manufacturer's instructions.

Finishing

1 Stand the cabinet upright. Refer to the photograph when placing the molding. If you're not skilled at cutting molding, refer to page 23. Carefully cut 3¹/₄ -inch-wide crown molding (T) to fit around the top of the cabinet. Use glue and 1-inch (2d) finish nails spaced every 5 inches. The bottom of the crown molding (T) should overlap the top of the cabinet by ¹/₂ inch.

2 Cut ³/₄-inch-wide cove molding (U) to fit around the bottom of the cabinet. Use glue and 1-inch finish nails spaced every 5 inches.

3 Fill all nail and screw holes, cracks, and crevices with wood filler.

4 Sand all surfaces of the completed wine cabinet.

5 Stain or paint the cabinet with the color of your choice. We chose a cherry stain, then sealed it with a clear polyurethane.

Adding the Tile

1 The last step is to install the tile on the top shelf. Following the manufacturer's directions carefully, spread an even coat of tile adhesive over the surface of the top shelf with a trowel.

2 Place the tiles on the adhesive one at a time, making sure that the tiles are straight. Do not slide tiles, or the adhesive will be forced up onto the sides of the tiles. Let the adhesive dry overnight.

3 Mix the tile grout according to the manufacturer's directions (or use premixed tile grout).

4 Using a rubber-surfaced float, spread the grout over the tiles with arcing motions. Hold the float at an angle so that the grout is forced evenly into the spaces between the tiles.

5 When the grout begins to set up, use a damp rag to wipe the excess from the tiles and joints. If you let the grout harden too long, it will be very difficult to remove. Use as little water as possible when removing the excess so that you don't thin the grout that remains. Let the grout dry overnight.

6 Use a damp rag to wipe the remaining film from the tile.

7 Apply grout sealer, following the manufacturer's directions. (You may need to wait several days before applying sealer to the project.)

Scrap-Wood Candlesticks

This project makes use of the scrap wood that may be lurking in your workshop. We simply cut squares from wood scraps to 1³/₄-, 2¹/₂-, and 3-inch sizes, painted them, and nailed the pieces together. The candlesticks are assembled in different arrangements: a simple stack, a star, and two free-form candlesticks. Either replicate one of our designs or come up with your own.

Materials

- Assorted scrap wood cut into squares (see cutting list below)

Hardware

- 20 1¼" (3d) finish nails (for all four candlesticks)

Cutting List

Code	Description	Qty.	Material	Dimensions
A	Stack (Small)	1	1" pine	1³/₄" square
B	Stack (Medium)	1	1" pine	2¹/₂" square
C	Stack (Large)	1	1" pine	3" square
D	Star (Small)	1	1" pine	1³/₄" square
E	Star (Medium)	2	1" pine	2¹/₂" square
F	Star (Large)	1	2" pine	3" square
G	Tall Free-Form (Small)	3	1" pine	1³/₄" square
H	Tall Free-Form (Medium)	2	1" pine	2¹/₂" square
I	Tall Free-Form (Large)	2	1" pine	3" square
J	Tall Free-Form (X-Large)	1	2" pine	3" square
K	Short Free-Form (Small)	2	1" pine	1³/₄" square
L	Short Free-Form (Medium)	3	1" pine	2¹/₂" square
M	Short Free-Form (Large)	3	1" pine	3" square

Making the Simple Stack Candlestick

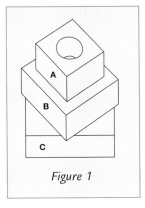

Figure 1

1 Cut squares to the following measurements from 1-inch-thick wood: one Small square (A) measuring 1³/₄ inches square, one Medium square (B) measuring 2¹/₂ inches square, and one Large square (C) measuring 3 inches squares.

2 Sand and paint each of the pieces, and allow them to dry thoroughly.

3 Refer to *figure 1* during assembly. Place the Large square (C) on a level surface. Center the Medium square (B) over it at a 45° angle, and nail the two pieces together using two 1¹/₄-inch nails.

4 Drill a ³/₄-inch-diameter hole in the center of the Small square (A) to accommodate the candle.

5 Center the Small square (A) over the assembly, and nail through the drilled hole into the assembly using two 1¹/₄-inch nails.

Making the Star Candlestick

1 Cut squares to the following measurements from 1-inch-thick wood: one Small square (D) measuring 1³/₄ inches, and two Medium squares (E), measuring 2¹/₂ inches.

2 Cut one Large square (F) from 2-inch-thick wood, measuring 3 inches.

3 Sand and paint each of the pieces, and allow them to dry thoroughly.

4 Refer to *figure 2* during assembly. Place the Large square (F) on a level surface. Center one Medium square (E) over it at a 45° angle, and nail the two pieces together using two 1¼-inch nails.

5 Center the second Medium square (E) over the assembly, again at a 45° angle, and nail the two pieces together using two 1¼-inch nails.

6 Drill a ¾-inch-diameter hole in the center of the Small square (D) to accommodate the candle.

7 Center the Small square (D) over the assembly, and nail through the drilled hole into the assembly using two 1¼-inch nails.

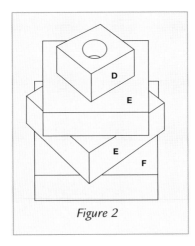

Figure 2

Making the Tall Free-Form Candlestick

1 Cut squares to the following measurements from 1-inch-thick wood: three Small squares (G), each measuring 1¾ inches; two Medium squares (H), each measuring 2½ inches; and two Large squares (I), each measuring 3 inches.

2 Cut one Extra-Large square (J) from 2-inch- thick wood, measuring 3 inches.

3 Sand and paint each of the pieces, and allow them to dry thoroughly.

4 Refer to *figure 3* during assembly. The assembly of the free-form requires two intermediate assembly processes. Place one Small square (G) on end on a level surface. Center one Large square (I) over the end of the Small square (G) at a 45° angle. Nail through the Large square (I) into the end of the Small square (G) using two 1¼-inch nails.

5 Turn the assembly over, and center one Medium square (H) over the end of the Small square (G) at a 45° angle. Nail through the Medium square (H) into the Small square (G) using two 1¼-inch nails.

6 Drill a ¾-inch-diameter hole ½ inch deep in the center of one Large square (I).

7 Repeat Steps 4 and 5 to complete a second intermediate assembly, making certain that the drilled hole on the Large square (I) ends up on the outside of the assembly.

8 Place the 2-inch-thick Extra-Large square (J) on a flat surface. Center the first intermediate assembly (without the drilled hole), Large square (I) down, at a 45° angle over the Extra-Large square (J). Nail through the edges of the Large square (I) into the Extra-Large square (J) using two 1¼-inch nails.

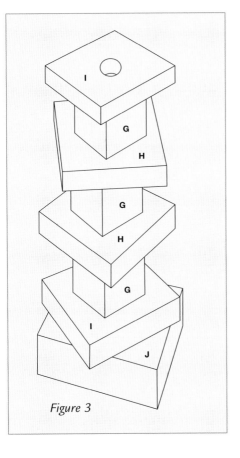

Figure 3

9 Center one Small square (G) over the assembly, again at a 45° angle, and nail through the Small square (G) into the Medium square (H) using two 1¼-inch nails.

10 Center the second intermediate assembly at a 45° angle over the Small square (G). Nail through the Medium square (H) into the Small square (G) using two 1¼-inch nails.

Short Free-Form Candlestick

1 Cut squares to the following measurements from 1-inch-thick wood: two Small squares (K), each measuring 1¾ inches; three Medium squares (L), each measuring 2½ inches; and three Large squares (M), each measuring 3 inches.

2 Sand and paint each of the pieces, and allow them to dry thoroughly.

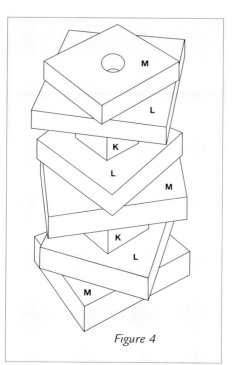

Figure 4

3 Refer to *figure 4* during the assembly. The assembly of the short free-form requires two intermediate assembly processes. Place one Small square (K) on end on a level surface. Center one Large square (M) over the end of the Small square (K) at a 45° angle. Nail through the Large square (M) into the end of the Small square (K) using two 1¼-inch nails.

4 Turn the assembly over, and center one Medium square (L) over the end of the Small square (K) at a 45° angle. Nail through the medium square (L) into the Small square (K) using two 1¼-inch nails.

5 Repeat Steps 3 and 4 to complete a second intermediate assembly, this time using one Small square (K) in the center, and two Medium squares (L) on the outside.

6 Place one Large square (M) on a flat surface. Center the first intermediate assembly (with the Large square [M] at the top), at a 45° angle over the Large square (M). Nail through the edges of the Medium square (L) into the Large square (M) using two 1¼-inch nails.

7 Repeat Step 6 to attach the second intermediate assembly.

8 Drill a ¾-inch-diameter hole in the center of the remaining Large square (M).

9 Center the Large square (M) (hole side up) over the assembly, again at a 45° angle, and nail through the drilled hole into the Medium square (L) using two 1¼-inch nails.

Corner Cabinet

The cheerful cabinet shown on page 203 will perk up any lonely corner in your house. The top and bottom both have storage shelves, so you can display lots of your favorite knickknacks with the doors open (or store lots of your un-favorite knickknacks with the doors closed). You can use fabric in the top doors to match a bedspread, but you could substitute glass or solid panels like those in the lower doors if you like. The finished cabinet is approximately 40" wide, 78" high, and 20" deep.

The upper and lower sections of the cabinet are built separately and then joined together in the final assembly. Just take your time and follow each step carefully. This project takes a lot of work, but it's well worth it. Countersink all nails and screws as you work so that the completed project is ready for finishing.

Special Tools & Techniques

- Hot-glue gun
- Router (optional)
- Beveling
- Dadoes
- Mitering
- Ripping

Materials

- 54 linear feet of 1x4 pine
- 15 linear feet of 1x6 pine
- 4 linear feet of 1x12 pine
- 8 linear feet of 2x2 pine
- 3 sheets of 3/4"-thick plywood, each 4'x8'
- 4 linear feet of 3½" beaded molding
- 4 linear feet of 3/4"x3/4" cove molding
- 5 linear feet of 4" crown molding
- 13 linear feet of 3½" fluted molding
- 1½ yards of fabric
- 6 yards of upholstery braid

Hardware

- Approximately 200 #6x1¼" flathead wood screws
- Approximately 50 #6x2" flathead wood screws
- Approximately 75 2d finishing nails
- Approximately 200 3d finishing nails
- Approximately 50 8d finishing nails
- 8 cabinet door hinges
- 4 cabinet door handles
- Tacks (optional)

*Notes on Materials

Because we intended to paint this cabinet, we used paint-grade 3/4"-thick plywood, and for each of the shelves, we simply filled the exposed plywood edges. If you intend to stain your cabinet, you should purchase stain-grade material. You should also buy some very thin wood veneer strips to match your plywood and glue them to the exposed edges of the cabinet shelves after they're installed.

Using careful planning, this project can be completed using 2½ sheets of plywood. To accomplish this, you must cut the narrowest pieces—the upper back (B), upper sides (C), and lower back (J)—from the half-sheet. Any other combinations require you to have three full sheets.

This cabinet requires extensive beveling and mitering, so we strongly recommend that beginners who want to tackle it enlist the help of an experienced woodworker. It's not that the cuts themselves are difficult, but setting blade angles can be confusing until you know what you are doing.

Cutting List

Code	Description	Qty.	Material	Dimensions
A	Upper Floor	1	³/₄" plywood	See *figure 1* (approx. 21"x42")
B	Upper Back	1	³/₄" plywood	13¹/₂"x40"
C	Upper Side	2	³/₄" plywood	17¹/₂"x40"
D	Upper Front	2	1x6 pine	40" long
E	Upper Shelf	2	³/₄" plywood	See *figure 5* (approx. 18"x36")
F	Upper Top	1	³/₄" plywood	Same as (E)
G	Upper Vertical Facer	2	1x4 pine, ripped	40" long
H	Upper Horizontal Facer	1	1x4 pine	25-5/8" long
I	Lower Top	1	³/₄" plywood	Same as (E)
J	Lower Back	1	³/₄" plywood	13¹/₂"x34¹/₂"
K	Lower Side	2	³/₄" plywood	17¹/₂"x34¹/₂"
L	Lower Front	2	1x6 pine	34¹/₂" long
M	Lower Shelf	1	³/₄" plywood	Same as (E)
N	Lower Floor	1	³/₄" plywood	Same as (E)
O	Lower Vertical Facer	2	1x4 pine, ripped	34¹/₂" long
P	Lower Top Horizontal Facer	1	1x4 pine	25⁵/₈" long
Q	Lower Bottom Horizontal Facer	1	1x4 pine	25⁵/₈" long
R	Panel	2	1x12 pine	9³/₈"x23¹/₂"
S	Lower Top/Bottom Frame	4	1x4 pine, ripped	8³/₄" long
T	Lower Side Frame	4	1x4 pine, ripped	26⁷/₈" long
U	Upper Top Bottom Frame	4	1x4 pine, ripped	8³/₄" long
V	Upper Side Frame	4	1x4 pine, ripped	36³/₈" long
W	Fabric Panel	2	fabric	23"x33¹/₂"
X	Back Reinforcement	1	2x2 pine	Approx. 13" long
Y	Side Reinforcement	2	2x2 pine	Approx. 17" long
Z	Front Reinforcement	2	2x2 pine	Approx. 5" long
AA	Facer Reinforcement	1	2x2 pine	Approx. 30" long
BB	Beaded Molding	3	3¹/₂" beaded molding	Cut to fit (approx. 45" total)
CC	Fluted Molding	4	3¹/₂" fluted molding	Cut to fit (approx. 142" total)
DD	Pine Trim	3	1x4 pine	Cut to fit (approx. 45" total)
EE	Cove Molding	3	³/₄"x³/₄" cove molding	Cut to fit (approx. 45" total)
FF	Crown Molding	3	4" crown molding	Cut to fit (approx. 50" total)

Constructing the Upper Section

1 Using *figure 1* as a guide, carefully measure and draw the outline for the upper floor (A) onto your ³/₄"-thick plywood; then cut out one upper floor (A).

2 Cut one 13¹/₂"x40" upper back (B) from ³/₄"-thick plywood.

3 Bevel both 40"-long edges of the upper back (B) at 22¹/₂ degrees. *figure 2* on page 203 shows the angle cuts for all of the beveled edges of the upper cabinet, back and sides.

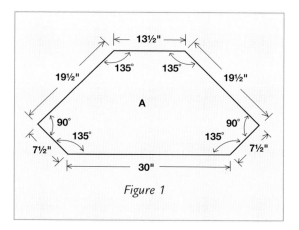

Figure 1

4 Cut two upper sides (C) from ³/₄"-thick plywood, each measuring 17¹/₂" by 40".

5 Bevel one of the 40"-long edges of each upper side (C) at 22¹/₂ degrees and bevel the opposite edge at 45 degrees, as shown in *figure 2*.

6 Cut two upper fronts (D) from 1x6 pine, each 40" long.

7 Bevel one of the 40"-long edges of each of the upper fronts (D) at 22¹/₂ degrees. Bevel the opposite edge at 45 degrees.

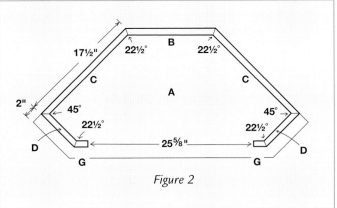

Figure 2

8 The assembly of the upper cabinet is shown in *figures 2* on page 203 and *3*. You would probably be wise to enlist the assistance of a willing helper (or two) to accomplish this task. Study both diagrams to familiarize yourself with how the pieces go together. Assembly won't be the best of times to have to say, "Hand me that book again—how does it fit together?"

As shown in *figures 2* on page 203 and *3*, the upper back (B), upper sides (C) and upper fronts (D) stand on end on top of the upper floor (A). The upper back (B) is set flush with the $13^1/_2$" edge of the upper floor (A), with its narrower face on the inside of the cabinet. The upper sides (C) are flush with the $19^1/_2$" edges of the upper floor, and their $22^1/_2$-degree beveled edges fit against the matching beveled edges of the upper back (B). Notice, however,

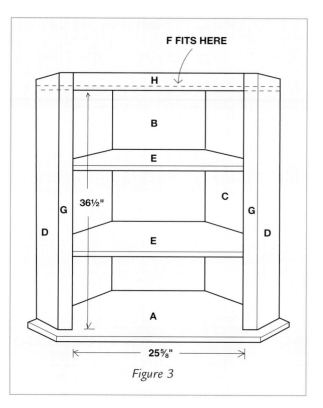

Figure 3

that the $17^1/_2$"-long end of each upper side (C) is 2" shorter than the corresponding $19^1/_2$" edge of the upper floor (A). The excess width of the upper floor (A) creates a small "shelf" between the upper and lower cabinet assemblies (see *figure 3*). This becomes an important design element in the finished project.

Begin by attaching the upper back (B) to the upper floor (A). Glue the parts together and insert $1^1/_4$" screws through the bottom of the upper floor (A) and into the edge of the upper back (B), spacing the screws about 3" apart.

9 Fit the $22^1/_2$-degree beveled edge of one upper side (C) against the matching beveled edge of the upper back (B), positioning the side (C) so that its outer face is flush with the edge of the upper floor (A). Glue the parts together and insert $1^1/_4$" screws through the upper floor (A) and into the edge of the upper side (C), spacing the screws about 3" apart. Then insert 3d finishing nails through the bevel in the upper back (B) and into the beveled edge of the upper side (C), spacing the nails about 4" apart.

10 Repeat Step 9 to attach the remaining upper side (C) to the upper floor (A) and the upper back (B).

11 The next step is to add the two fronts (D), using *figure 2* on page 203 as a guide. Note that the 45-degree beveled edge of each front (D) fits against the matching bevel on the adjacent upper side (C). Glue the parts together and insert $1^1/_4$" screws through the upper floor (A) into the edges of the upper fronts (D), spacing the screws about 3" apart. Secure the bevels with 3d finishing nails spaced about 4" apart.

Adding the Shelves and Top

1 *Figure 4* shows the dimensions of the two upper shelves (E) and the top (F). The shelves must fit exactly inside the assembly. To assure a good fit, first cut a cardboard pattern of an upper shelf (E), using the dimensions provided in *figure 4*. Position the cardboard pattern inside your assembly, check the fit, and alter the pattern as necessary. Then use the altered pattern to trace two upper shelves (E) and one upper top (F) onto ³/₄"-thick plywood, and cut out the plywood parts.

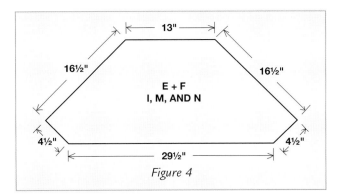

Figure 4

2 Place the assembly right side up on a level surface and decide where to place the shelves. I positioned the first shelf 12" above the floor and the second shelf 12" above that, but you may space the shelves as you like. Next, measure and mark both the upper back (B) and upper sides (C) with the desired locations of the shelves. The marks don't have to be exact—your job will be much easier if you use a level to position the shelves rather than relying on measurements.

3 Fit the lowest upper shelf (E) inside the cabinet assembly as close as possible to your marks. Place the level on the upper shelf (E) in several locations and facing in several directions, adjusting the position of the shelf until it is exactly level in every direction.

4 Use glue and 1¹/₄" screws placed about 3" apart to attach the shelf in place. Insert the screws through the upper sides (C), the upper back (B), and the upper fronts (D) into the upper shelf (E), counter sinking each screw as you go.

5 Repeat Steps 3 and 4 to attach the second upper shelf (E) inside the upper cabinet assembly.

6 Fit the upper top (F) inside the upper cabinet assembly as you did when adding the shelves, positioning its lower face 3¹/₂" from the top edges of the upper back, sides, and fronts (B, C, and D). Use your level again to make sure that the top (F) is even in all directions.

7 Glue the upper top (F) in place and insert 1¹/₄" screws, spaced about 3" apart, through the upper sides (C), the upper back (B), and both upper fronts (D) into the upper top (F).

Installing the Facers

1 Cut two 40"-long upper vertical facers (G) from 1x4 pine.

2 Rip each of the upper vertical facers (G) to 2¹/₄" in width.

3 Bevel one 40"-long edge of each upper vertical facer (G) at 22¹/₂ degrees, as shown in *figure 2* on page 203.

4 To avoid later problems with the doors, perform this next step without using any glue. Using *figures 2* and *3* on pages 203 and 204 as guides, attach one upper vertical facer (G) to

the left upper front (D), the two upper shelves (E), and the upper top (F). Note that the 22$\frac{1}{2}$-degree bevels on the upper vertical facer (G) and the upper front (D) face each other. Secure the meeting beveled edges of the upper front (D) and the upper vertical facer (G) by driving two 3d finishing nails just far enough in to hold the piece in place.

5 Repeat Step 4 to attach the remaining upper vertical facer (G) to the right-hand side of the cabinet assembly, again omitting the glue.

6 Check the width of the opening between the two upper vertical facers (G) along the exposed edge of the top (F). Also measure the width of the opening across the middle and bottom. The opening should measure exactly 25$\frac{5}{8}$", or the doors will not fit properly. To adjust the opening, remove the two upper vertical facers (G) and alter them as necessary. Then glue the adjusted facers in place and insert 1$\frac{1}{4}$" screws through the upper floor (A) and into the bottom edges of the upper vertical facers (G). Secure the meeting beveled edges of the upper front (D) and the upper vertical facer (G) with 3d finishing nails spaced about 6" apart. Also drive nails through the facers (G) and into the edges of the shelves (E) and the upper top (F).

7 Cut one 25$\frac{5}{8}$"-long upper horizontal facer (H) from 1x4 pine.

8 Fit the upper horizontal facer (H) between the two upper vertical facers (G) and position it so that its bottom edge is flush with the lower face of the upper top (F). Drive two 3d finishing nails through the upper horizontal facer (H) into the edge of the upper top (F), hammering them in only far enough to hold the piece in place.

9 Now measure the opening from top to bottom on the left and right sides and in the middle. It should measure exactly 36$\frac{1}{2}$", as shown in *figure 3* on page 204. If necessary, remove the upper horizontal facer (H) and alter it so that the opening conforms to these measurements.

10 Replace the upper horizontal facer (H), glue it in place, and secure with 3d finishing nails placed about 3" apart and driven into the edge of the upper top (F). Also toenail through the ends of the upper horizontal facer (H) into each of the upper vertical facers (G).

Constructing the Lower Section

1 The construction of the lower section is very similar to that of the upper section. There are several exceptions in the measurements of the parts and in the assembly process, however, so follow the directions carefully.
　　The lower top (I) has exactly the same dimensions as the upper shelves (E). Use your cardboard pattern again to cut one lower top (I) from $\frac{3}{4}$"-thick plywood.

2 Cut one 13$\frac{1}{2}$"x34$\frac{1}{2}$" lower back (J) from $\frac{3}{4}$"-thick plywood.

3 Bevel each of the 34$\frac{1}{2}$"-long sides of the lower back (J) at 22$\frac{1}{2}$ degrees, as shown in *figure 5* on page 207.

4 Cut two lower sides (K) from ³/₄"-thick plywood, each measuring 17¹/₂"x34¹/₂".

5 Bevel one 34¹/₂" edge of each lower side (K) at 22¹/₂ degrees. Bevel the opposite edge at a 45-degree angle (see *figure 5*).

6 Cut two 34¹/₂"-long lower fronts (L) from 1x6 pine.

7 Bevel one of the 34¹/₂"-long edges of each of the lower fronts (L) at a 45-degree angle. Bevel the opposite edge at 22¹/₂ degrees.

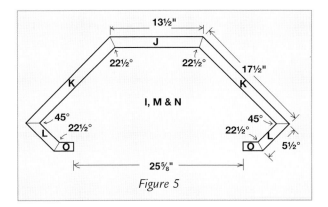

Figure 5

8 The assembly of the lower cabinet is shown in *figure 5* above and *figure 6* on page 208. Again, enlist the services of a helper and study the diagrams before beginning the assembly.

For ease of handling, the lower cabinet is assembled upside down, with the lower top (I) serving as a base. Note that the lower back (J) and lower sides (K) fit onto the edges of the lower top (I), not on its face. Make sure that the narrower faces of the beveled lower back (J) and lower sides (K) are on the inside of the cabinet and that the 22¹/₂-degree bevels are matched together.

9 Begin by gluing the lower back (J) to the lower top (I). Insert 1¹/₄" screws, spaced about 3" apart, through the lower back (J) and into the edge of the lower top (I).

10 Glue one lower side (K) to the lower top (I) and lower back (J), matching the 22¹/₂-degree bevels. Insert 3d finishing nails, spaced about 4" apart, through the lower back (J) and into the beveled edge of the lower side (K). Insert 1¹/₄" screws, spaced about 3" apart, through the lower side (K) and into the edge of the lower top (I).

11 Repeat Step 10 to attach the remaining lower side (K) to the lower top (I) and the lower back (J).

12 The next step is to add the two lower fronts (L), using *figure 5* above and *figure 6* on page 208 as assembly guides. Note that the 45-degree beveled edges of the lower fronts (L) and the lower sides (K) fit together. Glue the lower fronts (L) in place and insert 3d finishing nails spaced about 3" apart through their beveled edges and into the beveled edges of the lower sides (K). Also insert 1¹/₄" screws through the lower fronts (L) into the edge of the lower top (I).

Adding the Shelf & Floor

1 The lower shelf (M) and the lower floor (N) are the same dimensions as the lower top (I). Use your cardboard pattern again to cut one lower shelf (M) and one lower floor (N) from ³/₄"-thick plywood.

2 Place the lower cabinet assembly upside down on a surface that is exactly level. Position the lower shelf (M) inside it as you like. I positioned mine 13" from the lower top (I). Measure and mark both the lower back (J) and the two lower sides (K) with the desired shelf location.

3 Fit the lower shelf (M) inside the lower cabinet assembly as close as possible to your marks. Use your level to make sure that the lower shelf (M) is exactly level in all directions.

4 Glue the shelf in place and insert 1¼" screws, spaced about 3" apart, through the lower sides (K), the lower back (J), and the lower fronts (L) into the edges of the lower shelf (M).

5 Fit the lower floor (N) inside the lower cabinet assembly as you did with the shelf (M), positioning what will be its upper face (when the cabinet is turned right side up) 3½" from the exposed edges of the lower back, lower sides, and lower fronts J, K, and L). Again, level the lower floor (N) in all directions.

6 Glue the lower floor in place and insert 1¼" screws, spaced about 3" apart, through the lower fronts (L), the lower sides (K) and the lower back (J) into the lower floor (N).

Adding the Facers

1 Turn the lower cabinet assembly right side up. Cut two lower vertical facers (O) from 1x4 pine, each 34½" long.

2 Rip each of the lower vertical facers (O) to 2¼" in width.

3 Bevel one 34½"-long edge of each lower vertical facer (O) at 22½ degrees.

4 Note in *figure 5* on page 207 that the beveled edge of the lower vertical facer matches the beveled edge of the lower front (L). Attach one lower vertical facer (O) to the left lower front (L), the lower shelf (M), and the lower top (I), as shown in *figure 6*, using two 3d finishing nails driven in just far enough to hold the piece in place.

5 Repeat Step 4 to attach the remaining lower vertical facer (O) to the other side of the cabinet assembly.

6 Check the width of the opening between the two lower vertical facers (O) along the exposed edge of the lower floor (N), across the center of the opening, and across the top. The opening should measure exactly 25⅝". If necessary, remove the two lower vertical facers (O) and alter them to make the opening conform to this measurement. Then glue the two lower vertical facers (O) in place and drive 3d finishing nails, spaced about 4" apart, through the beveled edges of the lower fronts (L) into the edges of the lower vertical facers (O). Also insert 1¼" screws through the facers (O) into the edges of the lower floor (N) and lower shelf (M).

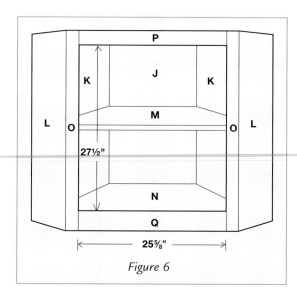

Figure 6

7 From 1x4 pine, cut one 25⁵/₈"-long lower top horizontal facer (P) and one 25⁵/₈"-long lower bottom horizontal facer (Q).

8 Fit the lower bottom horizontal facer (Q) between the two lower vertical facers (O), positioning it so that its top edge is flush with the upper surface of the lower floor (N). Glue the facer (Q) in place and secure it with 3d finishing nails driven through the facer (Q) and into the edge of the floor (N). Also toenail the ends of the facer (Q) to the edges of the lower vertical facers (O).

9 Fit the lower top horizontal facer (P) between the two lower vertical facers (O) so that it is flush at the top. Secure it temporarily by driving two 3d finishing nails through the facer (P) and into the edge of the lower top (I). Hammer the nails in only far enough to hold the piece in place.

10 Now measure the opening from top to bottom on the left, middle, and right sides. The opening should measure exactly 27¹/₂". If necessary, remove the lower top horizontal facer (P) and alter it so that the opening conforms to this measurement.

11 Glue the lower top horizontal facer (P) in place, securing it by driving 3d finishing nails through it and into the edge of the lower top (I). Space the nails about 3" apart. Also toenail the facer by driving nails through its edge and into the lower vertical facers (O).

Constructing the Lower Doors

1 Each of the two lower doors (see *figure 7*) consists of a center panel that is beveled on all four edges and inserted into a frame. This is not difficult to do, but it requires a certain amount of precision in cutting to obtain a professional-looking finished product. Don't hurry the process; be meticulous in your work. Start by cutting one 9³/₈" by 23¹/₂" panel (R) from 1x12 pine.

2 Set your saw blade to cut at 15 degrees off vertical and bevel all four edges of the panel (R), leaving a thickness of ¹/₈" on the outside edges. A diagram of the resulting cut is shown in *figure 8*.

3 Rip a total of 12 linear feet of 1x4 pine to 2" in width.

4 From the ripped 1x4 pine, cut two 8³/₄"-long lower top/bottom frame pieces (S) and two 26⁷/₈"-long lower side frame pieces (T).

5 Cut a dado ¹/₄" wide and ³/₈" deep down the center inside

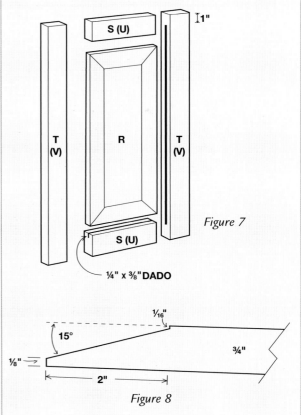

Figure 7

¼" x ⅜" DADO

15°

¹/₁₆"

¾"

⅛"

2"

Figure 8

edge of each of the four frame pieces (S and T) to accommodate the center panel (R). If you don't want your dadoes to show (what would the neighbors think?) on the outer edges of the doors, then start the dado 1" from one end of each lower side frame piece (T) and stop it 1" from the other end.

6 Place the panel (R) into the dadoes cut in the frame pieces to make sure that all of the pieces fit together properly. An optional step at this point is to rout a decorative design into the inside edges of the frame pieces. Because this is difficult to do with the panel installed, simply clamp the frame together securely and rout the inside edges. Then place the panel (R) inside the frame.

7 As shown in *figure 7* on page 209, the top and bottom frame pieces (S) fit between the side frame pieces (T). Glue and clamp the frame pieces together, with the panel (R) in place but not glued into the dadoes. Fasten the frame together by inserting 8d finishing nails at all four corners.

8 Repeat Steps 1 through 7 to assemble the second lower door.

Constructing the Upper Door Frames

1 The upper doors are constructed in the same manner as the lower doors, but they don't have raised panels in their centers. Instead, the upper doors are completed by adding fabric after the cabinet has been stained or painted. Start by ripping a total of 16 linear feet of 1x4 to 2" in width.

2 From the ripped pine, cut two $8^3/4$"-long upper top/bottom frame pieces, (U) and two $36^3/8$"-long upper side frame pieces (V).

3 Glue and clamp the four frame pieces (U and V) together as shown in *figure 7* on page 209, making sure to fit the upper top/bottom frame pieces (U) between the upper side frame pieces (V). Then drive 8d finishing nails into all four corners of the frame.

If you routed a decorative design onto the lower doors, you may want to rout one into the inside edges of the assembled frame at this stage.

4 Repeat Steps 1 through 3 to make the second upper door frame.

Hanging the Doors

1 Set the cabinet assemblies on their backs so that you don't have to support the weight of the doors while you hang them.

2 Set both of the upper doors inside the opening in the upper cabinet assembly. If you're using exposed hinges, position them equidistant from the top and bottom on the outside of each door and secure them in place using the screws provided by the manufacturer. For other kinds of hinges, follow the manufacturer's instructions for installation.

3 Repeat Step 2 to attach the two lower doors to the lower cabinet assembly.

4 Attach the four cabinet handles (one on each door), following the manufacturer's directions.

Completing the Base

1 The lower back (J), lower sides (K), lower fronts (L), and lower vertical and horizontal facers (O, P, and Q) form a 3½"-wide collar at the bottom of the lower cabinet. In order to support the weight of the cabinet, this collar must be strengthened with 2x2 pine reinforcements.

Cut the following pieces from 2x2 pine:

Code	Description	Qty.	Length
X	Back Reinforcement	1	13"
Y	Side Reinforcement	2	17"
Z	Front Reinforcement	2	5"
AA	Facer Reinforcement	1	30"

As you can see in *figure 9*, the reinforcements must be mitered to fit the beveled edges of the pieces they reinforce. The lengths specified above give you some excess for mitering room. Measure and miter carefully so that all of the reinforcements fit properly.

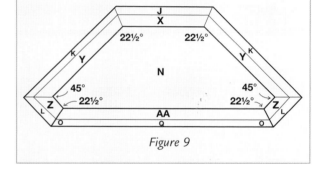

Figure 9

2 Start by mitering both ends of the back reinforcement (X) at 22½ degrees, as shown in *figure 9*.

3 Then miter each of the side reinforcements (Y) and front reinforcements (Z) to create a 22½-degree cut at one end and a 45-degree cut at the other end.

4 Finally, miter both ends of the facer reinforcement (AA) at 22½ degrees.

5 Fit the back reinforcement (X) against the lower back (I) and under and against the lower floor (N). Glue it in place and insert 2" screws, placed about 3" apart, through the back reinforcement and into the floor (N) and lower back (J).

6 Fit the two side reinforcements (Y) in place, matching the miters as you do. Glue them to the lower sides (K) and lower floor (N) and insert screws as in Step 5.

7 Fit the two front reinforcements (Z) in place, again matching the miters. Glue them to the lower fronts (L) and lower floor (N) and insert screws as in Step 5.

8 Fit the facer reinforcement (AA) in place. Glue it to both vertical facers (O), the lower bottom horizontal facer (Q), and the lower floor (N). Then insert screws as in Step 5.

Assembling the Cabinet

1 Place the upper cabinet assembly on top of the lower cabinet assembly, matching the upper and lower assemblies at the back and on the sides.

2 If you want to be able to separate the two assemblies (during a household move, for example), use only screws—not glue—so that you can unscrew the two halves for easier moving. Insert 1¼" screws through the lower top (I) into the upper floor (A). (You can reverse the direction of the screws, but the heads will be visible unless you countersink and fill them, making this a permanent attachment.) Use two or three screws across the back, two or three in the middle, and three or four across the front.

Adding the Trim

1 Study *figure 10*, which shows the pine trim (DD), cove molding (EE), and crown molding (FF) added to the cabinet top; the fluted trim (CC) added to both sides; and beaded molding (BB) added to the bottom. Because the back and sides of the cabinet fit against the wall, no molding is added to them.

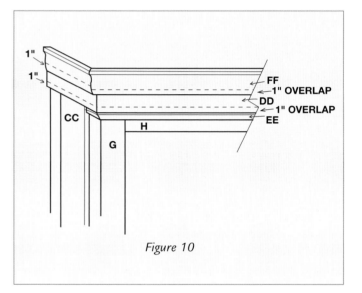

Figure 10

2 Carefully measure and cut two 6½"- long pieces of beaded molding (BB) to fit across the lower fronts (L) at the bottom of the cabinet and one 32"-long piece to fit across the lower facers (O and Q). Miter one end of each shorter piece and both ends of the longer piece at 22½ degrees. Glue the mitered pieces of beaded molding (BB) to the cabinet and secure with 3d finishing nails spaced about 3" apart.

3 Measure and cut two pieces of fluted molding (CC) to fit down the center of each of the lower fronts (L), between the upper floor (A) and the beaded molding (BB) that you just installed. Each piece should be approximately 31" long. Glue the pieces in place and secure with 2d finishing nails spaced about 4" apart. (Don't glue the end of the fluted molding (CC) to the upper floor (A) if you plan to separate the upper and lower assemblies at some future time.)

4 Measure the length of each upper front (D) along its center, starting at the upper floor (A) and extending 2½" higher than the top of the opening for the upper doors. This length should be approximately 39". Cut two pieces of fluted molding (CC) to this length. Glue the pieces in place and secure with 2d finishing nails spaced about 4" apart.

5 Following the same procedures described in Step 2, measure, cut, and miter 1x4 pine trim (DD) to fit around the top of the cabinet. The lower edges of the shorter trim pieces (DD) fit on top of the fluted molding (CC) that you attached in Step 4. Note that the pine trim (DD) will extend above the upper surface of the cabinet. Glue the trim in place and secure with $1\frac{1}{4}$" countersunk screws.

6 Again following the same procedures, measure, cut, and miter $\frac{3}{4}$"x$\frac{3}{4}$" cove molding (EE) to fit across the top of the cabinet. Use glue and 3d finishing nails to attach the cove molding just below the 1x4 pine trim (DD) that you added in Step 5. The ends of the cove molding (EE) stop at the edges of the fluted molding (CC).

7 The final addition is the crown molding (FF) that fits across the very top of the cabinet. Following the procedures in Step 5, attach the crown molding (FF) so that it overlaps the top of the 1x4 pine trim (DD) by 1".

Finishing the Wood

1 Fill all nail and screw holes with wood filler. If you want to be able to disassemble the cabinet for transport, don't cover the screw holes in the lower top (I), as these screws hold the two assemblies together.

2 Sand all the surfaces thoroughly.

3 Check the fit of each pair of doors. If they bind or scrape the edges of the opening, sand or plane them as necessary.

4 Stain or paint the cabinet and all four doors the color of your choice.

Adding the Fabric

1 Cut two 23"x33$\frac{1}{2}$" fabric panels (W) for the upper doors.

2 Sew gathering stitches $\frac{1}{4}$" from the edge along both 23"-long edges of one fabric panel.

3 Pull the gathering stitches until the panel measures 11$\frac{3}{4}$" across the top and bottom.

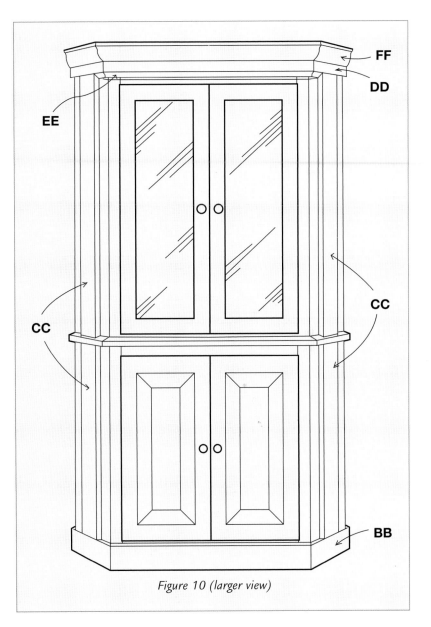

Figure 10 (larger view)

4 Hot-glue or tack the gathered panel to the inside of one upper cabinet door. Trim the gathered edges with scissors, then glue upholstery braid around all four edges of the gathered panel to conceal the gathering stitches.

5 Repeat Steps 2 through 4 to stitch and attach a fabric panel to the inside of the remaining upper door.

6 Now sit down, lean back, and admire your work!

Home Office
& Accessories

Desk Organizer with Drawers

It's always the small things in life that can drive anyone right over the edge—like hunting for a pencil and paper to write down an address or telephone number. After fumbling through every desk drawer, we used to record important information with a magenta crayon stub on the back of a water bill, but all that has changed since we made this desk organizer. It has three drawers for note pads, pens, and pencils, and a shelf large enough to hold a phone.

Special Tools & Techniques

- Router and roundover bit (optional)
- Mitering

Materials

- 8 linear feet of 1x4 pine
- 4 linear feet of 1x8 pine
- 6 linear feet of 1x10 pine
- 1 piece of ¼"-thick plywood, 14"x16"

Hardware

- Approximately 50 #6x1¼" flathead wood screws
- Approximately 50 3d finishing nails
- 1 small box of wire brads
- 3 decorative drawer pulls

*Notes on Materials

Before you shop for the necessary materials for this project, check your workshop for scrap pieces and compare what you find with the pieces in the "Cutting List." Most of the wood you need may be lying around on your workshop floor!

Cutting List

Code	Description	Qty.	Material	Dimensions
A	Top/Bottom	2	1x10 pine	26¼" long
B	Inner Divider	2	1x10 pine	3⅝" long
C	Side	2	1x8 pine	9¼" long
D	Back	1	1x8 pine	27¾" long
E	Drawer Front/Back	6	1x4 pine	8" long
F	Drawer Side	6	1x4 pine	7½" long
G	Drawer Bottom	3	¼" plywood	6¾"x7¾"

Making the Frame

1 Cut two 26¼"-long top/bottom pieces (A) from 1x10 pine.

2 Cut two 3⅝"-long inner dividers (B) from 1x10 pine.

3 Place the top/bottom pieces (A) on a level surface, parallel to each other, on edge, and 3⅝" apart. Fit the two inner dividers (B) between the two top/bottom pieces (A), spacing them 8¼" from each other and from the ends, as shown in *figure 1* on page 218. Glue the inner dividers (B) in place and drive three evenly spaced 1¼" screws through the top/bottom pieces (A) and into the edges of the inner dividers (B) at each joint.

4 From 1x8 pine, cut two 9¼"-long sides (C).

5 Position the sides (C) on the assembly as shown in *figure 2* on page 218. Note that the sides (C) are flush at the front, back, und bottom of the assembly, but extend above the top face. Glue the sides (C) onto the ends of both of the top/bottom pieces (A) and secure them in place with three 1¹/₄" screws at each joint.

6 Cut one 27³/₄"-long back (D) from 1x8 pine.

7 Attach the back (D) to the assembly, as shown in *figure 2*. Note that the back (D) is flush

with the assembly at the bottom and at the sides, but extends above the top/bottom piece (A). Glue the back (D) to the edges of the top/bottom pieces (A) and to the ends of both sides (C). Drive three 1¹/₄" screws through the back (D) at each joint.

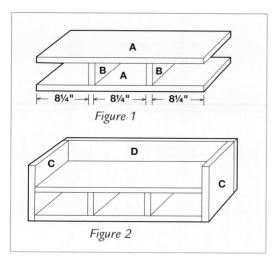

Figure 1

Figure 2

8 If you own a router and roundover bit, use them to round the upper edges of the sides (C) and back (D). If you don't own a router, simply sand the edges with very rough sandpaper and then finish with increasingly fine grades of sandpaper.

Making the Drawers

1 The three identical drawers for this organizer are constructed as shown in *figure 3*. From 1x4 pine, cut six 8"-long drawer front/back pieces (E) and six 7¹/₂"-long drawer sides (F).

2 To accommodate the plywood drawer bottoms (G), cut a ¹/₄"x¹/₄" dado on the inside of every drawer piece (E and F), ³/₈" from its lower edge.

3 Cut three 6³/₄"x7³/₄" drawer bottoms (G) from ¹/₄"-thick plywood.

4 Assemble one drawer as shown in *figure 3*. Note that the drawer front/back pieces (E) overlap the ends of the drawer sides (F). Use glue and 3d finishing nails at each end of the overlapping boards.

5 Repeat Step 4 two more times to assemble the remaining two drawers.

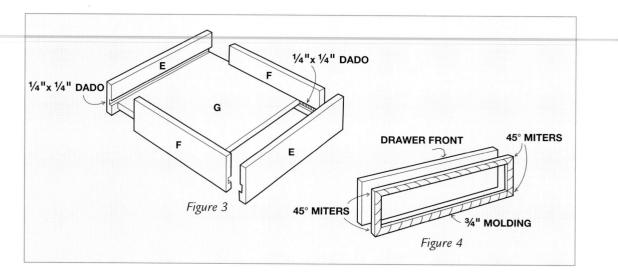

Figure 3

Figure 4

Adding the Drawer Trim

1 Each of the drawer fronts (E) is trimmed with $^3/_4$"-wide decorative molding. To trim the first drawer front, cut and fit pieces of molding, mitering the ends so that they fit perfectly flush with the outer edges of the drawer front (E), as shown in *figure 4* on page 218.

2 Glue the molding in place and use a tack hammer to drive tiny wire brads through the molding and into the drawer front (E). Recess the nails with a nail set.

3 Repeat Steps 1 and 2 twice more to trim the fronts of the remaining drawers with molding.

Finishing

1 Fill any holes or crevices with wood filler.

2 Sand all surfaces of the completed drawers and frame thoroughly.

3 Paint or stain the completed desk organizer the colors of your choice. I chose pale green and mauve to match the colors in the room where my organizer makes its home.

4 Follow the manufacturer's instructions to install a drawer pull in the center of each drawer front.

5 Insert the drawers into the frame and begin organizing!

Desk Organizer with Shelves

Too much work and not enough desk space? Make better use of your work surface with this handy/organizer. There's room for scores of desk necessities, and the top surface is large enough to accommodate books and even a clock.

Special Tools & Techniques

- Miter

Materials

- 12 linear feet of 1x12 pine
- 9 linear feet of 1x4 pine
- 6 linear feet of 3/4"-wide cove molding
- 6 linear feet of 3 1/4"-wide crown molding

Hardware

- 50 1 5/8" wood screws
- 20 1 1/4" wood screws
- 40 1" (2d) finish nails

Cutting List

Code	Description	Qty.	Material	Dimensions
A	Vertical Dividers	4	1x12 pine	9" long
B	Shelves	2	1x12 pine	11 5/8" long
C	Top/Bottom	2	1x12 pine	38" long
D	Front Trim	1	1x4 pine	40" long
E	Side Trim	2	1x4 pine	12 1/4219" long
F	Back Trim	1	1x4 pine	35" long
G	Cove Molding		3/4"x3/4"	cut to fit
H	Crown Molding		3 1/4" wide	cut to fit

Building the Center Compartments

1 Cut four Vertical Dividers (A) from 1x12 pine, each measuring 9 inches.

2 Cut two Shelves (B) from 1x12 pine, each measuring 11 5/8 inches.

3 Place two Vertical Dividers (A) on edge on a flat surface, parallel to each other and 11 5/8 inches apart. Center one Shelf (B) horizontally between the two Vertical Dividers (A), as shown in *figure 1.* Apply glue to the meeting surfaces, and screw through the Vertical Dividers (A) into the edges of the Shelf (B), using three 1 5/8-inch screws.

4 Repeat Step 3 to attach the remaining Shelf (B) to the remaining two Vertical Dividers (A).

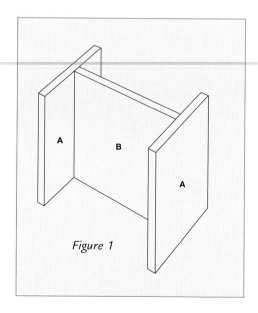

Figure 1

Adding the Top & Bottom

1 Cut two Top/Bottoms (C) from 1x12 pine, each measuring 38 inches.

2 Place one Top/Bottom (C) on edge on a flat surface. Place one shelf assembly (A and B) $1^1/_2$ inches from one end of the Top/Bottom (C), as shown in *figure 2* on page 222 Apply glue to the meeting surfaces, and screw through the Top/Bottom (C) into the ends of the Vertical Dividers (A). Use three $1^5/_8$-inch screws on each joint.

3 Repeat Step 2 to attach the remaining shelf assembly (A and B) $1^1/_2$ inches from the opposite end of the same Top/Bottom (C).

4 Center the remaining Top/Bottom (C) over the assembly. It should overhang the outermost

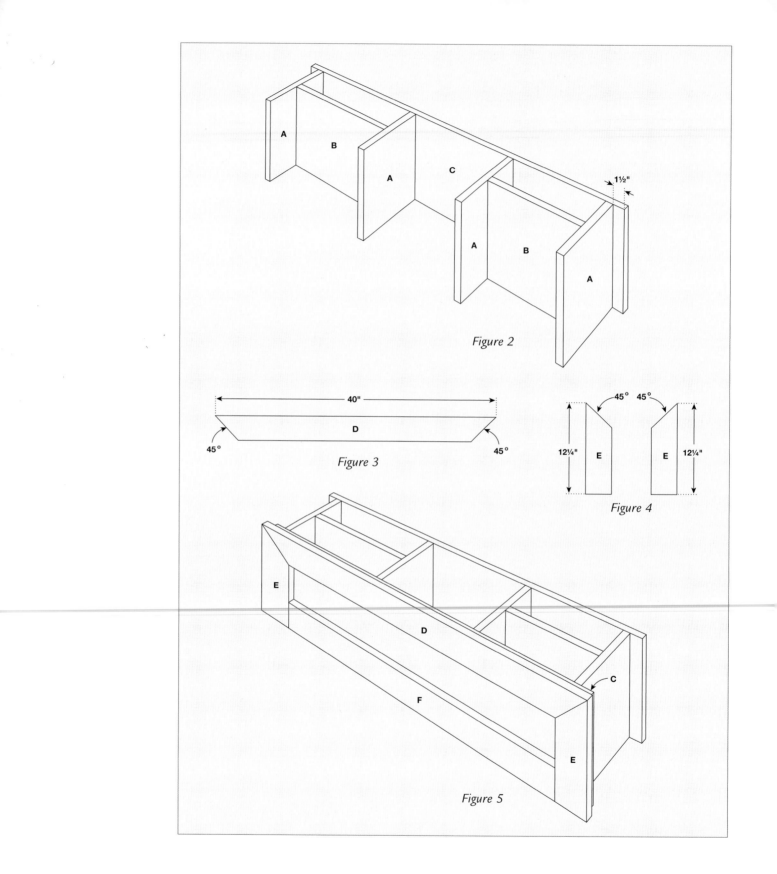

Figure 2

1½"

40"

D

45°   45°

Figure 3

45°   45°

12¼"   E   E   12¼"

Figure 4

E

D

C

F

E

Figure 5

Vertical Dividers (A) by 1¹/₂ inches on both ends. Apply glue to the meeting surfaces, and screw through the Top/Bottom (C) into each of the Vertical Dividers (A). Use three 1⁵/₈-inch screws on each joint.

Adding the Trim

1 Cut one Front Trim (D) from 1x4 pine, measuring 40 inches.

2 Miter each end of the Front Trim (D) at opposing 45° angles, as shown in *figure 3* on page 222.

3 Cut two Side Trims (E) from 1x4 pine, each measuring 12¹/₄ inches.

4 Miter one end of each of the Side Trims (E) at a 45° angle, as shown in *figure 4* on page 222.

5 Place the Front Trim (D) over the edge of the Top/Bottom (C), as shown in *figure 5* on page 222. The Front Trim (D) should overhang the Top/Bottom (C) by 1 inch on the front and both sides. Apply glue to the meeting surfaces, and screw through the Front Trim (D) into the Top/Bottom (C), using 1⁵/₈-inch screws spaced every 5 inches.

6 Place one Side Trim (E) over the ends of the Top/Bottom (C), with the miter toward the Front Trim (D), as shown in *figure 5* on page 222. The trims should overhang the sides by 1 inch. Apply glue to the meeting surfaces, and screw through the Side Trim (E) into the Top/ Bottom (C), using three 1¹/₄-inch screws.

7 Repeat Step 6 to attach the remaining Side Trim (E) to the opposite end of the Top/Bottom (C).

8 Cut one Back Trim (F) from 1x4 pine, measuring 35 inches.

9 Fit the Back Trim (F) between the two Side Trims (E), flush with the back edge of the Top/Bottom (C), as shown in *figure 5* on page 222. (This piece does not overhang.) Apply glue to the meeting surfaces, and screw through the Back Trim (F) into the Top/Bottom (C), using 1⁵/₈-inch screws spaced every 5 inches.

Adding the Molding

1 Turn the assembly so that the Front, Back, and Side Trims (D, E, and F) are against the work surface. Cut and fit ³/₄-inch Cove Molding (G) to cover the joints between the Top/Bottom (C) and the Front, Back, and Side Trims (D, E, and F). The molding should be cut at a 45° angle to fit the front corner, except the molding for the back of the organizer, which should be cut straight. Apply glue to the meeting surfaces, and nail through the Cove Molding (G) into the Top/Bottom (C), using 1-inch nails.

2 Cut and fit 3¼-inch Crown Molding (H) to fit around the remaining Top/Bottom (C), as shown in the photograph. Remember that the front corners are a compound 45° angle cut. Apply glue to the meeting surfaces, and nail through the Crown Molding (H) into the Top/Bottom (C), using 1-inch nails.

Finishing

1 Fill any holes, cracks, or crevices with wood filler.

2 Thoroughly sand all areas of the completed organizer.

3 Paint or stain the organizer with the color of your choice. We chose a honey maple stain, then sealed it with a satin polyurethane.

Birdcage

Here's a delightful fix for an uninteresting corner of the room. Although not designed for live birds, this birdcage is an attractive conversation piece with limitless decorative potential.

Special Tools & Techniques

- Dado
- Router with round-over bit

Materials

- 4 linear feet of 1x6 pine
- 20 linear feet of 1x2 pine
- 18 linear feet of 1x1 pine
- 2 linear feet of 1x4 pine
- 2-x-4-foot sheet of $^3/_4$" plywood
- 2-x-4-foot sheet of $^1/_4$" plywood

Hardware

- 30 $2^1/_2$" (8d) finish nails
- 10 $1^1/_2$" (4d) finish nails
- 15 2" (6d) finish nails
- 4 small metal L-angles
- 2 small drawer pulls
- 2 2" hinges
- 150 linear feet of 18-gauge wire rod
- Small spool of 28-gauge wire

Cutting List

Code	Description	Qty.	Material	Dimensions
A	Lower Sides	2	1x6 pine	$11^1/_4$" long
B	Vertical Sides	4	1x2 pine	43" long
C	Upper Sides	2	1x2 pine	$11^1/_4$" long
D	Back	1	$^3/_4$" plywood	29"x$13^1/_2$"
E	Bottom	1	$^3/_4$" plywood	$13^1/_2$"x$12^3/_4$"
F	Vertical Front	2	1x1 pine	43" long
G	Upper Front	1	1x2 pine	12" long
H	Middle Front	1	1x1 pine	12" long
I	Lower Front	1	1x4 pine	12" long
J	Door Vertical	2	1x1 pine	$25^3/_4$" long
K	Door Horizontal	2	1x1 pine	$11^3/_4$" long
L	Tray Front	1	1x1 pine	$11^7/_8$" long
M	Tray	1	$^1/_4$" plywood	$11^7/_8$"x13"
N	Top	1	$^3/_4$" plywood	$15^1/_4$"x$17^1/_4$"

Constructing the Sides

1 Cut two Lower Sides (A) from 1x6 pine, each measuring $11^1/_4$ inches.

2 Referring to *figure 1*, mark and cut out a semicircle on one $11^1/_4$-inch edge of each of the two Lower Sides (A). Our semicircle has a $6^1/_2$- inch radius, but cut to any radius you choose.

3 Cut four Vertical Sides (B) from 1x2 pine, each measuring 43 inches.

4 Cut two Upper Sides (C) from 1x2 pine, each measuring $11^1/_4$ inches.

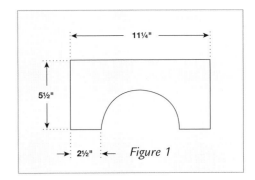

Figure 1

5 Place two Vertical Sides (B) on a level surface, parallel to each other and 11¼ inches apart.

Note: Because of the relatively thin wood used for this project and the depth that the nail must penetrate, we strongly suggest that you predrill all nail holes to avoid splitting the wood. Place one Upper Side (C) between the ends of the two Vertical Sides (B), as shown in *figure 2*. Apply glue to the meeting surfaces, and nail through the Vertical Sides (B) into the ends of the Upper Side (C), using two 2¹/₂-inch nails on each joint.

6 Fit one Lower Side (A) between the same two Vertical Sides (B), 26 inches below the Upper Side (C), as shown in *figure 2*. Apply glue to the meeting surfaces, and nail though the Vertical Sides (B) into the ends of the Lower Side (A), using two 2¹/₂-inch nails on each joint.

7 Repeat Steps 5 and 6 to construct another cage side using the remaining Lower Side (A), two Vertical Sides (B), and Upper Side (C).

Adding the Back & Bottom

1 Cut one Back (D) from ³/₄-inch plywood, measuring 29x13¹/₂ inches.

2 Place the Back (D) on a flat surface. Place one assembled side on edge, flush against one 29-inch edge of the Back (D), as shown in *figure 3*. Apply glue to the meeting surfaces, and nail through the Vertical Side (B) into the edge of the Back (D), using 1¹/₂-inch nails spaced about every 5 inches.

3 Repeat Step 2 to attach the remaining side assembly to the opposite 29-inch edge of the Back (D).

4 Cut one Bottom (E) from ³/₄-inch-thick plywood, measuring 13¹/₂x12³/₄ inches.

5 Fit the Bottom (E) between the two cage sides, 29 inches below the top of the Back (D).

6 Apply glue to the meeting surfaces, and nail through the sides and back into the edges of the Bottom (E), using 2-inch nails spaced every 5 inches.

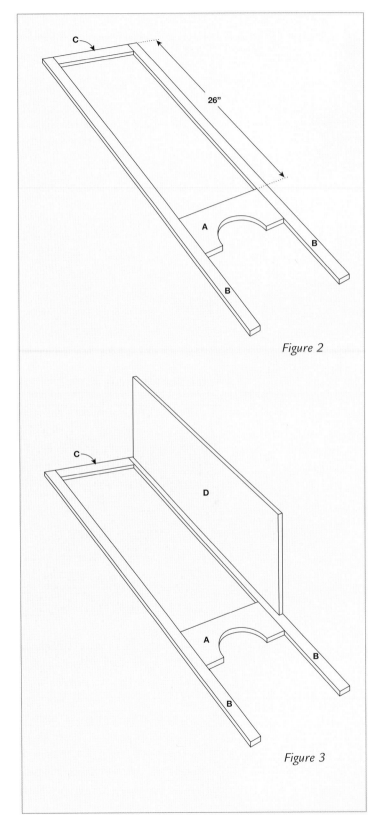

Figure 2

Figure 3

It should be flush at the back, and overhang the sides and front. Apply glue to the meeting surfaces, and nail through the Top (M) into the edges of the Upper Fronts (G) and Upper Sides (C), using 1¹⁄₂-inch nails spaced every 5 inches.

Installing the Door

1 Attach two 2-inch hinges to the left side of the Door Vertical (J). Fit the door inside the opening at the front of the birdcage, and secure the hinges to the Front Verticals.

2 Install a small drawer pull on the right side of the door.

Finishing

1 Fill any holes, cracks, or crevices with wood filler.

2 Thoroughly sand all areas of the completed birdcage.

3 Paint or stain the birdcage the color of your choice. We chose a pale yellow paint. After the paint dried, we applied a tropical wallpaper to the back of the birdcage, and random wallpaper cutouts to the front, sides, and top of the birdcage (photo, see above).

4 The bars of the cage are 18-gauge wire rods inserted into the Lower and Upper Sides (A and C). To install the rods, drill holes the diameter of the rods into the bottom of the Upper Sides (C), spacing the holes ¹⁄₂ inch apart. Drill corresponding holes (¹⁄₄ inch deep and ¹⁄₂ inch apart) into the top of the Lower Sides (A).

5 Insert the end of one wire rod in the first upper hole, and cut the wire rod to length (¹⁄₄ inch longer than the opening). Insert the cut end into the corresponding first hole in the top of the Lower Side (A).

6 Repeat Steps 4 and 5 to add wire rods across the entire opening, fitting the rods into each of the remaining corresponding holes.

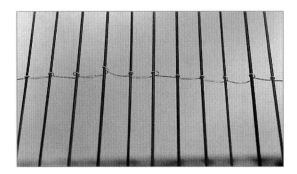

7 Repeat Steps 4 and 5 to add wire rod bars to the opposite side of the birdcage.

8 Drill corresponding holes ¼ inch deep every ½ inch into the inside edges of the Door Horizontals (K). Insert 18-gauge wire rods into the corresponding holes, using the same method described in Steps 4 and 5.

9 Wrap lengths of 28-gauge wire around each of the 18-gauge wire rods to hold the rods in position (see detail photo on page 230).

Display Box

This great accessory is both functional and decorative. The inside space is large enough for a variety) of storage purposes, everything from keeping remote controls together to serving as a jewelry box. The piece is also useful for displaying keep-sakes, such as photos, treasured collections, or (as shown on page 233) pretty shells.

Special Tools & Techniques

- Miter

Materials

- 4-"4-foot sheet of $^3/_8$" plywood
- 6 linear feet of $3^1/_4$"-wide crown molding
- 12"x11$^1/_4$" piece of clear plastic sheeting, $^1/_8$" thick
- 1 drawer pull
- 4 round curtain rod finials

Hardware

- 60 1" (2d) finish nails
- 4 1$^1/_2$" wood screws

Cutting List

Code	Description	Qty.	Material	Dimensions
A	Lower Box Side	4	$^3/_8$" plywood	5"x14$^3/_4$"
B	Lower Bottom	1	$^3/_8$" plywood	15$^1/_8$"x14$^3/_4$"
C	Lid Side	4	$^3/_8$" plywood	2$^1/_4$"x14$^3/_4$"
D	Lid Top	1	$^3/_8$" plywood	14$^3/_4$"x15$^1/_8$"
E	Long Top Trim	2	3$^1/_4$"-wide crown molding	15$^1/_8$" long
F	Short Top Trim	2	3$^1/_4$"-wide crown molding	14$^3/_4$" long
G	Inside Trim	4	$^3/_8$" plywood	2"x11$^1/_2$"
H	Clear Sheeting	1	Plastic	12"x11$^1/_4$"

Making the Lower Box

1 Cut four Lower Box Sides (A) from $^3/_8$-inch plywood, each measuring 15$^1/_8$x14$^3/_4$ inches.

2 Place two of the Lower Box Sides (A) on edge parallel to each other on a flat level surface and 14$^3/_4$ inches apart. Place the remaining two Lower Box Sides (A) between the ends of the first two Lower Box Sides (A), as shown in *figure 1*. Apply glue to the meeting surfaces, and nail the sides together, using three 1-inch nails on each joint. Nail through the face of the overlapping Lower Box Sides (A) into the end of the Lower Box Sides (A).

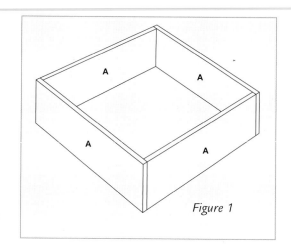

Figure 1

3 Cut one Lower Bottom (B) from $^3/_8$-inch plywood, measuring $5^1/_8$x$14^3/_4$ inches. Place the Lower Bottom (B) over the edges of assembled Lower Box Sides (A), as shown in *figure 2* on page 234. Apply glue to the meeting surfaces, and nail through the Lower Bottom (B) into the Lower Box Sides (A), using five 1-inch nails on each side.

Making the Upper Lid

1 Cut four Lid Sides (C) from $^3/_8$-inch plywood, each measuring $2^1/_8$x$14^3/_4$ inches.

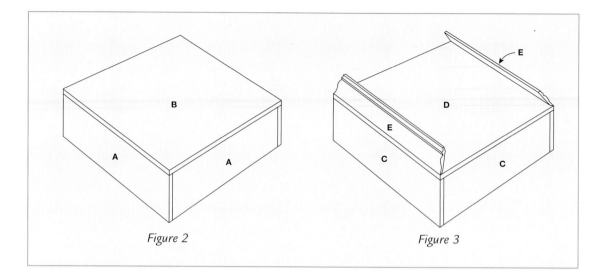

Figure 2

Figure 3

2 Place two of the Lid Sides (C) on edge, parallel to each other on a flat level surface and 14³/₄ inches apart. Place the remaining two Lid Sides (C) between the ends of the first two Lid Sides (C), as for the Lower Box Sides (A) (see *figure 1* on page 232). Apply glue to the meeting surfaces, and attach the sides, using 1-inch nails. Nail through the face of the overlapping Lid Sides (C) into the ends of the Lid Sides (C).

3 Cut one Lid Top (D) from ³/₈-inch plywood, measuring 14³/₄x15¹/₈ inches. Place the Lid Top (D) over the edges of Assembled Lid Sides (C), as for the lower box pieces (see *figure 2*). Apply glue to the meeting surfaces, and nail through the Lid Top (D) into the Lid Sides (C), using four 1-inch nails on each side.

Attaching the Top Holding

1 Place the assembled lid on a flat surface, with the Lid Top (D) facing up.

2 Cut two Long Top Trims (E) from 3¹/₄-inch crown molding at a compound 45° angle, each measuring 15¹/₈ inches. Attach the two Long Trims (E) on the long sides of the Lid Top (D), as shown in *figure 3*.

3 Cut two Short Top Trims (F) from 3¹/₄-inch crown molding at a compound 45° angle, each measuring 14³/₄ inches. Attach the two Short Trims (F) on the shorter sides of the Lid Top (D), as shown in *figure 4*.

4 Cut four Inside Trims (G) from ³/₈-inch plywood, each measuring 2x11¹/₂ inches.

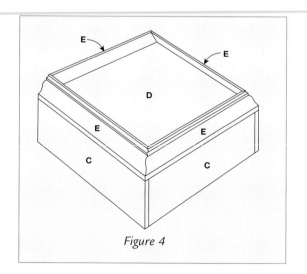

Figure 4

5 Place two of the Inside Trims (G) on edge, parallel to each other on a flat level surface and 11½ inches apart. Place the remaining Inside Trims (G) between the ends of the first two Inside Trims (G), as for the Lower Box Sides (A) (see *figure 1* on page 232). Apply glue to the meeting surfaces, and nail the sides together, using two 1-inch nails. Nail through the face of the overlapping Inside Trims (G) into the end of the Inside Trims (G).

6 Place the assembled Inside Trims (G) inside the crown molding frame, as shown in *figure 5*. Apply glue to the meeting surfaces. (Glue will be all that is needed to hold the Inside Trims (G) in place.)

Adding the Feet & the Plastic Top

1 Find the center of the 12-x11¼-inch piece of clear plastic sheeting (H). Use a ruler to draw two bisecting lines, each from opposing corners, as shown in *figure 6*. The center is the point at which the lines intersect. Drill a hole and attach the drawer pull. If you do not plan to change the decorative contents of the box, you can seal the plastic sheets with clear silicone.

2 Place the assembled lower box upside down on a flat surface so that the Lower Bottom (B) is facing up. Drill through all four corners of the Lower Bottom (B) in the locations shown in *figure 7*.

3 To attach the curtain rod finials to the Lower Bottom (B), screw through the inside of the lower box into the curtain rod finials using 1½-inch screws.

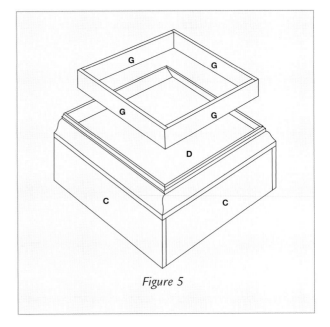

Figure 5

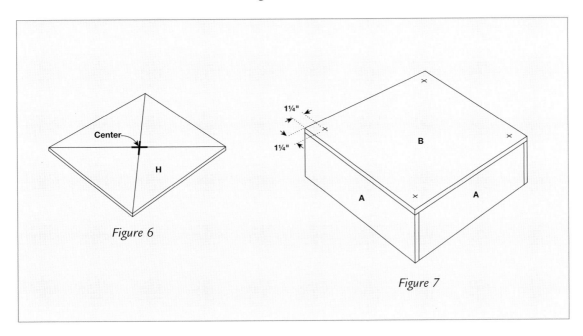

Figure 6

Figure 7

Finishing

1 Fill any nail holes, cracks, or imperfections with wood filler.

2 Sand all areas of the assembled display box.

3 Stain or paint your box the color of your choice. Here we've used a satin-finish maroon paint, and painted the feet white.

Folding Screen

Screens are wonderful accessories, and can block the afternoon sun, serve as a backdrop for a special table and chair, or even to divide a room in a crucial area. This pretty screen (see page 238) was first sponge-painted, then stamped with leaf motifs.

Special Tools & Techniques

- Miter

Materials

- 2 4-x-8-foot sheets of ³/₄" plywood
- 3- x4-foot piece of ¹/₄" plywood
- 65 linear feet of ³/₄"-wide rope molding

Hardware

- 400 small wire brads
- 9 2¹/₂" brass hinges

Cutting List

Code	Description	Qty.	Material	Dimensions
A	Main Panels	4	³/₄" plywood	16"x72"
B	Center Panel	16	¹/₄" plywood	6¹/₄"x9³/₄"
C	Vertical Molding	32	³/₄"-wide rope molding	13¹/₂" long
D	Horizontal Molding	32	³/₄"-wide rope molding	10" long

Cutting & Marking the Panels

1 Cut four Main Panels (A) from ³/₄-inch plywood, each measuring 16x72 inches. Fill the edges of each panel with wood filler, and sand the entire panel thoroughly.

2 Four smaller Center Panels (B) are attached to each of the Main Panels (A), then outlined with rope molding. The procedure is extremely simple, but requires exact measuring. For that reason, we suggest you carefully measure and mark each of the four Main Panels (A) with the position of both the Center Panel (B) and the Vertical and Horizontal Rope Molding (C and D). Begin at the top of one Main Panel (A) and, following the measurements in *figure 1*, draw the placement lines. Make certain that all of your lines are straight and squared.

3 Repeat the procedure outlined in Step 2 three times to draw the placement lines for the remainder of the Main Panel (A). At this point, the Main Panel (A) should appear as shown in *figure 2* on page 239. You should end with 6 inches remaining at the bottom of the Main Panel (A).

4 Repeat Steps 2 and 3 to mark the placement lines on each of the three remaining Main Panels (A).

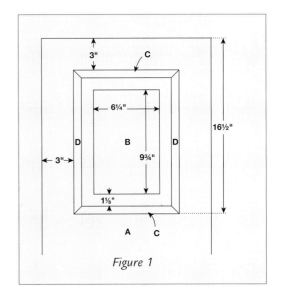

Figure 1

Adding the Center Panels

1 Cut 16 Center Panels (B) from ¼-inch plywood, each measuring 6¼x9¾ inches.

2 Thoroughly sand each of the 16 Center Panels (B).

3 Refer to the placement marks to attach one Center Panel (B) to the top of one Main Panel (A). Apply glue to the back of the center panel (B), and attach to the Main Panel (A) with small wire brads nailed through each corner.

4 Using the marks as a guide, repeat Step 3 three times to attach three additional Center Panels (B),

5 Repeat Steps 3 and 4 three times, attaching the remaining Center Panels (B) to the three remaining Main Panels (A).

Adding the Rope Molding

1 Cut 32 Vertical Moldings (C) from ¾-inch-wide rope molding, each measuring 13½ inches.

2 Miter each of the 32 Vertical Moldings (C) at opposing 45° angles, as shown in *figure 3*. Sand the cut edge lightly to remove any burrs.

3 Cut 32 Horizontal Moldings (D) from ¾-inch-wide rope molding, each measuring 10 inches.

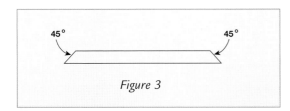

Figure 3

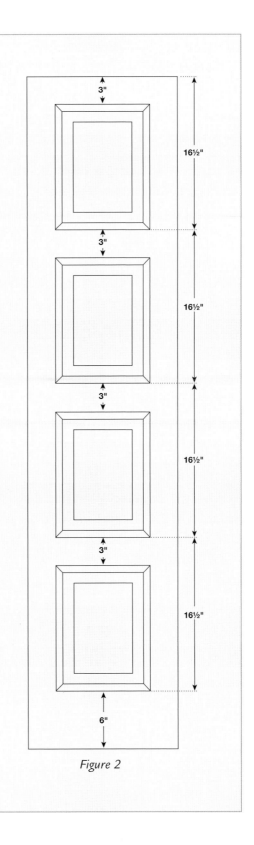

Figure 2

4 Miter each of the 32 Horizontal Moldings (D) at opposing 45° angles, as shown in *figure3* on page 239. Sand the cut edge lightly to remove any burrs.

5 Place one Main Panel (A) on a flat surface and position two Vertical and two Horizontal Moldings (C and D) to form a rectangle surrounding the first Center Panel (B), as shown in *figure 1* on page 237. Apply glue to the meeting surfaces, and use wire brads spaced about 3 inches apart to secure the Moldings (C and D) to the Main Panel (A).

6 Repeat Step 5 eleven times to attach the remaining Moldings (C and D) to the remaining Center Panels (B).

Finishing

1 The options for finishing the screen are limitless. We first painted our screen off-white, and then sponge-painted over it with peach. We then glazed it with a mixture of half glazing medium and half peach paint. After the paint dried, we stamped each of the center panels with leaf stamps, using a pale-green latex paint. (Craft supply stores have hundreds of stamps to choose from.) See page 24 for more information on decorative painting.

2 The last task is to attach the hinges. Use three hinges between each of the Main Panels (A). You will need to alternate the hinges to allow the screen to fold properly. The hinge peg should face the back of the screen between the two middle panels, and face the front of the screen on the outer panels.

CD Cabinet

If your CD collection could use a little order, you need this terrific shelf. Placed on a table or desk, or hung on a wall, it will hold your CDs—and you may even have room for storing tapes and displaying pictures.

Special Tools & Techniques

- Miter

Materials

- 19 linear feet of 1x6 pine
- 3 linear feet of 1x8 pine
- 4 linear feet of 3"-wide beaded molding

Hardware

- 50 2" (6d) finish nails
- 15 1¼" (3d) finish nails

Cutting List

Code	Description	Qty.	Material	Dimensions
A	Shelf Sides	2	1x6 pine	34½" long
B	Shelves	6	1x6 pine	24" long
C	Shelf Top	1	1x6 pine	27" long
D	Base Front	1	3"-wide beaded molding	26⅝" long
E	Base Sides	2	3"-wide beaded molding	6" long

Making the Frame

1 Cut two Shelf Sides (A) from 1x6 pine, each measuring 34½ inches.

2 Cut six Shelves (B) from 1x6 pine, each measuring 24 inches.

3 Place the two Shelf Sides (A) on edge, parallel to each other, and 24 inches apart. Using *figure 1* as a guide, place the Shelves (B) between the Shelf Sides (A). Position two of the Shelves (B) flush with the ends of the Shelf Sides (A), and the remaining four Shelves (B) inside the first two, spaced 6 inches apart. Apply glue to the meeting surfaces, and nail through the Shelf Sides (A) into the ends of the Shelves (B), using three 2-inch nails on each joint.

4 Cut one Shelf Top (C) from 1x8 pine measuring 27 inches.

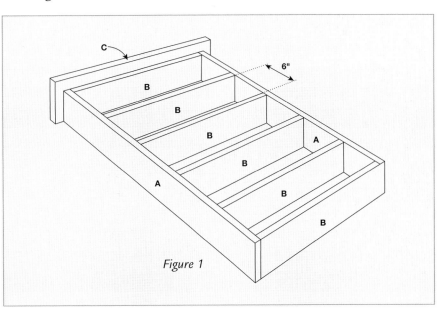

Figure 1

5 Place the Shelf Top (C) over one end of the assembled Shelves (B) and Shelf Sides (A) as shown in *figure 1* on page 241. Apply glue to the meeting surfaces, and nail through the face of the Shelf Top (C) into the ends of the Shelf Sides (A), using three 2-inch nails on each joint.

Adding the Base

1 Cut one Base Front (D) from 3-inch-wide beaded molding, measuring 26$^5/_8$ inches. Using *figure 2* as a guide, miter both ends of the molding at opposing 45° angles.

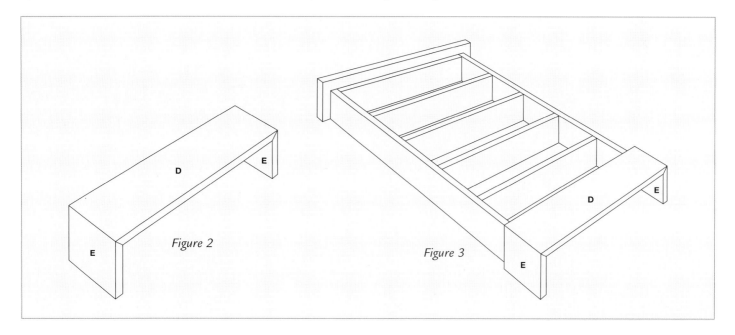

Figure 2

Figure 3

Making the Desktop

1 Cut one 23¹/₂"x35³/₄" desktop (A) from laminated pine.

2 Cut two 6"-long desktop braces (B) from 1x3 pine.

3 Attach one desktop brace (B) to the desktop (A), as shown in *figure 1* on page 247, using glue and two 1¹/₄" screws. Note that the ends of the desktop brace (B) and the desktop (A)

are flush and that the 6"-long edge of the desktop brace (B) is flush with the 35³⁄₄"-long edge of the desktop (A).

4 Repeat Step 3 to attach the remaining desktop brace (B) to the opposite end of the desktop (A).

5 Each of the desktop braces (B) must now be drilled to accept a dowel rod (C). Using the placement dimensions given in *figure 2*, drill a ³⁄₈"-diameter hole, ¹⁄₂" deep, in the end of one desktop brace (B).

6 Repeat Step 5 to drill a ³⁄₈"-diameter hole, ¹⁄₂" deep, in the end of the other desktop brace (B). The second hole must be drilled as a mirror image of the first hole.

7 Using a router and roundover bit, round the 35³⁄₄"-long edge of the desktop (A) to which the desktop braces (B) are attached, as shown in *figure 3*.

8 Cut two 1"-long pieces of ³⁄₈"-diameter dowel rod (C).

9 Apple glue to one end of each dowel rod (C) and insert the rods into the holes drilled in the desktop brace (B). Each rod should protrude ¹⁄₂" from its hole.

10 Cut one 35³⁄₄"-long desktop front (D) from 1x4 pine.

11 Glue the desktop front (D) to the unrouted 35³⁄₄"-long edge of the desktop (A), as shown in *figure 4*. Secure the desktop front (D) by driving 1¹⁄₄" screws, spaced about 6" apart, through its face and into the edge of the desktop (A).

12 Cut two 2³⁄₄"-long desktop supports (E) from 1x4 pine.

13 Glue one desktop support (E) flush with the ends of the desktop front (D) and the desktop (A), as shown in *figure 4*. Drive two 1¹⁄₄" screws through the face of the desktop (A) into the edge of the desktop support (E) and two more screws through the face of the desktop front (D) into the end of the desktop support (E).

14 Repeat Step 13 to attach the remaining desktop support (E) to the opposite ends of the desktop front (D) and the desktop (A).

15 Cut one 34¹⁄₄"-long desktop inner support (F) from ³⁄₄"x³⁄₄" pine.

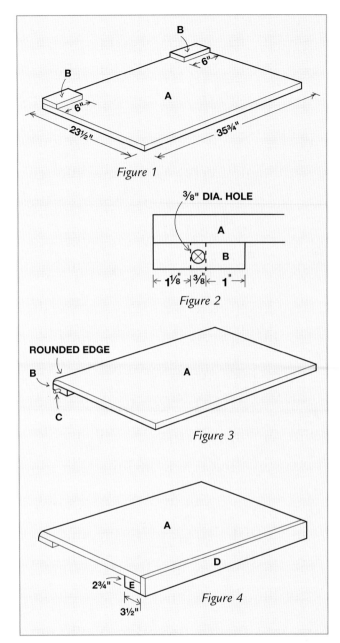

Figure 1

³⁄₈" DIA. HOLE

Figure 2

ROUNDED EDGE

Figure 3

Figure 4

16 Glue and nail the desktop inner suppo_ _ F) between the two desktop supports (E), over the joint formed by the desktop (A) and the deskiop front (D). Secure the support (F) to both the desktop (A) and desktop front (D) by inserting 1¼" nails, spaced about 4" apart, along its length.

Constructing the Outer Cabinet

1 Cut two 15"x29½" sides (G) from laminated pine.

2 A dado must be cut in each of the two sides (G) to accommodate the dowel rods (C) in the desktop assembly. Using *figure 5* as a placement guide, cut a ⅝"-wide dado, ½" deep, 1" from one 29½" edge of one side (G). Note that the dado stops 1" from the upper end of the side (G), turns 90 degrees, and proceeds 1⅛" further.

3 Repeat Step 2 to dado the remaining side (G), keeping in mind that the two dadoed sides (G) must be mirror images of each other when you're finished.

4 Cut one 37½"x29½" back (H) from ¾"-thick plywood.

5 At this point, you should perform what's known as a "dry assembly"—a temporary assembly using screws but no glue—to make certain that the desktop assembly will fit and slide easily inside the dadoes cut into the two sides (G). This particular step will be easier if you can find a willing helper to assist.

First, using only as many screws as needed to hold the parts together, attach the back (H) over the edges of the two sides (G), as shown in *figure 6*, with the mirror-image dadoes in the sides (G) placed at the back of the assembly. Insert the screws through the back (H) and into the edges of the sides (G). Now turn the assembly upside down.

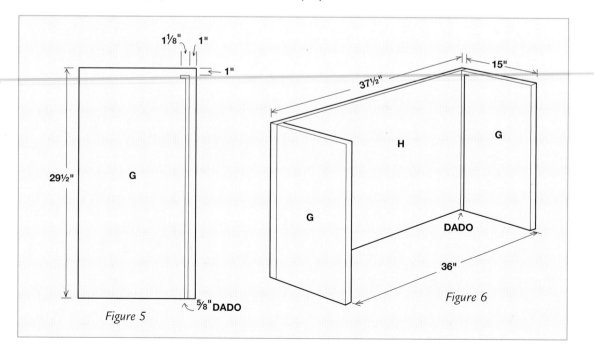

Figure 5

Figure 6

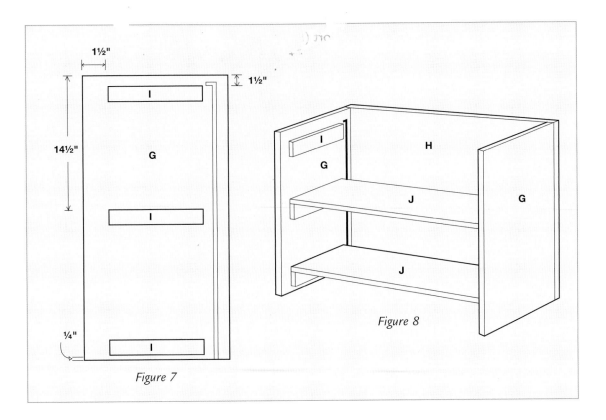

Figure 7

Figure 8

6 To hold the open front edges of the sides (G) exactly 36" apart, attach two pipe clamps to them.

7 Now you need to test-fit the desktop assembly by slipping the dowel rods (C) protruding from its ends into the dadoes in the sides (G) of the cabinet. To do this, hold the desktop assembly vertically over the partly assembled cabinet, with the top face of the desktop (A) facing the inner surface of the cabinet back (H) and the desktop front (D) facing down. Fit the dowel rods (C) into the dadoes in the two sides (G), and gently lower the desktop assembly into the cabinet.

8 Carefully turn the entire assembly right side up. Pull the desktop front (D) upward and forward towards the open front of the cabinet, making certain that the dowel rods (C) glide easily within the dadoes, and that the desktop assembly will rotate from a vertical to a horizontal position when you reach the top of the dadoes. If the movement isn't smooth, now is the time to correct it. You may have to enlarge the dadoes at places where the dowel rods (C) bind, sand down the rods slightly, or further round the back edge of the desktop assembly.

9 When the assembly works to your satisfaction, disassemble the structure, set the desktop assembly aside, and reassemble the back (H) and two sides (G), this time using glue and inserting 1¹/₄" screws about 6" apart along the length of each joint.

10 Cut six 9³/₄"-long inner supports (I) from 1x3 pine.

11 Using *figure 7* on page 249 as a placement guide, glue three of the inner supports (I) to one side (G). Position the first inner support (I) 1½" from the upper end of the side (G); the second inner support (I) 14½" from the same end; and the third inner support (I) ¼" from the bottom end. Note that all three supports (I) should be 1½" from the front edge of the side (G); they do not cover the dado at the back edge.

12 Repeat Step 11 to attach the remaining three inner supports (I) to the other side (G).

13 Cut two 36"-long shelves (J) from 1x12 pine.

14 Install one shelf (J) between the two sides (G) and over the middle inner supports (I), as shown in *figure 8* on page 249, placing the shelf (J) 1½" from the front edges of the sides (G). Glue the shelf (J) in place and insert three 1¼" screws through its face and into the edge of each inner support (I). Also insert screws through the side (G) and into the ends of the shelf (J).

15 Repeat Step 14 to attach a second shelf (J) over the lowest pair of inner supports (I), as shown in *figure 8* on page 249.

16 Cut one 36"-long top (K) from 1x12 pine.

17 Cut one 34"-long top support (L) from 1x4 pine. Set this piece aside; you'll add it to the top (K) during final assembly.

18 Attach the top (K) over the top inner supports (I), between the two sides (G) and flush with their front edges (see *figure 9* on page 251).

Adding the Trim

1 Cut three 36"-long trim pieces (M) from 1x4 pine.

2 Glue one trim piece (M) to the front ends of the upper inner supports (I), between the two sides (G), as shown in *figure 10*. Secure the trim (M) by driving two 1¼" screws through its face and into the end of each inner support (I). Also insert 1¼" screws, spaced about 6" apart, through the top (K) and into the trim piece (M).

3 Glue the second and third trim pieces (M) to the two shelves (J) and the front ends of the middle inner supports (I), between the two sides (G), as shown in *figure 10* on page 251. Secure with two 1¼" screws inserted through the face of each trim piece (M) and into the inner support (I) at each joint. Also insert 1¼" screws, spaced about 6" apart, through each trim piece (M) and into the edge of each shelf (J).

4 Cut one 36"-long bottom trim piece (N) from 1x3 pine.

5 Attach the bottom trim piece (N) between the two sides (G), flush with the bottom edge of the lower trim piece (M) and with the bottom of the cabinet, as shown in *figure 10* on page 251. Insert 1¼" screws, spaced about 6" apart, to secure the bottom trim piece (N).

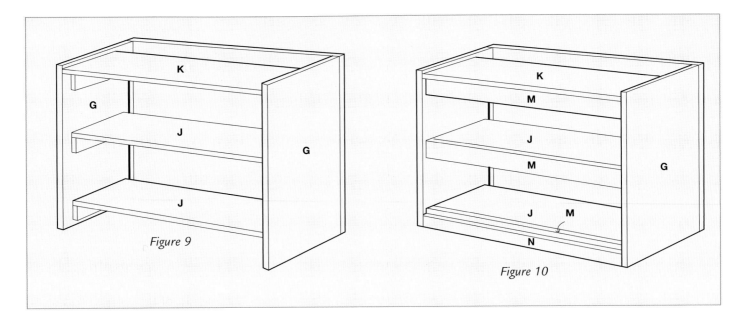

Figure 9

Figure 10

Installing the Desktop

1 Turn the completed desk/cabinet upside-down. Fit the assembled desktop, with the desktop front (D) facing down, into the opening in the back of the cabinet, fitting the dowel rods attached to the desktop assembly into the dadoes in the sides (G).

2 Now you'll attach the top support (L) to the top (K). The top support (L) serves to keep the desktop assembly from dropping all the way down into the cabinet when the desktop isn't in use. With the desk/cabinet still upside down, place the top support (L) on the 36"-long edge of the top (K) that is closest to the desktop assembly. Note that the top (K) is 1" longer than the top support (L) at each end. Make certain that the top support (L) overlaps the top (K) by 1$^1/_2$" as shown in *figure 11*. Then glue the top support (L) in place and insert 1$^1/_4$" screws, spaced about 4" apart, through it and into the top (K). Be sure to attach the top support (L) only to the top (K) and not to the desktop front (D).

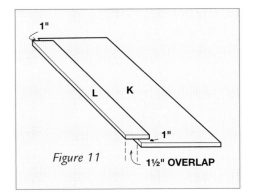

Figure 11

3 Turn the desk/cabinet right side up.

Making the Cabinet Doors

1 Cut two 25$^1/_4$"x17$^3/_4$" cabinet doors (O) from laminated pine.

2 Using a router and roundover bit, rout all four edges on what will be the front face of each door (O).

3 Fit the doors (O) into the opening at the front of the desk/cabinet, and check their fit. Then attach two concealed cabinet hinges to each of the doors (O) and to the inside of the desk/cabinet.

Finishing

1 Using a router and roundover bit, round both edges of the sides (G) and back (H) of the cabinet.

2 Fill all holes, cracks, and crevices with wood filler. Pay particular attention to the routed edges of the back (H) of the cabinet; because it is plywood, it will require more filler than the rest of the cabinet.

3 Sand all surfaces of the desk/cabinet thoroughly.

4 Paint or stain the project the color of your choice.

5 Install recessed drawer pulls on the desktop front (D).

6 Install one cabinet knob on each of the doors (O), being careful to align them with one another.

Metric Conversion Chart

Inches	CM		Inches	CM
$\frac{1}{8}$	0.3		25	63.5
$\frac{1}{4}$	0.6		26	66.0
$\frac{3}{8}$	1.0		27	68.6
$\frac{1}{2}$	1.3		28	71.1
$\frac{5}{8}$	1.6		29	73.7
$\frac{3}{4}$	1.9		30	76.2
$\frac{7}{8}$	2.2		31	78.7
1	2.5		32	81.3
$1\frac{1}{4}$	3.2		33	83.8
$1\frac{1}{2}$	3.8		34	86.4
$1\frac{3}{4}$	4.4		35	88.9
2	5.1		36	91.4
$2\frac{1}{2}$	6.4		37	94.0
3	7.6		38	96.5
$3\frac{1}{2}$	8.9		39	99.1
4	10.2		40	101.6
$4\frac{1}{2}$	11.4		41	104.1
5	12.7		42	106.7
6	15.2		43	109.2
7	17.8		44	111.8
8	20.3		45	114.3
9	22.9		46	116.8
10	25.4		47	119.4
11	27.9		48	121.9
12	30.5		49	124.5
13	33.0		50	127.0
14	35.6			
15	38.1			

Volumes

1 fluid ounce	29.6 ml
1 pint	473 ml
1 quart	946 ml
1 gallon (128 fl. oz.)	3.785 l

Inches	CM
16	40.6
17	43.2
18	45.7
19	48.3
20	50.8
21	53.3
22	55.9
23	58.4
24	61.0

Weights

0.035 ounces	1 gram
1 ounce	28.35 grams
1 pound	453.6 grams

Acknowledgments

From Previous Editions:

Great Looking 2x4 Furniture

Editor: Chris Rich
Art Director: Kathy Holmes
Photography: Evan Bracken
Production: Elaine Thompson
Illustrations: Orrin Lundgren

This book is dedicated to twelve remarkable women, each of whom has made an immense difference in my life. One I have known for over fifty years; some are new friends. They are (in alphabetical order): Ellen Mahoney Biondolillo, Cheri Cetto, Patrice Connolly, Sandra Fisher, Patti Kertz, Barbara McMahon-Ritzhaupt, Anita Miller, Linda Milstead, Jackie Nelson, Virginia Newby, Diane Thompson, Bette Wood-Hall.

Although each of these women is unique, they all share some of the same wonderful traits. Their courage has inspired me, their accomplishments have astounded me, their minds have challenged me, their hearts have nurtured me, their humor has cheered me, their common sense has guided me, and their compassion has consoled me.

The world is a better place because these women exist. I am grateful to call them my friends.

Stevie Henderson

Many thanks to:
Mark Baldwin (Bradenton, FL), who shared equally in the design and production of all the projects in this book, who cheerfully took on the heavy stuff, and who always came up with brilliant solutions to difficult problems. He's a wonder!
Chris Rich (Altamont Press, Asheville, NC), our editor and friend, who spent hundreds of hours checking and rechecking and who exhibited patience throughout the preparation of this manuscript. Cheers, Chris!
Evan Bracken (Light Reflections, Hendersonville, NC) and Leslie Dierks (Altamont Press, Asheville, NC), who "shot till they dropped" during our marathon photo shoot. You made a huge chore enjoyable.
Kathy Holmes and Elaine Thompson (art director and typesetter at Altamont Press, Asheville, NC), for their inspired and careful work.
Orrin Lundgren (Asheville, NC), for his illustrations.
Rob Pulleyn (Altamont Press, Asheville, NC), world's finest publisher, for his professional and personal support.
Patti Kertz (Longboat Key, FL) and Craig Weiss (Asheville, NC), for their generous help with photography.

Great 2x4 Accessories for Your Home

The authors would like to gratefully acknowledge the assistance of those who helped ensure the successful production of this book.

Many thanks to:
Laura Dover Doran (Lark Books, Asheville, NC), our editor, who accomplished miracles on an incredibly tight deadline, and who, on a person-al basis, showed compassion and kindness.
Chris Bryant (Lark Books, Asheville, NC), art director for the photo shoot, whose talent, skill, and humor always get us through it.
Evan Bracken (Light Reflections, Hendersonville, NC) whose photographic genius is only exceeded by his patience and expertise.
Eric Stevens (Portland, Oregon), who created the illustrations and designed the book-thanks for your efficiency and skill under deadline pressure!

In Loving Memory of: John Andrew Thompson
18 December 1914—25 January 1999

Index

Subject Index

Adhesives, 13–14
Band clamps, 19, 20
Band saw, 21
Bar clamps, 19, 20
Belt sanders, 20
Bevels, 24
Brads, 15
Brushes, 13
Butt joints, 22
C clamps, 19, 20
Chisels, 18, 19, 20
Circular saws, 17, 20
Clamps, 18–19, 20
Combination saw, 20
Combination square, 17, 20
Crosscut saws, 17, 20
Crown molding
  cutting, 24
  miters, 23–24
Cutting
  bevels, 24
  crown molding, 24
  lumber, 21
Cutting list, 29
Cutting tools, 17–18, 20, 21
Dado, 23
Drilling holes, 15, 16
Drill press, 21
Drills, 17, 20
Dust masks, 20, 27
Ear protection, 27
Edge-to-edge joints, 22–23
Eye protection, 27
Fasteners (hardware), 14–16, 29
Finishes. See Paint; Stains
Finishing sanders, 20
First-aid kits, 26
Framing square, 17, 20
Glazing, 25
Goggles, 20, 27
Hammers, 18, 20
Hardware. See Fasteners
  (hardware)
Hardwood, 9, 12

Hearing protection, 27
Jigsaws. See Saber saws
Joints
  butt, 22
  edge-to-edge, 22–23
  miter, 23–24
Lumber, 9–12
  buying, 9–10
  cutting, 21
  grades, 10–11
  hardwood, 9, 12
  measuring, 21
  normal and actual sizes, 10
  plywood, 12
  selecting, 11–12
  softwood, 9
Materials, 9–16. See also Lumber
  adhesives, 13–14
  brads, 15
  brushes, 13
  fasteners, 14–16
  nails, 14–15
  paints and stains, 12–13
  project list of, 28–29
  screws, 15–16
  staple guns and staples, 16
Measuring lumber, 21
Measuring tools, 17, 20
Metric conversion chart, 253
Miter box, 20
Miter joints, 23–24
  basic, 23
  on crown moldings, 23–24
Miter saws, power, 18
Nails, 14–15, 29
Nail sets, 15, 18, 20
Orbital sanders, 20
Paint, 12–13
  buying, 13
  glazing, 25
  pros and cons of, 12
  sponge painting, 25
  stamping with, 25–26
Pipe clamps, 19, 20

Planes, 18, 19
Plywood, 12
Power miter saws, 18
Projects. See also Projects Index
  cutting lists, 29
  hardware for, 29
  making mistakes, 30
  materials lists, 28–29
  preparing for, 29–30
  skill level, 28
  special tools/techniques, 28
Rip saws, 17–18, 20
Routers, 17, 20
Rulers, 17
Saber saws, 18, 20
Safety equipment, 20
Safety precautions, 26–27
Sanding tools, 19–20
Saw blades, 18, 20
Saws. See Cutting tools
Screwdrivers, 18, 20
Screws, 15–16, 29
Softwood, 9
Sponge painting, 25
Spring clamps, 19
Squares, 17
Stains, 13
Stamping, 25–26
Staple guns and staples, 16
Straightedges, 17
Table saw, 21
Toenailing, 15, 16
Tools. See also specific tools
  advanced, 21
  checklist, 20–21
  essentials, 20
  optional, 20
  project list of, 28
Vises, 20
Web (band) clamps, 19, 20
Wide steel tape rules, 17
Wood clamps, 19
Wood plugs, 16
Work surface, 16

Project Index